# THE ART PUBLIC

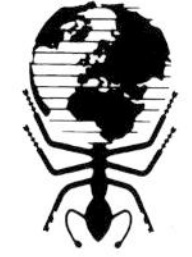

# THE ART PUBLIC
## A SHORT HISTORY

OSKAR
BÄTSCHMANN

TRANSLATED BY NICK SOMERS

REAKTION BOOKS LTD

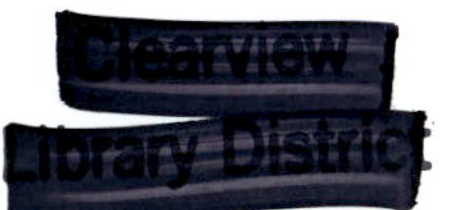

*For MTh*
*G & K & L*

Published by
REAKTION BOOKS LTD
Unit 32, Waterside
44–48 Wharf Road
London N1 7UX, UK
www.reaktionbooks.co.uk

First published 2023


The translation of this book has been supported by the Ernst Göhner Stiftung

**ERNST GÖHNER** STIFTUNG



Printed and bound in India by Replika Press Pvt. Ltd

A catalogue record for this book is available from the British Library

ISBN 978 1 78914 694 3

# CONTENTS

He [Apelles] placed his works in a gallery in the view of passers-by, and he himself stood out of sight behind the picture and listened to hear what faults were noticed, rating the public as a more observant critic than himself.

PLINY THE ELDER, first century CE

This outstanding work [the Ghent altarpiece] was only opened and shown on occasion to grand gentlemen or if someone gave the doorkeeper a good tip. It was also shown sometimes on certain high holidays. The people crowded to see it to such an extent that it was almost impossible to get close, because the chapel where it could be seen was full throughout the day with all kinds of people.

CAREL VAN MANDER, 1606

Annibale Carracci, he [Bernini] repeated, claimed that a painting should be exposed to public criticism immediately on completion, because the public did not delude itself and never flattered but did not fail to say that something was dry or hard, and so on.

GIAN LORENZO BERNINI, 1665

It is not only the educated and respectable people, who are most probably always the most reasonable and who pride themselves on their knowledge, but also the common people, who interfere with their opinions, so that it would appear that it [painting] is in some way an affair for everyone.

ROLAND FRÉART DE CHAMBRAY, 1662

As for Bernini's *Daphne*, I can only say that as soon as it was completed and displayed, there was such clamour that all of Rome rushed to admire this miracle.

FILIPPO BALDINUCCI, 1682

The word 'public' includes only those who are enlightened either by reading or world knowledge.

JEAN-BAPTISTE DUBOS, 1733

Just as the approval of an enlightened public confirms the true value of all genres of work, the [artist's] reputation is formed by this collective approval.

ANONYMOUS, *Explication des peintures, sculptures, et autres ouvrages de messieurs de l'Academie Royale* (1742)

Or do we desire that the public be as learned as the expert with his books, that it should be well acquainted and familiar with every scene of history and of fable which can yield materials for a beautiful picture?

GOTTHOLD EPHRAIM LESSING, 1766

If ever a picture caused a sensation, this was it. People flocked in procession for several days. The nobility travelled there to see it; cardinals and prelates, monsignori and priests, burghers and workers, all made their way there.

JOHANN HEINRICH TISCHBEIN, 1786

I myself know no greater honour than to be judged by the public. I do not fear either passion or partisanship. The rewards are the voluntary contributions demonstrating the public's taste for art. Its praise is a free expression of the pleasure it experiences, and such rewards certainly outweigh those from the time of the Academy.

JACQUES-LOUIS DAVID, 1800

In terms of solemnity, a painting exhibition is like a theatre performance: it is the public that brings them both to life. Without a public, everything is dead. If a play is performed in front of an empty house, even the best drama will receive no applause.

HILAIRE SAZERAC, 1834

Place ten people of sufficient intelligence in front of a new and original painting and they will all behave like children; they will nudge one another and joke about the work. The onlookers will come and join the group, and soon there will be mayhem, an outbreak of stupid madness.

ÉMILE ZOLA, 1867

The time of alienation of the artist from the public should come to an end. The inseparable inner band between these two elements must also find a form in which it can proclaim itself.

WASSILY KANDINSKY, 1910

It is vital to remind the public of its unworthiness as a judge and to teach it that neither painting nor sculpture nor architecture are 'entertainment arts' but sources of infinite torment and considerable annoyance.

ANDRÉ LHOTE, 1944

The public wanted more. The stadium was filled with an image, but they wanted even more. They wished new wishes. They had new anxieties. A new longing. The painter had to start again. New cans of paint were rolled in. The paint sprayed in the air, the people cheered.

MARTIN DISLER, 1983

In a realm as chockablock with legerdemain as the art world, what matters, at the end of the day, is that the audience enjoyed the show. With his star turn at Sotheby's, Banksy gave us all a command performance.

LENNY SCHACHTER, 2018

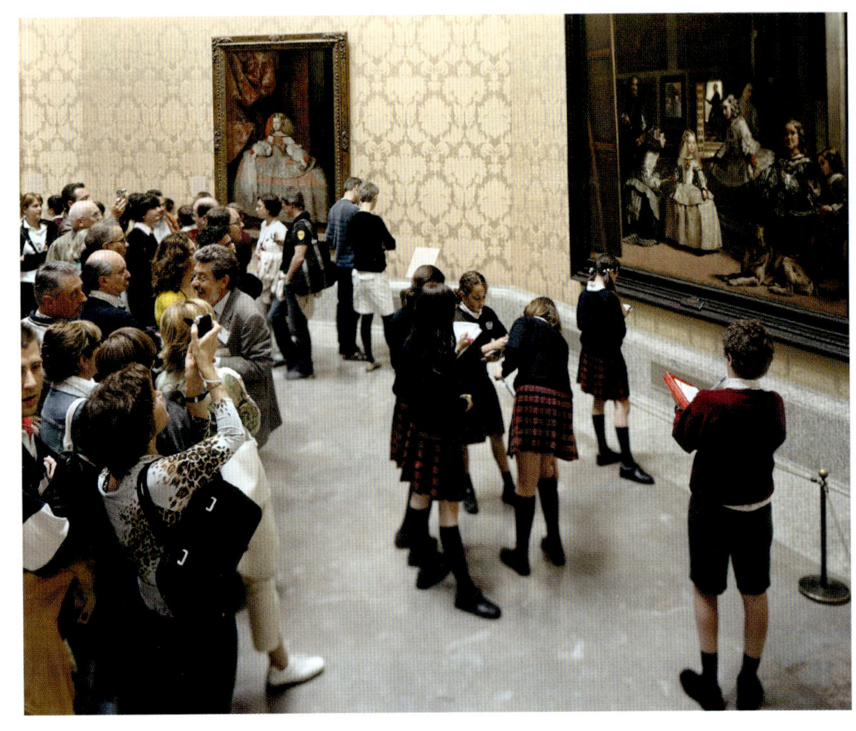

1 Thomas Struth, *Museo del Prado 7*, 2005, chromogenic print.

# PROLOGUE

Art history has still to discover the art public. Usually, it is seen as a passive and silent recipient whose opinions can be attributed at will, as the need arises. After production and distribution, the reception of a work of art is the third major area of research in art history. The recipient or viewer is referred to almost exclusively in the masculine form (spectator, beholder, viewer, *spettatore*, *spectateur*) and as a collective noun that is supposed to include female viewers. A distinction is hardly ever made between the public and the viewer.[1] In production, the public is largely ignored, since artists and those commissioning works of art are the exclusive focuses of attention, and their anticipation of any public demands is of secondary interest. Research into distribution, which focuses on the art market and collections, usually manages without any reference to the public and at best includes museum, exhibition and auction statistics.[2]

Art historians are happy to leave the analysis of the public to sociologists who conduct surveys to investigate the relationship between art and society. In the 1950s, Arnold Hauser provided the model for the sociology of art, and in the 1960s the analyses by Pierre Bourdieu and Alain Darbel became the paradigm for research into the art public.[3] In 1997, a representative cross-section of the field was published under the title *Soziologie der Kunst*, containing essays on art producers, mediators and recipients.[4] A statistical survey of museum visitors was conducted in Germany from 1984 to 1989, recording age, origins, gender, group affiliation and so on.[5] Museum and exhibition visitor research collects data on origins, education, behaviour and the course of a visit. The evaluation looks at the opinion of the museum and exhibition content by visitors.[6] The many surveys are already considered to be a detailed mapping of the public.[7] Knowledge of '(potential) consumers of culture' is required for culture policy and management so as to determine the 'need for legitimation' and to develop 'targeted' content.[8] Following on from Bourdieu, a research group from the University of St Gallen published a detailed sociological analysis of Art Basel.[9]

Can and should art historians be asking their own questions regarding the art public, distinct from sociological studies and statistical surveys? The public has always been present in the art world, drawing attention to itself, observing and being wooed, admired, painted, mocked and despised by those excluded. The attitude to the public is ambivalent: artists take account of it in the creative process, or else they believe that they can ignore it; they present it respectfully, praise or mock it, reject it or ally with it. Art lovers are either irritated by the masses who visit museums and exhibitions or welcome them for popularizing an interest in art.[10] In the mid-eighteenth century the appearance of a wider public disturbed art lovers, who thought their expertise assured them of a privileged access to art. In 1747, the great painter Charles-Antoine Coypel sought to make a distinction between the reliable judgement of an exclusive public and that of the fickle masses.[11] But the public is neither uniform nor organized, and its behaviour often comes across as erratic, as Paul Gauguin wrote in 1900 to Prince Emmanuel Bibesco: 'that strange and irrational public that demands the greatest originality of the painter but then only accepts him if he is like the others'.[12]

It might have been expected that a book such as Umberto Eco's *The Open Work* – written in 1962 – would have mentioned the contribution of the public, at least in the visual arts, but here too the objects and their authors are the main focus and the viewers are subordinate.[13] In the literature of art history the public is frequently referred to in passing, and more detailed considerations tend to focus on a restricted period and a defined territory.[14] For example, in *Legend, Myth and Magic in the Image of the Artist* of 1979, Ernst Kris and Otto Kurz devoted a section to the public but did little more than to indicate the primacy of the artist.[15] Some pictorial and literary material on the art public and on the relationship of other actors to the public is to be found. In 2009 Charlotte Klonk published her major study of the organization of and visitors to galleries and museums, focusing in particular on the experience of men and women and the interaction between visitors and the works displayed. The study is confined to Western Europe and North America and extends over a period from 1800 to 2000.[16]

The attempt in this book to examine the history of the art public concentrates mainly on the early modern and modern period. A more intense material and methodological study will be required to move beyond a brief history of the art public in the form of an *histoire anecdotique*. An analysis of the collection of written and pictorial documents would seem to be a useful starting point. The time frame and the geographical and language limits are defined by both the available texts and images and the author's work and linguistic capacities.

# 1

# THE PUBLIC COMPONENT

In 1989, the photographer Thomas Struth discovered the museum public in Vienna and started documenting groups of visitors and individuals in front of paintings and sculptures.[1] In 1990, photographs were taken in the Vatican Museums, including pictures of visitors in front of Raphael's *Fire in the Borgo*.[2] The photographer looks down on the members of the group, whose backs are to the camera and who cannot thus be identified; only the guide and two other persons are shown in profile. Except for one woman wearing a fur cape, the visitors all look similar in their undistinctive coats. The clothed mass contrasts with the vivid naked figures on the painted plinth. The photographer is the unseen observer of the public, waiting for an opportune constellation for his picture. As we look at his photos, we assume the role of observers.[3]

A number of photos were taken in the Museo del Prado in Madrid from an angle, so that Velázquez's painting *Las Meninas* was at the edge of the picture and the public in the centre (illus. 1). As on many of Struth's photos, the public is mixed. Schoolgirls in uniform standing in front of the *Meninas* discuss their homework and take notes on the painting. One girl is standing alone in front of the picture, suggesting a comparison with the Infanta Margarita Teresa and her ladies-in-waiting in the picture. On the left is a crowd of male and female visitors, including a woman with a camera, an art scholar and a female guide. Further back, a man is lifting his camera. A couple are studying the museum commentary on the painting. The public is focused completely on the *Meninas*, and no one is looking at the painting of the Infanta to its left. As in many of Struth's museum photos, the subjects are interested museum visitors and not tourists who spend twenty seconds in front of a painting before moving on to the next one.

Sometimes Struth photographs an individual. A 1989 photo, for example, shows a man in the Kunsthistorisches Museum in Vienna looking at two paintings by Rembrandt.[4] He is wearing a dark blue raincoat, and his hands are behind his back, the right hand holding three fingers of the left hand. The concentrated observer inevitably brings to mind the surly Reger, the alter ego of another Thomas and his growing contempt for Austria and the world as he looks at Tintoretto's *White-Bearded Man* in the Kunsthistorisches Museum.[5] In the Alte Pinakothek in Munich, a man stands in front of Albrecht Dürer's *Self-Portrait* of 1500, shown directly on the wall, while all that can be seen of the observer is his blue jacket and left arm, the top of his trousers and his chin.[6] The observers of the portraits by Rembrandt and Dürer remain anonymous, as in the group photos. For the pictures taken in 2004 in the Galleria dell'Accademia in Florence, by contrast, the photographer turns towards the public grouped in wonder in front of Michelangelo's colossal *David*.[7] Their clothing – the men in shorts, the women in jeans and shirts – reveals them to be tourists.

Sometimes Struth uses extras, as in the Pergamon Museum in Berlin, where they are placed in small groups sitting, standing or pretending to be in conversation. In a photo taken at the Art Institute in Chicago, seven people are standing before the cordon in front of *Grande Jatte* by Georges Seurat, replicating the disconnectedness of the figures in the painting. All of the pictures show the same respect of the public in front of paintings and sculptures. Visitors are controlled in all museums by rules and things that they are allowed or not allowed to do. Museums in Italy still demand suitable clothing and respectful behaviour.[8] These rules are relics of the past, when women wore two-pieces, hats and gloves and men wore suits and ties to visit museums. The *Règlement de visite* for the Louvre, issued by the Président-Directeur, has 36 articles, of which number 3 gives a detailed list of activities that are not allowed, such as eating and drinking, smoking, shouting, running or touching the art objects. In both Italy and the Louvre it is forbidden to carry weapons, and all major museums have a security check; photography is allowed but not with a flash, tripod or stick; the attention of visitors is drawn to the anti-theft alarm and video surveillance; coats and bags must be left in the cloakroom and so forth. Everywhere there are rules and threatened sanctions for disobeying them.

Struth does not imply that the visitors are behaving improperly, nor does he caricature them. His objective photographs of individuals and groups beg the question as to whether we regard the art public as a multiplicity of viewers: can 'viewers' be seen collectively as a 'public' or do we have to break it down by gender, ethnicity and dynamic? Reception aesthetics identifies the viewer component as one of perception and sensibility. It conceives a work of art as the 'result of an interaction of the work and the viewer' and analyses the means that 'trigger this dialogue behaviour'.[9] Can a public component be inferred in the same way? Can a crowd standing in front of a painting exhibit 'dialogue behaviour', and how would this be understood? When we speak of viewers, do we mean individuals or a collective, and is collective or private consumption of a work implied? Private consumption can be intended by the client or desired by the owner, as is the case with erotic depictions, for example. The Ottoman diplomat Khalil Bey in Paris is known to have acquired erotic paintings by Gustave Courbet, which he concealed underneath a removable landscape.[10] By contrast, Courbet's exhibition pictures are meant for the public: 'le public' or 'le grand public'.[11]

In a frantic action over several days and nights in 1981, Martin Disler, who worked ceaselessly as a painter, sculptor, writer and poet before dying of a stroke in 1996 at the age of 47, created the colossal 4.4 × 140 metre (14 × 460 ft) panorama *Die Umgebung der Liebe* for the Württembergischer Kunstverein in Stuttgart.[12] In 1983, he wrote two parables on the relationship between the public and the artist and a fairy tale about the people as artists. In the parables, the art public behaves exactly like crowds at sporting events.[13] The fairy tale tells of a painter who is under public pressure and obsessed by paint, forcing him to work ceaselessly; otherwise, the material will dry up for ever. The people are enthusiastic about the billions of pictures that flood the country, but the king and his ministers feel threatened and order 5,000 riders to trample on the pictures. The attack distracts the artist, the paint dries up, and art is over. The painter flees, the king triumphs, but the people mourn and transform themselves into the painter. The transformation of the people as a collective into the painter follows the idea of the State as a composite entity, as shown in the frontispiece to Thomas Hobbes's *Leviathan* of 1651: a giant, wearing a crown and holding a sword and crosier, representing the power of the Church and State, made of countless composite human bodies.[14]

The parables are about a star artist. In one he puts on a supershow in a sports arena before 50,000 spectators, and in the other the bloodthirsty public hound the artist-gladiator to death. The artist runs around the stadium with five huge brushes and reacts at lightning speed to the wishes, longings and fears of the spectators. The crowd goes wild, and their millions of wishes and anxieties are broadcast by more than eighty television stations:

> The painter processed millions and millions of wishes of half of mankind. He ran around with the red brush, with the black brush, with the yellow, blue and white. The public howled. The tension mounted unbearably. The wishes poisoned the air. The painter was shrouded in a mist of longing. The anxiety of millions lit up the stadium.

Following the parable of the painter as a star cheered by the howling crowd comes the parable of the artist whom the public condemn to death. The painter is connected to a computer, and his eyes are covered with a black blindfold. Like a Kafka victim, he doesn't know that he is to be killed. Then he struggles with the electrodes and stumbles over the cans of paint, while the public bloodlust reaches a crescendo and hounds the painter to death in the arena:

> The public wanted more. The stadium was filled with an image, but they wanted even more. They wished new wishes. They had a new anxiety. A new longing. The painter had to start again. New cans of paint were rolled in. The paint sprayed in the air, the people cheered. The painter couldn't breathe. The paint flowed all over his body. The reporters gesticulated wildly. Their voices crackled. The paints mixed together in the stadium. A grey sauce spread out. The painter's movements became more sluggish. He was stuck in to the paint and lost his footing in the puddles. He looked like a soaked poodle. Chequered with paint. The public gasped for breath. The artist could no longer lift himself out of the paint.

The painter in the stadium is a slave of the masses, who drive the artist-athlete to ever greater efforts or to destruction. Disler took as his model the spectators at boxing or football matches whose fanaticism drives the athletes to perform violent acts. Can the behaviour of the public in stadiums, music halls or theatres really be applied to the art public? Does the public at an exhibition work itself up to a fever pitch of rage, violence or cheering as in sports stadiums; is it torn from its seats; does it wave its arms, dancing like the public at pop concerts; does it clap wildly?[15] An art event would never attract the crowds of fans like the 1998 World Cup final, said to have been watched on television by 1.7 billion people, a million of whom celebrated the victory frenetically through the night on the Champs-Elysées.

Dionysian effects are known to be triggered by music, but hardly by paintings or sculptures. Natalie Bauer-Lechner observed: '[Gustav] Mahler told me of a performance of Beethoven's Seventh Symphony, the last movement of which had a Dionysian effect on the audience, who left the concert as if drunk.'[16] In 1913, the public in Paris was stupefied and aroused by the heathen dances, thrilling rhythms and bold dissonances of Igor Stravinsky's *Sacre du Printemps*. And in *Cock and Harlequin*, written in 1918, Jean Cocteau recalls from memory the compulsive reaction of the public during the premiere in the Théâtre des Champs-Élysées on 29 May 1913:

> The audience behaved as it ought to; it revolted straight away. People laughed, boo-ed, hissed, imitated animal noises, and possibly would have tired themselves out before long, had not the crowd of aesthetes and a handful of musicians, carried away by their excessive zeal, insulted and even roughly handled the public in the loges. The uproar degenerated into a free-fight.[17]

The public reacted as expected to the provocation. Cocteau recalls the old Countess de Pourtalès flourishing her fan and shouting, scarlet in the face, that it was the first time in sixty years that anyone had dared to make a fool of her. That the countess should come at the age of 77 to a performance of Stravinsky's *Sacre du Printemps* is worthy of the greatest respect.[18]

It is hardly conceivable that the public would react as tumultuously to an exhibition or a museum as it did in the Théâtre des Champs-Élysées in 1913. There is no shortage of provocation of the art public: for example, in the form of the Futurists' *Grande Serate*, which was performed in theatres, or the various actions and performances since the 1950s. The organizers claimed that the Futurists had a triumphant success in the Teatro Verdi in Florence on 12 December 1913: the irritation of the public, the sympathies aroused, the momentary conversions and subsequent mockery of the fainthearted stupidity of the audience.[19] With their actions and performance, artists sought to attract public interest among passers-by for a limited event.

What happens to a group of exhibition or museum visitors when they enter a building and collect in front of artworks? Is there a curiosity that spreads from one participant to the next? Do they want to have part of what the others are seeing or does a 'feeling of participation' in the extraordinary events and things develop?[20] Is a similar enthusiasm evoked as in a theatre or concert hall, stimulating the actors or musicians and the public alike, or are such reactions limited to performances? Do individuals in the art public react independently or is there a transfer from one participant to the next? Answers to these questions have been sought for over a thousand years. The Roman poet Horace demanded more from poetry than formal elegance; he said it must 'captivate', pointing out that the human face smiles at a smile and echoes those who are weeping.[21] In 1435–6, Leon Battista Alberti wrote in the treatise *On Painting* that 'we cry with those who cry, we laugh with those who laugh, we grieve with those who suffer.'[22] Neither Horace nor Alberti limits the transfer of sensitivities to the effect on the public of a painting, play or reading. On the contrary, they assume a transfer of emotional reactions among the listeners or viewers. But how can such phenomena be explained? Is there an invisible substance, a metaphorical 'Fluidum'?[23] Or is it 'infectious', as Gustave Le Bon sought to explain the transfer of reactions? These metaphors are somewhat older than the 'mirror neurons', a modern explanation for psychic transmission.[24] Compared with earlier metaphors, the latest iteration has the advantage that the transfer of physical and mental motions, voices or odours can be measured through the activation of similar regions in the brain.[25]

The various forms of performance art that have developed since the 1960s use the presence of artists and public to achieve simultaneous creation and reception.[26] As in a play, it can be assumed in performances that the audience reactions rebound on the performers through stimulation, empathy, emotion, noises or boredom and unrest. Marina Abramović became world-renowned, proposing her first idea for a performance to the Cultural Centre in Belgrade in 1969, then in the 1970s had an idea for public self-mutilation, which she herself described as 'completely insane'.[27] On 14 March 2010 she commenced the performance 'The Artist Is Present' at the Museum of Modern Art in New York, for which she had three long woollen dresses made in blue, red and white, which kept her warm and gave her the appearance of a high priestess.[28] As always, she imposed rules on the public: anyone could sit opposite her, eye contact would be maintained at all times, and no one was allowed to speak or touch. The artist wrote that this exposure made her 'extremely receptive', enabling her to understand the state of mind of Van Gogh, and that she felt that every person sitting across from her left 'a specific energy' behind. She sensed the incredible emotional energy of the people who sat opposite her alone in front of the spectators lined up against the walls. Many were overcome by strong emotions and were in tears, which also made the artist cry. Scientists wanted to measure the brain wave patterns triggered by this mutual gaze. A simple experiment was conducted in 2011, and a more extensive measurement of non-verbal communication during eye contact was conducted with Abramović and Daria Parkhomeno in 2018 at the Laboratory for Neurophysiology and Neuro-Computer Interface in Moscow.[29] In 'The Artist Is Present', individuals from the public isolate themselves in a direct confrontation with the artist and thus become much more central than in other performances.

# 2

# HIERARCHICAL CATEGORIES

The 'art public' may be described as that part of the population that spends a defined amount of time with art objects or shows an interest in art by reading, studying, writing, listening or acting. *Lexikon zur Soziologie* describes the 'public' as follows: 'A formally non-organized group whose members have the same interests, of which they are aware through non-personal communication and contact, and who select and receive information on the basis of these interests.'[1]

The long article in the *Oxford Latin Dictionary* defines *publicus* as 'of public life', 'of the state or nation', 'common', 'of the people'. In English, the word 'public' has a wider meaning than the German *Publikum*, as it is also the opposite of 'private' and refers to a collective that shares cultural, social or political interests. The listening or reading public is called an 'audience'.[2] In French, *public, publique* refers in addition to something that is shared, as in *bruit public* or general gossip. It can also apply to all of the people who read a book or attend an event; furthermore, a distinction is made between 'grand public' or general public, as opposed to the chosen few.[3] In Italian, *pubblico* can refer to everyone who attends a cultural or political event.[4]

Like other publics, the art public is neither homogeneous nor a self-contained unit. In 1962, Jürgen Habermas referred to the 'basic non-exclusivity of any public' that can 'never completely shut itself off and form a clique' and is always 'part of a larger public'.[5] Practically all museums divide their public into ordered categories. The Museum of Modern Art in New York, mentioned here as a first example, works with a strict hierarchy. The base is formed by the 'general public', who pay admission and have access only during the regular opening hours. They are followed by 'Ordinary Members' with free admission and discounts in the museum store, and 'Supporting Members', who for a higher subscription enjoy further benefits. Above them is the 'Patron Program' with various levels, the highest of which is a 'Leader'. This category, which costs $15,000 per year, offers all kinds of benefits, including personal meetings with the director. An important consideration for Leaders is that $14,776 of the $15,000 is tax-deductible, so that in fact the general public recompenses these patrons.[6] 'Leader' is the second-highest category. The highest category on the website is 'Director's Council' for 'generous philantropists', who donate at least $25,000 per year, all but $776 of which is tax-deductible. But above them in reality are the major patrons, whose donations entitle them to a seat on the board of trustees and to the highest social recognition at the black-tie receptions. The largest public category is the millions of anonymous 'Followers' in the no-man's land of Instagram, who have only free Internet access.[7] Few art museums have such a strict hierarchy as the Museum of Modern Art in New York, but all make a distinction between the general public and members of an association or group of supporters, and all reward sponsors, patrons and donors with increased attention and exclusive recognition.

The National Gallery in London offers only 'membership' for an annual fee of £60 in return for free admission (which is available in any case to all visitors), events for members and exhibition previews. The main argument for membership is solidarity, because the subscription enables the National Gallery to remain accessible to everyone: 'Art for everyone // By supporting us you'll be supporting free art for everyone. Not only can art benefit your own wellbeing, you are helping others too.'[8]

The third example is the Van Gogh Museum in Amsterdam. It calls on its website for public support and offers three categories for individuals. The lowest level is the 'Sunflower Collective' with a minimum annual contribution of €1,000 (£865) in return for an annual pass, a dinner, invitations to exhibition openings and 10 per cent discount in the museum shop. The next level, 'Theo van Gogh Circle' with a minimum annual contribution of €5,000 (£4,315), is intended for young curators and restorers. Admission to 'The Yellow House', the highest category for collectors and art lovers, costs €15,000 (£13,000) and offers additional benefits, such as previews or private guided tours by the directors. There is a further group, 'Vincent's Friends', which supports the museum by means of an annual donation. Contributions in all categories are tax-deductible in the Netherlands.[9]

This categorization of the public by museums is one of the numerous hierarchies existing on the basis of different criteria in the art world. The hierarchy in the art trade is based on the most recent auctions, anticipated results and the purchasing power of the clients, at the peak of which are those who can afford more than U.S.$100 million for a work, whereas those who are only willing to spend U.S.$1 million are nothing more than foot soldiers.[10] As another example of such hierarchies, in their heyday, publishing companies used limited numbered editions with original illustrations, cloth or leather binding and gold lettering, for example.

Wassily Kandinsky presented a hierarchical classification of the public with associated artists in Munich in 1912. Having written his doctoral thesis in Moscow in 1893 on workers' wages, he devised a hierarchical order in intellectual life in the form of a mystical triangle based on 'spiritual' capital: 'A large acute triangle divided into unequal segments, the narrowest one pointing upwards, is a schematically correct representation of spiritual life. The lower the segment, the larger, wider, higher and more embracing will be the other parts of the triangle.'[11]

Kandinsky saw the mystical triangle as a means of ascending from low to higher understanding. With great pathos he describes the lonely visionary at the apex, called a 'knave or fool' by his enemies. In the many segments are various artists with their own public. Some, like prophets, look beyond the limits of their present stage and offer their contemporaries 'spiritual food'. Others misuse their art to feed lower needs, deceiving the public and destroying the spiritual triangle as creators of a 'large deadly black spot'.[12]

Apart from the hierarchical categorization of the public by institutions, there is a worldwide ranking of art museums and exhibitions based on visitor numbers. At the head of the 2017 Wikipedia list of the most-visited art museums was the Louvre with 8.1 million visitors, followed by the Chinese National Museum in Beijing with 8.06 million, and the Metropolitan Museum of Art in New York with 6.7 million. The 2020 Statista ranking was headed by the Louvre, followed by the Chinese National Museum with around 8 million visitors, the Vatican Museums, which in 2019 registered 6.75 million visitors, in fourth place the Metropolitan Museum of Art in New York and in fifth place the British Museum in London with 5.86 million.[13] The Staatliche Museen zu Berlin reported a total of 111.6 million visitors to the 6,800 or so museums in Germany in 2019.[14] The *Art Newspaper* magazine published a list of the most popular exhibitions with photographs of queues. No indication is given of how the data for these rankings are obtained, nor of the role of assumptions, projections and estimates. All of these rankings are used for political and financial purposes and for or against institutions, and also to motivate sponsors and donors.

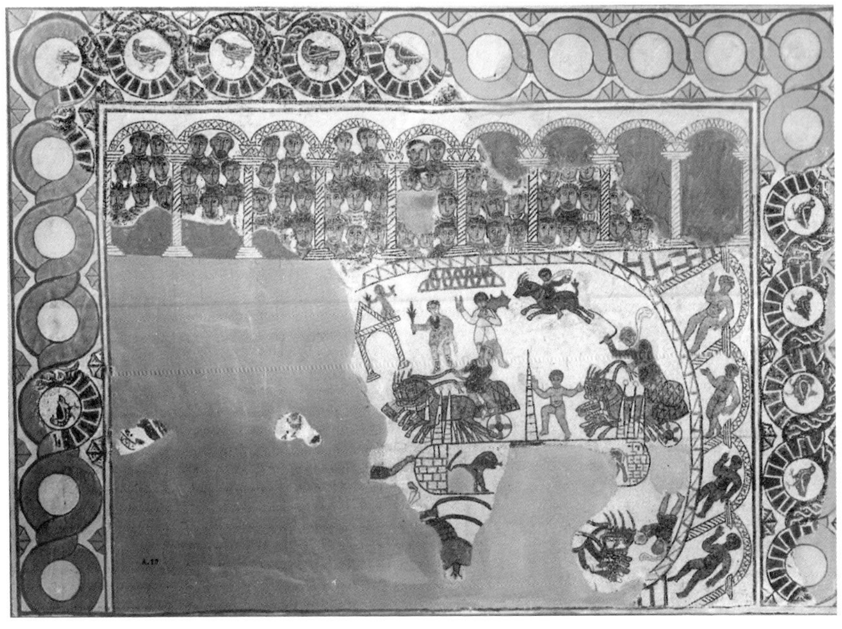

2 Arena of an amphitheatre with horse racing and spectators, mosaic from Gafsa (Capsa), Tunisia, 6th century CE.

# 3

# THE APELLES PROBLEM

Pliny the Elder, who wrote his encyclopaedic *Natural History* in the first century CE, described the legendary Greek painter Apelles from the fourth century BCE as an artist who consistently sought perfection. Every day he practised drawing a line and competed with Protogenes as to who could draw the finest line. In spite of his fame, however, he remained modest and bowed to the judgement of others.[1] Apelles created a public for his work from random passers-by and called for their judgement: 'Another habit of his was when he had finished his works to place them in a gallery in the view of passers-by, and he himself stood out of sight behind the picture and listened to hear what faults were noticed, rating the public as a more observant critic than himself.'[2]

Pliny called the public *volgus* or *vulgus*, which Georges translates in his Latin–German dictionary as 'people, crowd, mean person' and also pejoratively as 'heap, mob' or 'the large mass, the commonplace'.[3] According to the Roman way of thinking hinted at here by Pliny, the passers-by must be plebeians, servants, handworkers and merchants. The public remain silent except for a shoemaker, who points out a mistake in a sandal and the next day criticizes the leg, for which Apelles rebukes him.[4] Thus one of the first texts about the art public already alludes to the rivalry between the artist's judgement and that of the public. I call it the Apelles problem, one that has already been addressed in countless historical and pictorial approaches.

Apelles' public behaves differently to a sports public, for example, whose ecstasy is described by Philostratus in the third century CE in his essay in *Imagines* about a painting showing spectators watching a wrestling match at Olympia. Some shout, some jump up from their seats or throw their clothing in the air, and some imitate the wrestlers and grapple with their neighbours. The spectators are upset because Arrichion has just been killed in the wrestling match.[5] A mosaic in Gafsa in Tunisia shows the spectators densely packed and wide-eyed in an amphitheatre as they watch a chariot race (illus. 2).[6] The behaviour of two refugees admiring new artworks in Carthage is completely different, as the Roman poet Virgil describes in Book I of the *Aeniad* written towards the end of the first century BCE. Aeneas and his companion Achates, who have fled from Troy and

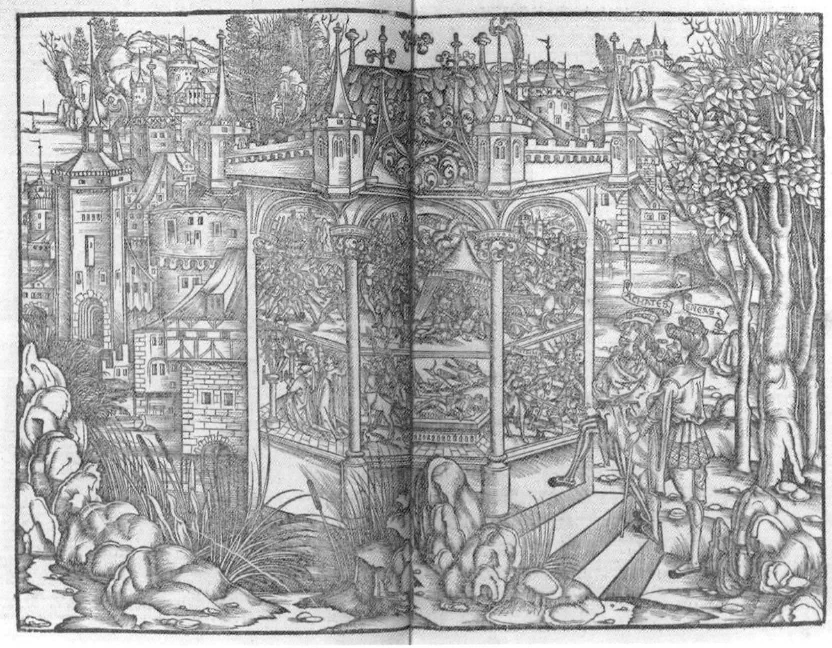


3 Aeneas and Achates observing the images of the Trojan battles in Carthage, woodcut illustration from Publius Vergilius Maro, *Opera* (1502).

are waiting in a temple for Queen Dido, admire pictures and are surprised to recognize depictions of the recent battles between the Greeks and the Trojans, which have already become legendary.[7] Tearful and sobbing, Aeneas relates the events to his companion and cites the names of the gods and heroes. The illustrator of the Strasbourg edition of 1502 (illus. 3), presumably on instructions from the publisher Sebastian Brant, shows Aeneas and Achates on the building steps discussing, admiring and re-enacting the battle scenes with Hector, Achilles and Penthesilea, and also the women pleading to Pallas Athene.[8] Virgil's description of Aeneas and Achates reflects typical public behaviour: an explanation of the images by a knowledgeable expert and the emotional reactions to the events that they themselves have experienced. This is stereotypical behaviour by an art public, where one person in the crowd is willing to instruct the others, who are in ignorance.

Around 1610 to 1615, Frans Francken the Younger offered an interesting interpretation of Apelles' public (illus. 4). He shows a back view of the shoemaker in his red jacket and yellow trousers at the side of the painting pointing to the knee of Mercury, whose head is raised to the naked pair above him. On the left, four men and a boy form the public. One of the men is wearing a red beret with an agraffe, a fur-trimmed coat and the chain of office of the mayor. He is inclining his head towards a man in profile, who is whispering something in his ear, pointing at the boy in front of him and placing his left hand on the shoemaker's shoulder. To the right behind the mayor are two heads, one of which has a turban. On the square in the background are market stalls and crowds of market-goers, forming a contrast to the art public in the foreground. Apelles, who appears from behind the painting, points with his left hand at the boot and rebukes the shoemaker. A male figure with a plumed beret and cloak and his back to the viewer appears to be talking.

Francken places a young woman with child, shown from behind, in the foreground pointing at the shoemaker, while her smile calls on the viewers to laugh at what they are seeing. The mayor is instructing a boy with his back to the viewer, who is raising his arms and pointing to the shoemaker. In this way, Francken creates a public for Apelles consisting of various people who discuss the painting.

In his fifteenth-century treatise on the art of painting, the scholar Leon Battista Alberti derives a piece of advice for contemporary artists from the Apelles anecdote. After instruction on geometry and composition in the first two books, in the third book he advises artists to seek the opinion of their friends and even to invite passers-by to pass judgement on a work in progress. He explains: 'The painter's work will be pleasing to a great number of people.'[9] The advice is supported by the authority of Apelles, who wishes to hear the unbiased judgement of his work by the public. Alberti refers to friends, passers-by and the general public, and not an adviser or spectator in the singular. To date, the frequent use of the plural for advisers or the public – *multitudine* – has not been commented on or felt to be important. Alberti already talks of the multitude in his second book, referring to the recipients of art in the plural, as when he states that the *historia* moves the souls of those beholding it, adding the famous dictum by Horace of the infectiousness of emotive depictions.[10] In the sections on mental expression, Alberti uses the plural Latin word *spectatores*. He recommends that there should be a person in the *historia* showing the public what is happening, highlighting the most important aspects and telling the spectators how they should be reacting. Andrea Mantegna achieved this, for example, in his copper engraving *The Entombment of Christ* completed around 1470.[11]

The most surprising sentence by Alberti is his reference to the interaction between the figures in the painting and the spectators:

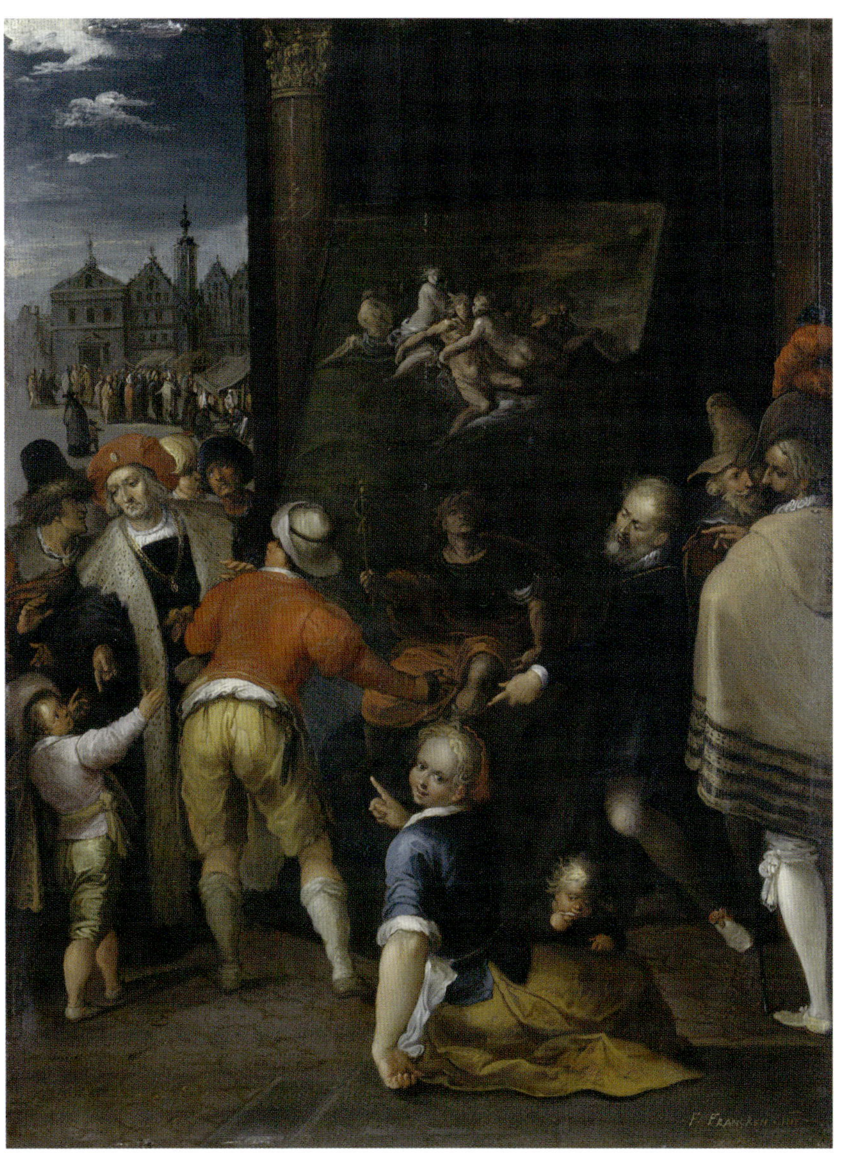

4 Frans Francken the Younger, *Apelles and the Shoemaker*, 1610–15, oil on copper.

'It is necessary in the end that also all [the occurrences] that those painted [characters] made with the spectators and with themselves concur to realize and explain the *historia*.'[12] This important sentence demonstrates that Alberti conceived a lively interplay between the figures in the painting and their reflection in the spectators on the model of theatrical plays and their audience. He himself was involved in the theatre. In 1424 he wrote the allegorical comedy *Philodoxeus fabula* in Latin prose, with a *Commentarium* to it around 1434 to 1437.[13] In Book 8, chapter 7, of *De re aedificatoria* he spoke in detail about the theatre and scenery.[14] In *On Painting* he admonishes painters who believe that their figures are most lively when they gesticulate wildly like performers might in a juggling show or *ars saltandi* but in doing so lose all their dignity.[15] The *spectatores* are the conceptual and physical link to the way dramas and paintings are seen. 'Movements of the soul and body' are required for the interaction between actors and spectators, but moderation is called for.

For Alberti, artists are as much interested in success and recognition by the masses as they are in their constant search for perfection in any activity. In his autobiographical *Vita* he advocates self-edification, from physical exercise to the sciences and arts.[16] But why did Alberti suggest that artists should seek approval from the masses and not from the clients, when he had discovered through the banishment of his own family that he lived in a city full of scheming citizens? Alberti probably visited Florence for the first time in the second half of the 1420s and saw the astounding works of the new artists, whom he praises to the highest in the Prologue to *On Painting* as the revelation of new arts and sciences. He cites the frescos in the Brancacci Chapel by Masolino and Masaccio. In the magnificent picture *Raising of the Son of Theophilus* (illus. 5), Masaccio confronts the inhabitants of Florence and the ruler of

Antioch. The composition is divided into four parts. On the left, a group of five men comment on what is happening; in the centre the public mass around St Peter and the disciples; on the right is the enthroning of St Peter with three clerics; and on the far right are three Florentines. The heathen enemy is depicted as Gian Galeazzo Visconti from Milan, and it has been suggested that the three men on the far right are Masaccio, Alberti and Brunelleschi. The members of the crowd – *multitudine* – are shown by Masaccio as being of the same social status with similar clothing, behaviour and gestures. The fresco was completed about 1485 by Filippino Lippi.

Alberti states in his autobiography that the public can be formed only by those, like himself, who were raised as free men and thus deserve to be appreciated as honourable men. He explicitly excludes slanderers, whom he describes as the greatest evil in human life, who ruin the reputation of righteous people.[17] No account should be taken of those who do not appear 'honourable'. The Apelles problem is thus solved by a Florentine patrician who had only recently been permitted to return from exile. In a passage on the writing of *Intercenales* – table talk – Alberti assures us that he acts the same way as Apelles: 'He thanked those who criticized his writings providing they gave their personal opinion, and was grateful for many a criticism, as he believed that as a result of the rebukes by his critics he could become better himself.'[18]

Painters should, of course, listen to everyone, but they should follow only those who are knowledgeable. Alberti wants to show that he is an expert who can offer advice to artists and also instruct them on how to distinguish a competent judgement from a misleading one as a result of ignorance or envy. As artistic rivalry was commonplace in Florence, Alberti believed it necessary to dispel the fear of enviers and slanderers by affirming that a well-finished work would still safeguard the artist's reputation. But in his *Vita* he

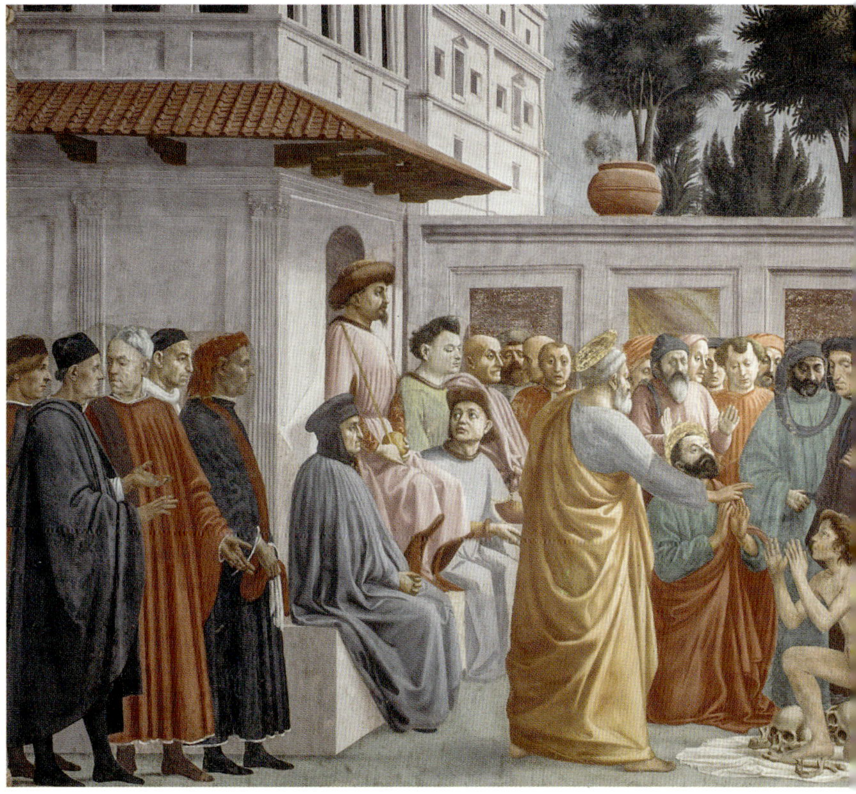

describes how he suffered from hate, enmity, intolerable insults and conspiracies, not least by his own relatives. As a reward for his advice, he merely hopes that the artists will paint his portrait in their *historiae*, which was not a modest request, since his contribution to the creation of the work would then be publicly documented.[19]

In 1502 Leonardo da Vinci took Apelles' and Alberti's advice in Florence and invited the inhabitants of the city to view his model for *The Virgin and Child with St Anne and St John the Baptist* for two days in his studio. Heinrich Wölfflin, whose book *Classic Art*, originally published in 1899, was aimed at the educated public, wrote of the furore caused by Leonardo's cartoon: 'Yet the cartoon alone, in its day (1501), aroused tremendous excitement in Florence

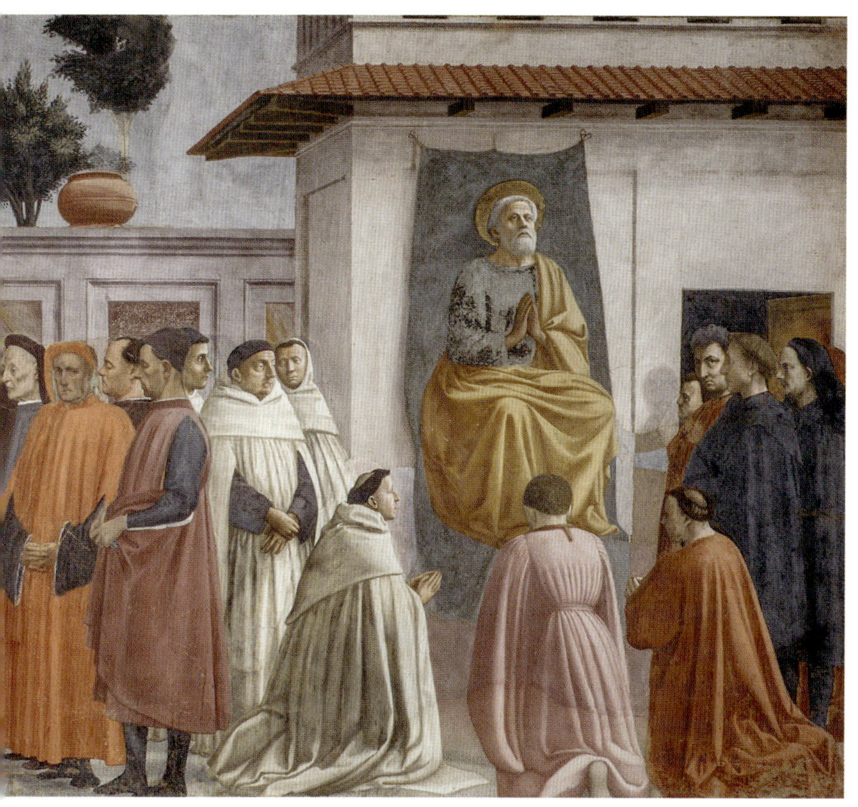

5 Masaccio and Filippino Lippi, *Raising of the Son of Theophilus and St Peter Enthroned*, 1427–8 and c. 1485, fresco, Brancacci Chapel, Florence.

and caused a general pilgrimage to the convent of the Annunziata, where Leonardo's latest miracle could be seen.'[20]

Leonardo showed a cartoon that was prepared for transfer to a canvas. The subject was the same as the cartoon (illus. 6) in the National Gallery in London, completed a little earlier but with no trace of having been transferred. Giorgio Vasari wrote of the viewing in the studio in Florence in the 1550 and 1568 versions of *Le vite*:

> Finally he showed a cartoon of Our Lady and Saint Anne with the figure of Christ, which not only amazed all the artisans

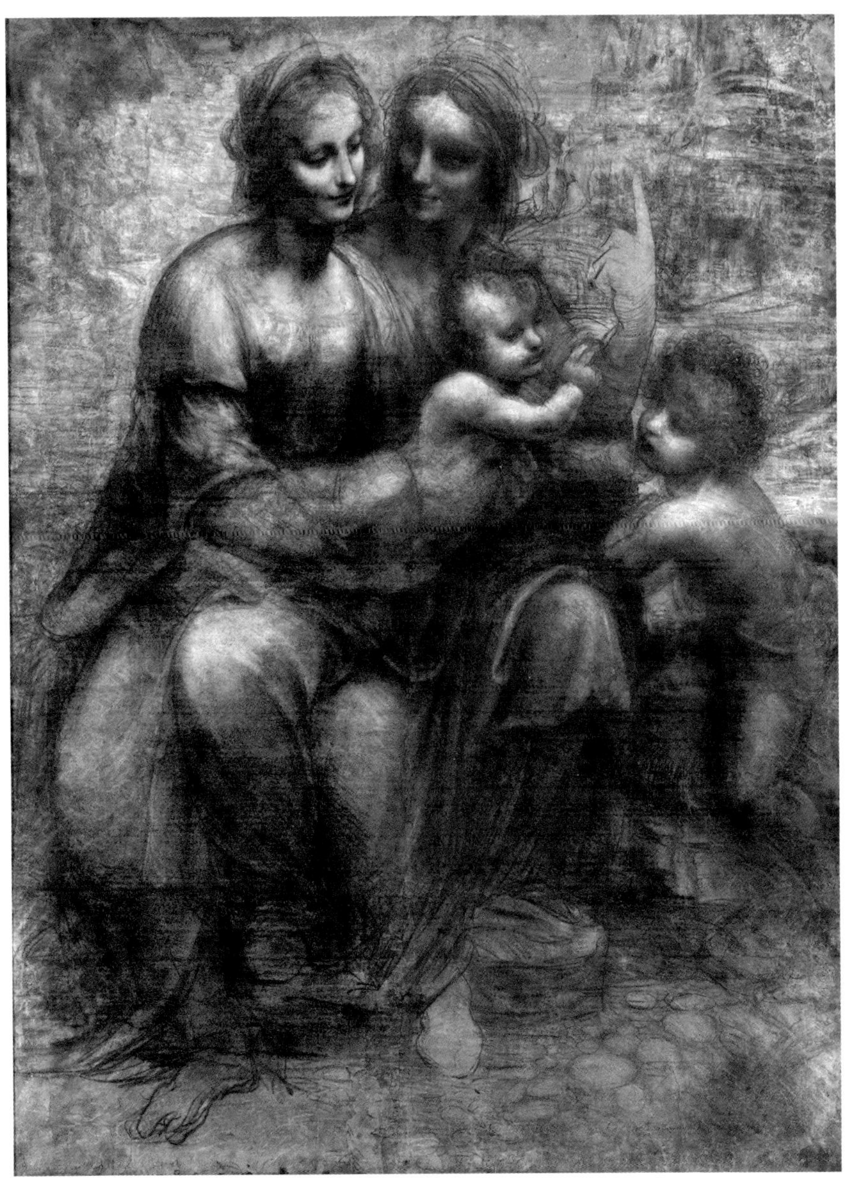

6 Leonardo da Vinci, *The Virgin and Child with St Anne and the Infant St John the Baptist* (*The Burlington House Cartoon*), 1499–1500, charcoal and white highlights on paper, mounted on canvas.

> but, once completed and set up in a room, brought men, women, young and old to see it for two days as if they were going to a solemn festival in order to gaze upon the marvels of Leonardo which stupefied the entire populace.[21]

Vasari, who wrote his text almost fifty years after this public event, used the expression *tutto quel popolo* – 'the entire populace', a reference to Pliny's *volgus* or *vulgus* used by Apelles for the public. The rush by the people of Florence to Leonardo resembles the crowds who flocked to see the miraculous painting of the Virgin in SS Annunziata whenever a cardinal opened it to the public.[22] According to a contemporary record, there was such a crush that a woman started giving birth and could only be taken out of the crowd with difficulty.[23] Matteo Bandello, a contemporary of Leonardo, describes the artist's interest in allowing everyone to give their opinion freely on all of his pictures.[24] Like Alberti, Leonardo urges painters to listen patiently to the opinions of everyone, even if they are not artists themselves. He was aware of the possibility of self-delusion and therefore recommended verification by means of a mirror that made the picture look as if it was by someone else and permitted analysis from a greater distance. He believed that the majority of people perceived nature correctly and hence also its representation by the painter. The virtue that Leonardo urged artists to emulate was thus the very same modesty attributed to Apelles.[25]

Pietro Perugino had a sad experience of a negative opinion by the art public in 1507, when his work *The Assumption of the Virgin* in SS Annunziata in Florence was unveiled. Vasari, who did not have a high opinion of Perugino, is said to have asserted that artists were critical of the new work because they recognized figures that the painter had already used in earlier works. Perugino was accused of complacency and greed and was derided by the public. Perugino replied that he had not understood that repetitions were no longer in fashion and that the modern era demanded new inventions: '"I painted the same figures," replied Pietro, "that had elsewhere been met with praise and acclaim. What can I do if you no longer like or acknowledge them?"'[26] The incident had a precedent, however: Perugino was jealous of Michelangelo and had maligned him, with the result that some artists rudely insulted him and Michelangelo himself called him a fool.

For artists who do not appear to have sufficient education, scholars – *letterati* – take over the function of advisers on the mythological, philosophical and theological content.[27] The instructions to the illustrators and woodcarvers by Sebastian Brant for the Strasbourg Virgil edition of 1502 were mentioned earlier. A well-known example of scholarly advice is Raphael's *Camera della Segnatura* in the Vatican. In 1855, Jacob Burckhardt wrote in *Cicerone* of the presumptions of the time:

> Apart from the fact that Raphael hardly possessed enough learning to place and to give the right characteristics of the personages of the Disputa or of the school of Athens, and that here the assistance of some important person of the court of Julius II is clearly felt; apart from this, art had long before lent itself to such attempts.[28]

The assumption of a scholarly adviser implies that the artist's intellect is inadequate. Burckhardt avoids this by referring to the artist's iconographic achievements. But his own activity as a friendly adviser to Arnold Böcklin ended in a serious dispute, owing to the fact that he was not only Böcklin's friend but represented his clients.[29]

# 4

# PUBLIC JUDGEMENT

The Apelles problem was kept alive for centuries by artists, non-experts, educated laypersons, scholars and the nobility. In the mid-seventeenth century, the class-privileged and educated public regarded itself as knowledgeable and qualified to judge art and rejected the judgement of the 'common people' as unqualified. An incident in Rome in 1646 caused astonishment, when the judgement of a woman from the people agreed with that of a scholarly painter from France. Giovan Pietro Bellori reported on Nicolas Poussin's assessment of the frescos painted by Guido Reni and Domenichino in 1608–9 in the Oratorio di Sant'Andrea near Piazza S. Gregorio Magno in Rome. The inhabitants raved about Guido Reni, and young artists rushed to copy his fresco, but only Poussin had a good word for Domenichino's painting: 'He was so able to appreciate the parts and the beauties of this wonderful work that the others, convinced and persuaded by his example, also turned to study Domenichino.'[1]

The Roman biographer Bellori and the Frenchman André Félibien cite this anecdote to demonstrate the superior artistic judgement of the painter from France.[2] In 1843, François-Marius Granet painted a picture showing the supporters of Reni and Domenichino (illus. 7). The clerics, young people and the rest of the public are looking at Guido Reni's fresco. A prelate with his servant turns his back on the painting by Domenichino and looks through a telescope at Reni's work, while Poussin points to Domenichino's painting and persuades his companion of its merits. We have already seen this type of public instruction with Aeneas and Achates.

An anecdote circulated in Rome in 1646 about the artistic judgement of a lowly woman of the people. The great painter Annibale Carracci, who cannot decide whether he prefers Reni or Domenichino, is tutored by an old woman who says nothing about Reni's work but talks in detail to her granddaughter about the figures, action and affects in Domenichino's painting.[3] This Vecchiarella anecdote suggests first that an uneducated woman of the people can judge an artwork better than an artist, and second that the quality of a work is measured by the degree to which the public is interested and responsive enough to talk about it.

In 1649 the engraver Abraham Bosse stated that the distinction between originals and copies and the attribution of works were

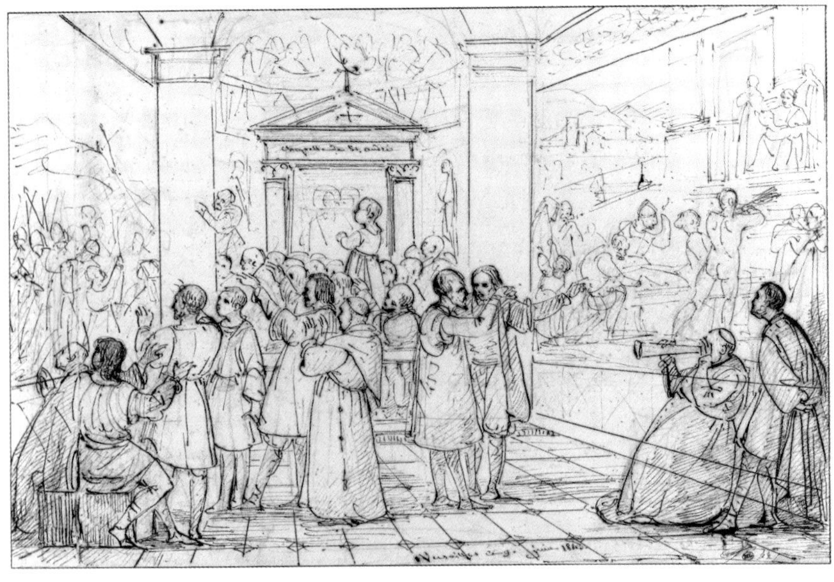

7 François-Marius Granet, 'Public and Poussin in Front of Works by Reni and Domenichino', 1843, pen, brown ink and black pencil.

matters for experts. He called their activities *connaissance et curiosité*, spoke of the necessary qualifications, and with his own assessments of Raphael, Leonardo da Vinci, Nicolas Poussin and other artists also introduced those who did not themselves paint to an appreciation of art.[4] The Apelles problem as to whether laypersons can assess works of art or whether such assessments should be reserved for artists will continue to divide artists, experts, critics and the public. The public assessment was given a boost by Gian Lorenzo Bernini, who visited the Académie royale de peinture et de sculpture on 5 September 1665 and spoke about the teaching of art, copying and advising artists. Asked whether a painter should show his work to the public before it was completed, Bernini replied: 'Annibale Carracci . . . claimed that a painting should be exposed to public criticism immediately on completion, because the public did not delude itself and never flattered nor did it hold back from saying that something was dry or hard, and so on.'[5]

Carracci's claim that public opinion was infallible and unerring was based on the contentious sentence *vox populi vox dei* – voice of the people, voice of god – but Bernini confined the public assessment to secondary aspects. Carracci's view that the purpose of public presentation was to correct mistakes was inspired by Apelles, while Bernini's opinion that Raphael's incomparable compositions benefited from his scholarly friends Pietro Bembo and Baldassare Castiglione raises questions as to how competent the public is to judge.[6]

The question of competence to assess works of art was discussed in France during the seventeenth century by art lovers such as Paul Fréart de Chantelou, who was in the service of Louis XIII, like his brother Roland Fréart de Chambray and their cousin François Sublet de Noyers, the superintendent of the royal buildings. In 1639, the two brothers were sent to Rome to fetch Nicolas Poussin, who was now working as a freelance artist, back into the king's service. After the death of Cardinal Richelieu in 1642, Louis XIII accused Sublet of financial irregularities, leading to his resignation and withdrawal (or banishment?). It is likely that Cardinal Mazarin, Richelieu's successor, managed to get rid of Sublet by intrigue, thereby also removing the court protection for the Fréart brothers.[7] Roland Fréart concentrated on scientific activities, translated Andrea Palladio's theory of architecture, drafted a comparison between antique and modern architecture, had his translation of Leonardo's *Trattato della pittura* (Treatise on Painting) printed in 1651, and in 1662 in Le Mans published his layman's essay on perfection in painting.[8] These writings came out in Normandy and not in the capital and bore the dedication 'Monseigneur Le Duc d'Orléans, frère unique de sa Majesté', indicating the backing of the king's brother, Philippe I of Bourbon. The author hoped that through the mediation of Philippe I of Bourbon, painting, which had been regarded in antiquity as the queen of arts, would have a worthy reception in the court of Louis XIV.[9]

The foreword to *Idée de la perfection de la peinture* contains a criticism of the way painting was talked about and the glorification of the past in contrast to the present decadence and popular judgement:

> There is hardly that man living, but has some inclination for *PAINTING*, and that does not even pretend sufficient abilities to control the *Works* which it produces: for not only *Learned men*, and persons of *Condition*, who are ever probably the most rational, are emulous of this knowledge; but the very *Common People* will adventure to spend their Judgements too; so as it seems, this art is in some sort, the *Universal Mystery*.[10]

Fréart de Chambray makes a concession to the general public but at the same time disparages the interest of the 'common people', calling it interference, as they can only express opinions but are not qualified to make judgements. He was obviously unaware of the Vecchiarella anecdote in Rome. But, he continues, the veneration of antiquity makes it impossible to maintain a general disdain for the common people.

> Neither is this presumption a vice peculiar to the French alone, or of this Age of ours only; 'tis as old as *Painting* itself, and sprung from her very Cradle in *Greece*. This is evident by that which *Pliny* has recorded of *Apelles*; who before he gave the last touches to his *Pieces*, was wont to expose them in *Publique* to the *Censure* of all the *Passengers*, whilst he conceal'd himself behind them, that he might hear what everyone said, and make use of it accordingly; whence the Proverb, *Apelles post Tabulam*.[11]

Fréart de Chambray continues by saying that painters still invite visitors to their studios for their opinion but claims that this is merely a hypocrisy, because if they were to perform this service honestly, the artists would feel insulted, as in truth they only want to hear compliments and flattery.[12] He attributes this to the corruption of artists, who are interested not in mastering their art but in demonstrating their supposed skill. The accusation of dishonesty, pretence and feigned skill is made here by a courtier with first-hand experience of the artificiality and insincerity of courtly behaviour. The suggestion that an artist deceived the public and could be false and fraudulent was transported in this way from the court to the art world and could be used thereafter as a cheap way of discrediting artists.

Fréart de Chambray compared his corrupt contemporaries with the noble artists of antiquity, who presented their works not only to philosophers and scholars but to the common people, and accepted criticism even from artisans.[13] Painters of his day, by contrast, were neither geniuses as in olden times nor did they seek fame and immortality, but rather abandoned their ideals and favoured *peinture libertine* or frivolous painting. Chambray locates one of the causes of the decadence and corruption of painting in his own class of 'gens de lettres & de condition', educated and respectable people:

> Even *Painting* itself, whose *diminution* and *decadency* we so much deplore, and which seems not to have been born for times of Peace and Tranquility, was happily never in higher esteem amongst us, not more sought after than it is at present; which may partly be the occasion of its Corruption and decay.[14]

Artists, says the author, are spoiled by the blind adulation and exaggerated flattery but above all by the growing demand. As a remedy, he recommends that his principles be followed, but Nicolas Poussin, to whom he sent a copy of his book in Rome, politely disagreed.[15]

Fréart de Chambray respects the public of antiquity but accuses the contemporary public of interfering in art matters. The ignorant conceit of *gens de lettres et conditions* is evident, because how could the common people have spoken about art and how could Fréart de Chambray have heard about it? The presumed attitude of the ignorant masses to art is a pure fiction employed by a provincial aristocrat and his like-minded contemporaries to set themselves apart. Fréart de Chambray's brother, Paul Fréart de Chantelou, who had a significant painting collection, kept a diary during a visit by Gian Lorenzo Bernini in Paris, which reveals something of the accessibility of art collections.[16]

Like Fréart de Chambray, Roger de Piles, also a provincial aristocrat, evokes the primacy of art experts.[17] He studied philosophy and theology and attended painting courses. For his treatise on expertise, he presents a fictional public, which includes Pamphile, who has some knowledge; Damon, who can distinguish painting styles; and the author.[18] Thus the first conversation is conducted by an expert, an art lover and a scholar. For the second conversation he adds a further three persons to this exclusive group. After a lengthy discussion, the group views the collection of the Duc de Richelieu, and the conversation continues in front of the pictures. Roger de Piles first describes a private discussion and then offers a gallery conversation. Damon arranges to meet Pamphile, bringing his friends Caliste and Leonidas with him. They are joined by Philarches, who has just returned from England and has already met Caliste and Leonidas in Rome and Venice. They each present their cases. The numismatist Caliste insists on the primacy of antiquity, Leonidas presents the dispute about colour and drawing, and Pamphile opposes the critics of drawing in the paintings. The group of non-artists agree on a presumptuous claim, which the experts then refer to: 'The spectator is not obliged to have the same knowledge as the painter and need only rely on his common sense to judge what he sees.'[19]

The comparison between sculpture and painting is continued with the familiar arguments until Damon proposes a visit to the collection belonging to the Duc de Richelieu, whose expertise he highly praises. Then the group goes to Place Royale (now Place des Vosges, probably no. 21), where they are granted access to the collection, because Pamphile had been of service to the duke with a description of paintings by Peter Paul Rubens.[20] The discussion of artistic problems is not continued in the exhibition rooms; the group is distracted by the life of St George and only returns to Rubens, whom Philarches knew, at the subsequent reception.[21]

In discussion, the public cannot reach agreement on questions of aesthetics and art theory. The point being made is that, unlike the textbook, the function of dialogue in art theory has always been to question authority and decisions.

In *Réflexions critiques*, the scholar Abbé Jean-Baptiste Dubos bases an understanding of art on sensitivity – *sentiment* – the instinctive feeling that all people possess, and attributes to poetry and painting the ability to touch (*toucher*).[22] This sounds at first as if the distinction between different types of art recipients is being abolished. Dubos claims that the public can judge poetry and painting well and without self-interest. But his 'public' is not the masses or the 'common people' but people with education and distinction, in other words *les gens de lettres et de condition*:

> The word 'public' includes only those who are enlightened either by reading or world knowledge. They are the only ones capable of recognizing the status of poems and paintings, although it can happen that outstanding works possess a beauty that can be felt and applauded by common people.[23]

This point of view is taken up by the writer Friedrich Gottlieb Klopstock in Hamburg in 1758. His attitude to the public and its competence to judge art uses almost exactly the same wording as part 2, section 22, of Dubos' *Réflexions critiques*.[24] Klopstock makes a distinction between the public 'that merits this great name' and the 'broad mass' and its claim also 'to belong to the *publico*'. Once again, an invented 'presumptuousness' of the masses serves uncritically to distinguish different publics. There are fewer members of this limited public than might be expected, and furthermore the public for the fine arts and sciences is different from the scholar public. It is made even more exclusive through the use of the term 'true public', which according to Klopstock is made up of judges (of art) and experts, while all others belong to the 'large mass', which out of ignorance is always on the wrong side. 'Judges' are capable of defining the principles underlying beauty and of demonstrating reliable taste. Experts, on the other hand, have stood still 'in the practical exercise of their innate ability to consider taste' and must bow to the conclusions of those capable of judging. Klopstock sketches the usual way in which a new work is received. The judges embark on an assessment, a few experts give their opinion, and the ignorant masses almost always condemn it. The true public ignores the presumptuousness of these hundred minor censors, and an increasing number of judges and experts appear whose judgements are disseminated 'in good society'. The writer is rewarded and the large mass who still criticize become an intellectually 'insignificant pile of panegyric copiers'.[25] However, 'the taste of a nation must be fully formed'; otherwise the process of recognition takes longer.

In spite of the gradual opening of galleries and collections, the attitude of artists and experts in France remained unchanged with regard to the public, whose main problems were access to art and their credentials for judging it. In 1747, Charles-Antoine Coypel, 'first painter of the king', published a dialogue about the Salon between the fictional characters Dorsicour and Celigni. Dorsicour wishes first to do away with the preconceptions associated with name and distinction. The question of publications that disseminate judgements and opinions prompts him to criticize the public and those who presume to speak on its behalf:

> But Celigni, you must agree that in these little works the writer seeks to present himself as a competent judge by humbly but falsely claiming to speak on behalf of the public. The great Corneille used to ask where the public was. I would venture to

> say that in the Salon where the paintings are exhibited the public changes twenty times a day. What the public admires at 10 o'clock in the morning will be publicly criticized at noon. I tell you, in a single day this place can offer you twenty publics of different character and mood. A simple public at certain times, and this public should not be listened to less for all that: a biased public, an easy public, an envious public, a public slave to fresh air that in order to decide wants to see everything and does not look closely at anything.[26]

Coypel is extremely sceptical of crowds, who he believes rush to exhibitions, loudly proclaim their opinions, then moderate their tone with time and become more reasonable. This was the case with the plays by Racine and Molière, which were disapproved of by the masses but rescued by a more understanding public. The masses judge wrongly and are mistaken, and only experts are capable of judging. Celigni defends his reference to the pamphlets with the argument that he is describing only an exclusive group of five or six 'true' experts as the public.

5

# SENSATIONAL ATTRACTIONS

When lots of people go to visit a work of art or a miraculous image and draw in others in this way, it becomes an attraction, and the class differences disappear in the crowd. There are few early reports of such attractions. One example is the large and widely known altarpiece by the brothers Hubert and Jan van Eyck in Ghent.[1] The work, made up of multiple panels, was installed in 1432 in the chapel of St John the Baptist, renamed St Bavo in 1540 and transformed into a cathedral in 1559. On the frame is a Latin inscription identifying Hubert and Jan van Eyck as the artists and Jodocus Vijd as the person commissioning the altarpiece, but not his wife, Lysbette Borluut. The assessment, dating and interpretation of the inscription are contested. Some say that it dates to 1432 and that the inscription is an invitation to the public to admire the work: 'Versu sexta Mai vos collocat acta tueri' (With this verse he calls on you to gaze at this work). Others put the date of the inscription at the end of the sixteenth century and understand *tueri* as 'defend', arguing that the altar in the church tower and then in the town hall should be defended from iconoclasts.[2] But neither of these interpretations explains the date, 6 May, or the encrypted year 1432.[3] Whichever interpretation is preferred, the public is invited to do something with the work, namely *tueri* – admire or defend.[4]

The court public in the 1430s was able to see the life-size portrait of the donor on the outside of the altarpiece, the artistically painted stone statues, above them the grey-brown chamber with the Annunciation to Mary by the Archangel Gabriel, both in billowing white robes, and in the upper register the prophets and prophetesses. The panels open to reveal the resplendent Garden of Eden with Adam and Eve coyly hiding their nakedness.[5] The altarpiece was closed again after the mass. It was reconstructed for public viewing in a *tableau vivant* outdoors on the occasion of the entry into Ghent of Duke Philip the Good on 23 April 1458, as reported by the *Kronyk van Vlaenderen*.[6]

In 1606, the painter and writer Carel van Mander wrote in his *Schilder-Boeck* about access to the altarpiece. Grand and munificent gentlemen were allowed private viewings, while the public were only admitted on high holidays, when people came in large numbers to the chapel:

> This outstanding work was only opened and shown occasionally to grand gentlemen or if someone gave the doorkeeper a good tip. It was also shown sometimes on certain high holidays. The public crowded to see it to such an extent that it was almost impossible to get close, because the chapel where it could be seen was full throughout the day with all kinds of people. Painters young and old and all art lovers thronged around the picture, just as bees and flies cluster around fig and grape baskets seeking their sweetness.[7]

The first description of the altarpiece is provided by the Nuremberg humanist, doctor and geographer Hieronymus Münzer, who arrived in Ghent in late March 1495 during his travels through Western Europe. His report mentions the precious painting and the persons and scenes represented.[8] Albrecht Dürer visited Ghent in 1521 and noted in his diary the honourable reception, the good food and the view from the tower of the church of St John the Baptist. Finally, he praised the altarpiece: 'Afterwards I saw the Jan [van Eyck] picture, which is a very splendid, deeply studied painting, and especially the "Eve", the "Mary" and "God the Father" were very good.'[9] But Dürer attached greater importance to the honourable receptions by notables and many colleagues and people in Antwerp, Bruges and Ghent and the good food, meticulously noting all of his expenditures and receipts.[10] By 1521, the renown of Dutch painting had spread beyond the German-speaking world to northern and central Italy. In connection with their commercial and banking relations with the Netherlands, princely collectors became more and more interested in works by Flemish painters. In 1456 the scholar Bartolomeo Facio wrote in *De viris illustribus* (Concerning Illustrious Men) about four famous painters, the Flemish artists Jan van Eyck and Rogier van der Weyden and the Italians Gentile da Fabriano and Pisanello.[11]

There are reports of the great public acclaim given to Gian Lorenzo Bernini's group *Apollo and Daphne* in Rome in 1624 and to Jacques-Louis David's painting *Oath of the Horatii* in Rome in 1786. The descriptions of this public fascination are probably exaggerated, even in the knowledge of the great enthusiasm for art in cities such as Rome after the sixteenth century, which extended beyond the educated classes and the nobility to other segments of the population.

Crowds gathered everywhere for various reasons: in Rome for papal benedictions, in Florence for Medici festivals, in the European courts for many celebrations, and in London, Vienna or Leipzig for public executions.[12] Ambrogio Brambilla made an engraving of the papal benediction on St Peter's Square to celebrate the victory at the Battle of Lepanto in 1571. An interesting feature of the representations of these events is the need that was felt to include armed sentries keeping the crowds in check. Brambilla shows riders

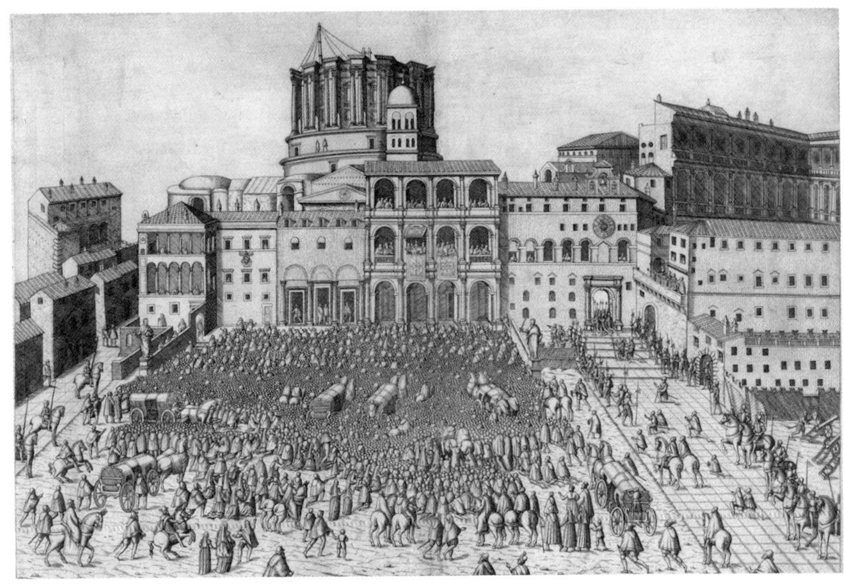

8 Ambrogio Brambilla (attr.), *Speculum Romanae Magnificentiae: Papal Benediction*, late 16th century, engraving.

with lances and guards with halberds on St Peter's Square. In the foreground are a number of men and women seen from the back and then circles to denote the countless heads. Four horse-drawn carts are stuck in the crowd. Brambilla gives an idea of how a mass gathering in Rome was perceived.

There is no contemporary report confirming the attraction of Bernini's *Apollo and Daphne* (illus. 9). Cardinal Scipione Borghese commissioned the work immediately after Bernini had completed the sculpture *The Rape of Proserpina*.[13] Daphne's pursuit by Apollo is known from Ovid's *Metamorphoses* and many pictures. Apollo defeats a swollen python with his giant bow and mocks Cupid for his tiny bow, whereupon Cupid shoots a golden arrow at Apollo and a lead one at the nymph Daphne. The golden arrow makes Apollo fall in love and pursue Daphne, while the lead arrow makes her repulse the god. Before she is caught, her father, the river god Peneus, transforms her into a laurel tree, which Apollo acquires.[14] Ovid commences this story of vanity, revenge, pursuit, flight, transformation and empowerment with Cupid's mockery by Apollo.

In his 1682 biography of Bernini, dedicated to Christina, former Queen of Sweden, the Florentine scholar Filippo Baldinucci gives an insight into the enthusiastic reception of an art miracle, a *miracolo dell'arte*: 'As for Bernini's Daphne, I can only say that as soon as it was completed and displayed there was such clamour that all of Rome rushed to admire this miracle.'[15] Baldinucci goes on to say that wherever Bernini, not yet eighteen years old (in reality he was 26), went in the city he was followed and admired as a wonder by young and old alike. Bernini shows Apollo running and standing still at the same time: the left leg is raised, the right leg on the ground, his left arm embraces Daphne's body, while his right arm is swinging freely in step with his left leg. Daphne is pulling away from him, her left leg already transformed into marbled wood, the other leg moving parallel to Apollo's raised leg. Daphne's upper body is turned away to escape Apollo, and she stretches out her hands, already transformed into laurel leaves.

But did Bernini's miraculous work really create such a clamour that all of Rome rushed to see it? Baldinucci was born in Florence a year after this sensation in Rome, and his report was written over fifty years after the event. We do not know who told him about the sensation and its effect on the young Bernini. In reality, the Romans were relatively indifferent to Bernini's *Apollo and Daphne*. Filippo de' Rossi's guide to Rome, *Ritratto di Roma*, in 1652 makes no mention of it, and Giovan Pietro Bellori includes it briefly in his 1664 list of Roman collections, but makes no mention of Bernini in his main work, *Le vite* of 1672.[16] Were Romans at the time unmoved by Bernini's work, particularly after the loss of patronage following the death of Urban VIII?[17]

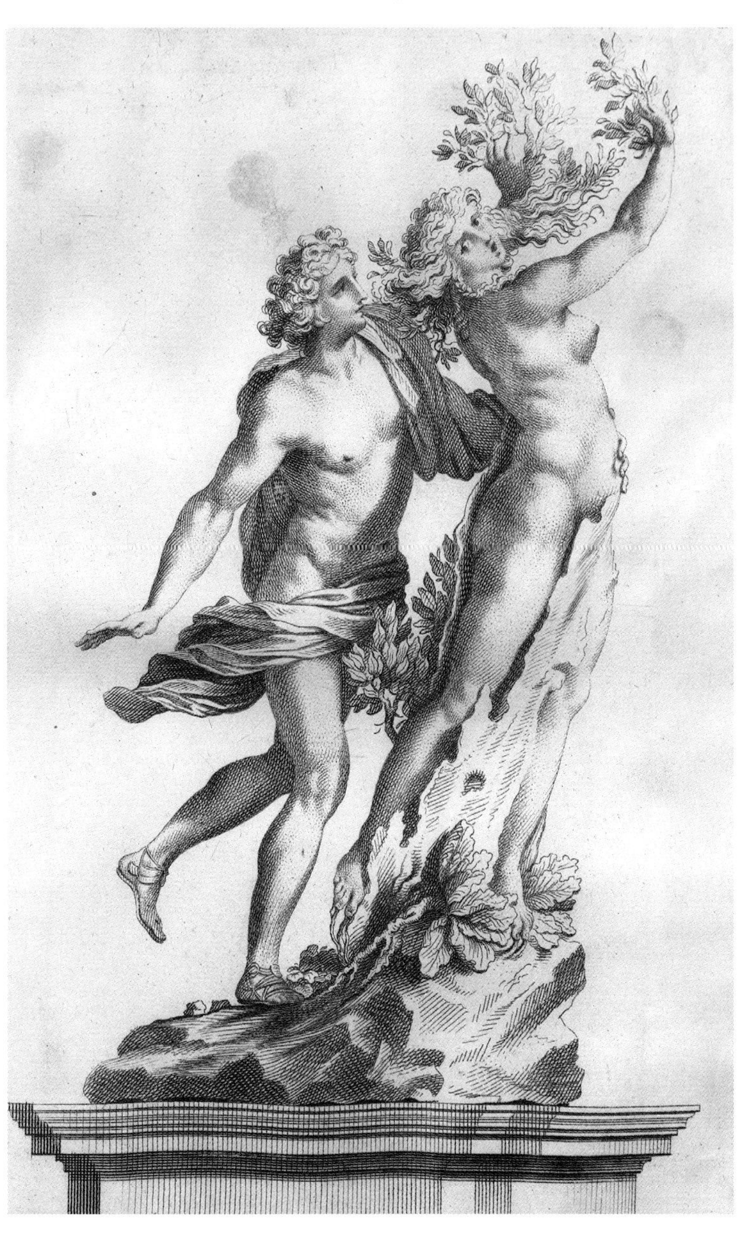

9 Gian Lorenzo Bernini, *Apollo and Daphne*, 1624, engraving in Domenico de Rossi and Paolo Alessandro Maffei, *Raccolta di statue antiche e moderne* (1704).

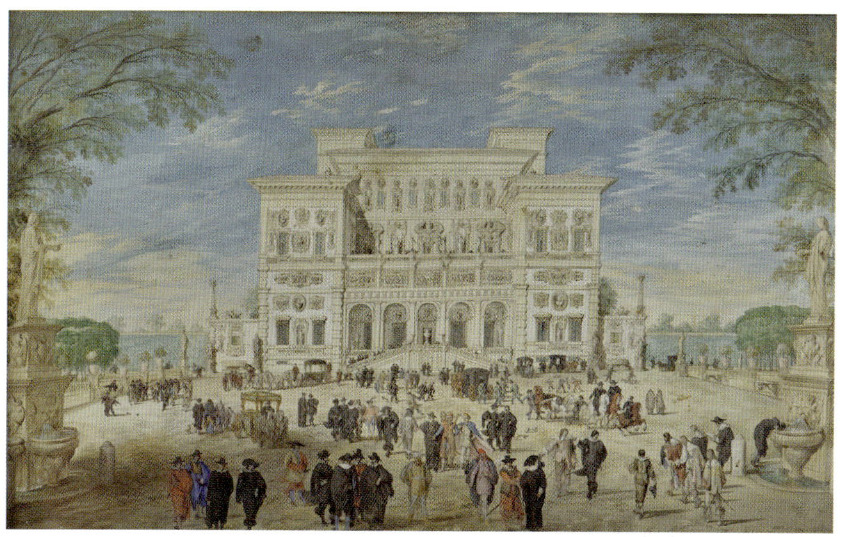

10 Johann Wilhelm Baur, *View of Villa Borghese*, 1636, tempera on parchment.

It was not until the publication of Baldinucci's monograph that the guide to Rome by Pier Vincenzo and Michelangelo Rossi in 1708 drew attention to the quality of Bernini's work in Villa Borghese, extolling the 'artificio mirabile' (wonderful artistry) and 'maggior industria' (outstanding skill) of the artist's *Apollo and Daphne*.[18] The view of Villa Borghese (illus. 10) by Johann Wilhelm Baur in 1636 shows the crowd assembling on the large square in carriages, on horseback and on foot. There are only men, from all countries, some doffing their hats and bowing to the noblemen, evidently 'grand tourists': wealthy travellers to Italy from England and the Netherlands in particular, élite visitors to the country and its art treasures.[19] The 'common people' are represented by coachmen and grooms looking after the horses. The gardener has placed an edict in Latin, as an invitation and warning to visitors, on the gateway of the entrance to the gardens, which Wölfflin reproduced in 1888:

> [I], guardian of the Villa Borghese/ On the Pincio declare:/ Whoever you may be, if free,/ Fear here no regulations./ Go where you wish, pluck what you wish,/ And stay indeed as long as you wish./ This garden is intended more for strangers than for the master of the house./ In a golden age, when peaceful times/ Have made all things seem golden,/ The owner declines to post up rules:/ Let your goodwill be here the friendly law./ Yet, if someone deceitfully,/ wilfully, knowingly/ Breaks the golden laws of courtesy,/ Let him beware lest a displeased gardener/ Withdraws the token of his friendship.[20]

Filippo de' Rossi's guide to Rome in 1652 encouraged visitors to see the wonderful Villa Borghese as 'una delle maraviglie del Mondo' (one of the wonders of the world) but failed to mention Bernini's sculptures.[21] Perhaps Bernini, who died world famous in 1680 at the age of 82, invented the sensational public acclaim in 1624 for his biographer. 'Grido' (cry) recalls the caprices of fame in Dante's *Divine Comedy*, Purgatory XI, verses 94–6: while Cimabue thought that he still held sway in painting, Giotto was the talk of the town, the 'cry', a term that covers rumour, gossip, acclaim and fame. Baldinucci writes in detail of Bernini's interest in the public, and his stupendous inventions for the theatre that amazed, deceived or frightened audiences with their artificial devices and machines. His most humorous invention was to duplicate the audience in a second room, so that the real audience was confronted by a fake mirror image of itself.[22]

A few years before Bernini's appearance in Rome, the inspired engraver Hendrick Goltzius completed a picture of the colossal statue *Hercules Farnese* (illus. 11) installed in the courtyard of Palazzo Farnese. It shows the statue from behind with two spectators at its feet looking up in admiration. The torso was found without head and

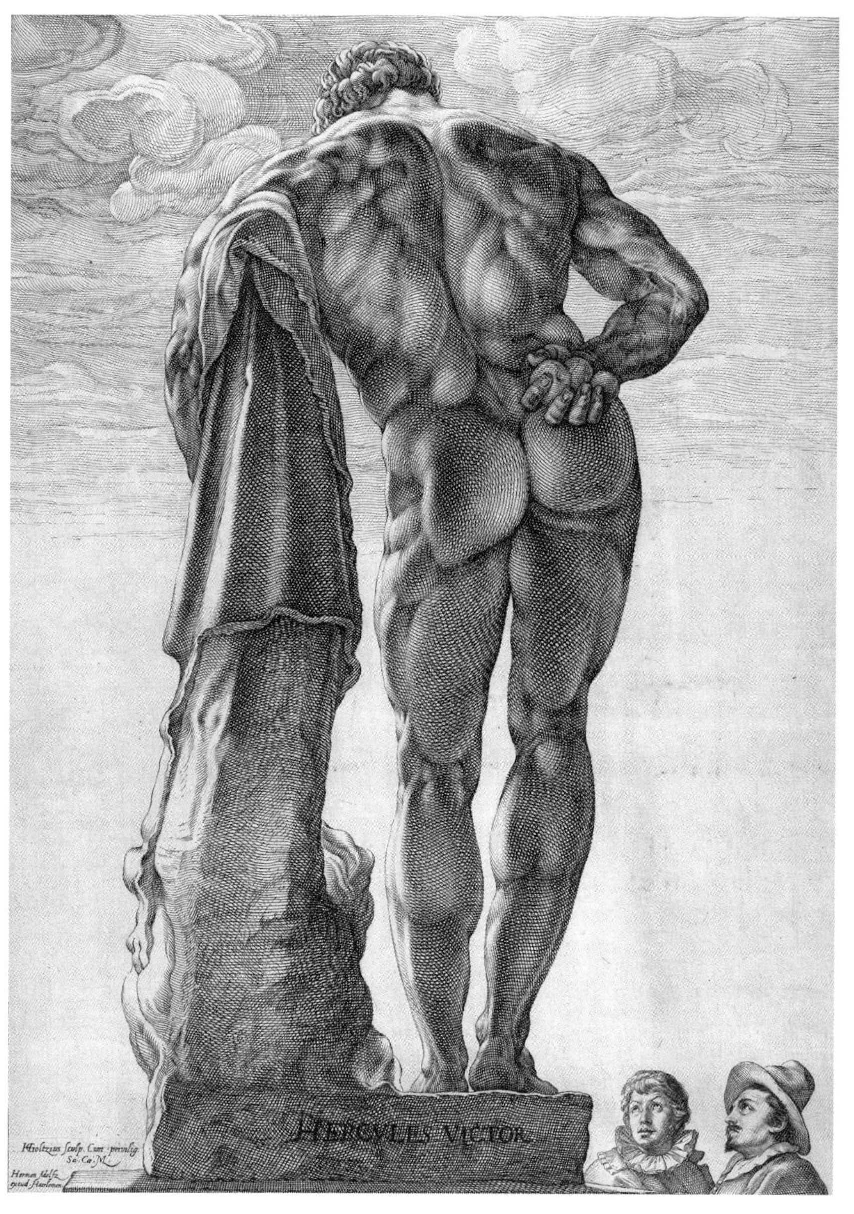


11 Hendrick Goltzius, *Hercules Farnese*, c. 1592, engraving dated 1617.

feet in 1546 in the Baths of Caracalla and subsequently completed by Guglielmo della Porta, an assistant of Michelangelo.[23] Goltzius shows the back of the restored statue backlit from below, with the head in the clouds and the eye level in line with the pedestal, so that only the head and chest of the observers can be seen.[24] They are much smaller than the statue, and the position of their heads and their gaze is reminiscent of the saints who, as in Raphael's *Ecstasy of St Cecilia* (1515–16), gaze upwards in rapture.[25] In Goltzius's engraving, the tiny representations of the present day, in the form of his companions Jan Matthijs Ban and Philips van Winghe, look up at the might of antiquity.[26]

Goltzius shows the admiration of the colossus with two people from the art milieu. According to Baldinucci, a crowd of indeterminate size and composition came to see Bernini's miracle work, driven to *Apollo and Daphne* by curiosity, emulation and jealousy, manufacturing the sensation through their infectious curiosity, which encouraged others to come and see it. As we can see from Baldinucci's description, the fact that a work attracts large crowds increases its reputation immensely.

A German artist reported in Germany on the astonishing sensation caused by a French painting in Rome, and the painter himself did the same in France. The report by Johann Heinrich Tischbein on the presentation of *Oath of the Horatii* (illus. 12) by Jacques-Louis David in his studio in Rome appeared in the first quarter of 1786 in the magazine *Der Teutsche Merkur*, and was published by Christoph Martin under the title 'Briefe aus Rom, über neue Kunstwerke jeztlebender Künstler' ('Letters from Rome, about New Works by Contemporary Artists'). It was the third letter in a series that began in 1785 with a report on Angelica Kauffmann and continued with an essay on landscape painting in Rome.[27] The third letter, dated February 1786, reported on the sensational public interest in David's large painting exhibited in 1785 in his studio in Casa Costanzi not far from Piazza del Popolo in Rome.[28] Tischbein described the general interest in the new painting, stating explicitly that it attracted not only 'artists, art lovers and experts but also droves of "common people"'. He also attempted to compare the collective behaviour of the different nationalities.

Tischbein, who was born in Hesse in 1751 as the son of a joiner, visited Rome for the first time in 1779. During a further visit he met Jacques-Louis David, who arrived there in October 1784, after having spent five years on a scholarship from 1775 to 1780.[29] In his recollections, Tischbein describes a visit to David's studio and the 'ice-cold shower' that the painting triggered.[30] He wrote

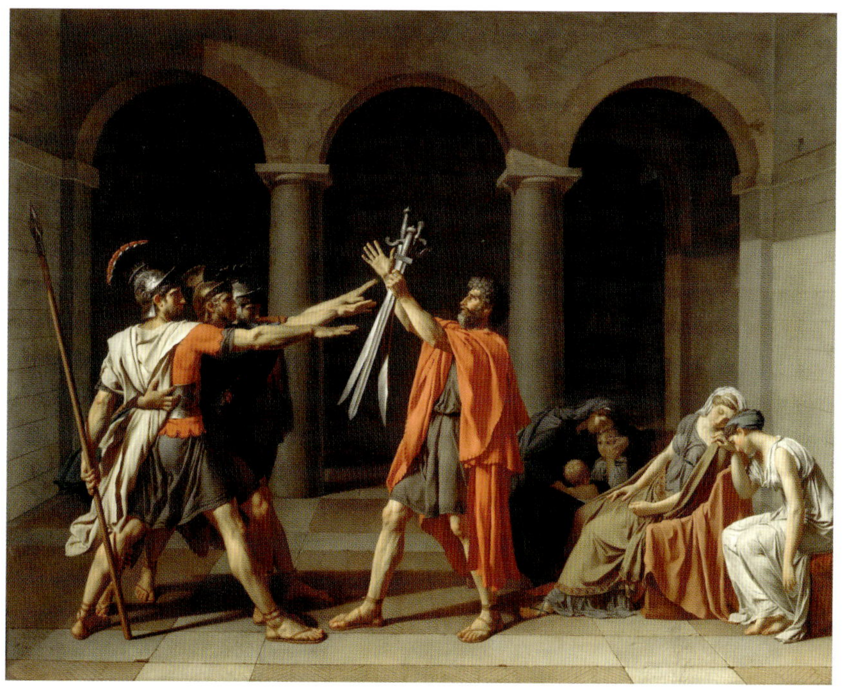

12 Jacques-Louis David, *Oath of the Horatii,* 1784, oil on canvas.

enthusiastically of the sensation caused when David opened his studio to the public and then withdrew, as Apelles had done:

> If ever a picture caused a sensation, this was it. People flocked in procession for several days. The nobility travelled there to see it; cardinals and prelates, monsignori and priests, burghers and workers, all made their way there. As all Romans are used from their youth to seeing pictures in churches, they develop a certain taste. The people met in taverns. Some said: 'The picture is better than Raphael'; others 'It bears no comparison with Raphael.' Inflamed by the wine, they would fight and stab with daggers. Educated and non-educated, academics and non-academics, experts and non-experts disputed the value of the picture.[31]

Tischbein emphasized the fiery enthusiasm of the public in Rome, including the common people, whose good taste and judgement are explicitly mentioned. The painter from Germany was amazed at the partisan passion:

> Not only artists, art lovers and experts but also the common people troop from morning to evening to see the painting. The enthusiasm is widespread. People are called on to take sides, whether they want to or not, and no one is allowed to have an opinion of his own. The plain judgement that good is good and mediocre is mediocre doesn't apply here. The people either praise something to the sky or imperiously reject it as the most wretched thing. And it is one or the other of these judgements of David's three Horatii that is heard in society, in coffeehouses, and on the streets.

Tischbein concludes with a remark about the 'extraordinary ferment' that the painting produced among the people in Rome and predicts that it will be no different in Paris:

> The opinions of the public here are strange, and nothing is more diverse than the opinions of those who, as artists or art lovers, lay claim to the highest seat of judgement. The French artists and their factions will rush to praise the three Horatii over anything that has ever been done in modern times.[32]

In a letter of 8 August 1785 to the Marquis de Bièvre, David reported on the great interest in Rome in his painting:

> I should like to inform you, honourable marquis, of the unexpected success of my painting, not least as the people of Rome have difficulty in acknowledging any merit in French painters. But this time they proved generous, and the throngs of people who came to see my painting were almost as numerous as those coming to see the comedy *Le Séducteur* [The Seducer].[33] As an admirer of my work, you would have enjoyed being here, and I owe you at least a description. It started with the foreign artists, then the Italians, whose excessive praise attracted the attention of the nobility, who came in large numbers. All Rome is talking of nothing but the French painter and the Horatii. I have an appointment this morning with the Venetian Ambassador. The cardinals want to see this rare animal and are all coming to visit me, and as it is known that the painting will be leaving soon, everyone is hurrying to see it.[34]

The artist described the enthusiastic public in Rome while noting the social hierarchy, starting at the bottom with French artist acquaintances, then Italian colleagues, then the nobility, then the Venetian envoy, then the cardinals, with only the top of the pyramid missing, but of course the pope could not visit an artist in his studio. This only became possible with Canova and Thorvaldsen. David's impressions of the public and its interest in his picture differ from Tischbein's in that there is no mention of the burghers and workers. Tischbein offers a selective description for the educated readers in Germany, while David's description is tailored to the recipient, a member of the middle French aristocracy.

In 1800, David published a leaflet on the occasion of the exhibition of his huge painting *The Intervention of the Sabine Women* in the Louvre, in response to the accusation of exorbitant enrichment and greed.[35] The painter justified himself by pointing to the tradition of exhibitions in antiquity and the recent examples of Benjamin West and John Singleton Copley in England. David claimed that it was an artist's natural right to stage an exhibition against payment and it was something that benefited everyone. In the first place, it gave the artist freedom and autonomy, making him independent of princely or ecclesiastical commissions. Second, he repeated the Apelles–Alberti argument that the artist can learn from the public. Third, the admission fee protected artists from poverty and prostitution and art from privatization and export. And finally, the revenue from an exhibition was no less honourable than the fees paid to poets and musicians. David paid tribute to the public and assured it of his highest respect:

> I myself know no greater honour than to be judged by the public. I do not fear either passion or partisanship. The rewards are the voluntary contributions demonstrating the public's taste for art. Its praise is a free expression of the pleasure it

> experiences, and such rewards certainly outweigh those from the time of the Academy.[36]

David's prostration before the public is somewhat suspicious, all the more so as he insists that the most flattering reward for him is to see the public lining up to enjoy his painting and to encourage young artists to imitate him in the interests of progress in art and raising morale. But there was also the matter of freedom from dependence on the court and submission to the public, as in the cases of Asmus Jakob Carstens, who felt answerable only to humanity and God, and Friedrich Schiller, who, as a 'citizen of the world', recognized only the public as addressee and sole judge.[37]

An informative document explaining David's admiring public is provided by Louis-Léopold Boilly with the painting *The Public Viewing David's 'Coronation' at the Louvre.*[38] Most of the numerous

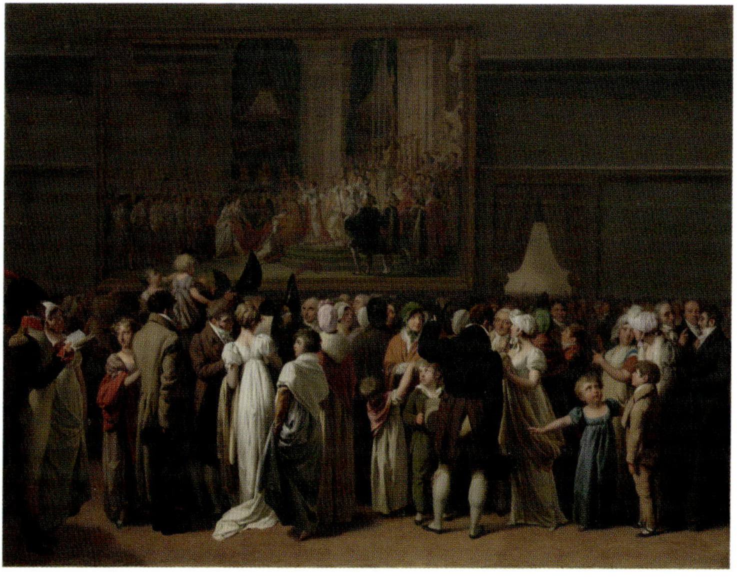

13 Louis-Léopold Boilly, *The Public Viewing David's 'Coronation' at the Louvre*, 1810, oil on canvas.

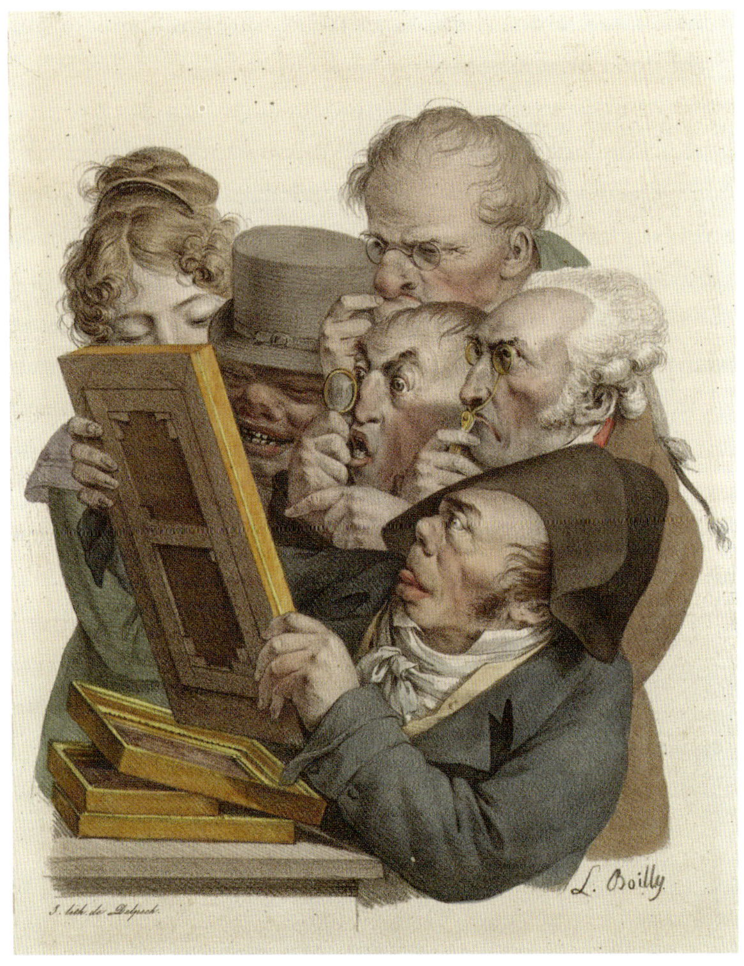


14 Louis-Léopold Boilly, *The Picture Enthusiasts*, 1823, hand-coloured lithograph.

spectators are shown from behind. The man on the left in profile is holding a catalogue with the key plate and is telling his partner and a young woman turning round the names of the persons portrayed in the painting. The woman in the white dress and her partner are also studying the key plate, while a male figure painted from behind is pointing in explanation with his index finger. A young woman is making an inquisitive gesture with her finger, as is a young girl in a blue dress looking up to a somewhat older boy. A group of men, among them the artist, are gathered on the far right. Two children are lifted up to see David's huge depiction of the ceremony in Notre Dame and hats are doffed in greeting, as if the painted characters were present in person. There is no trace in this painting of Boilly's tendency to caricature the public, as is the case in his depictions in 1819 of men and women fighting to enter a theatre or the densely packed crowds in a theatre atrium in the late 1820s. His lithograph *The Picture Enthusiasts* (illus. 14) from the 1820s makes fun of art lovers. Six heads are pressed close together, the two hat-wearers extremely ugly, particularly in contrast to the female face, whose beauty can only be imagined from the bridge of the nose upwards. Then there are the magnifying glass and spectacles as ridiculous accessories. Curiously, the object of the onlookers' enthusiasm cannot be seen. Boilly's extensive collection of caricatures, *Recueil des Grimaces* (Collection of Grimaces), to which this sheet belongs, contains heads and distorted physiognomies repeated and transformed scores of times.[39]

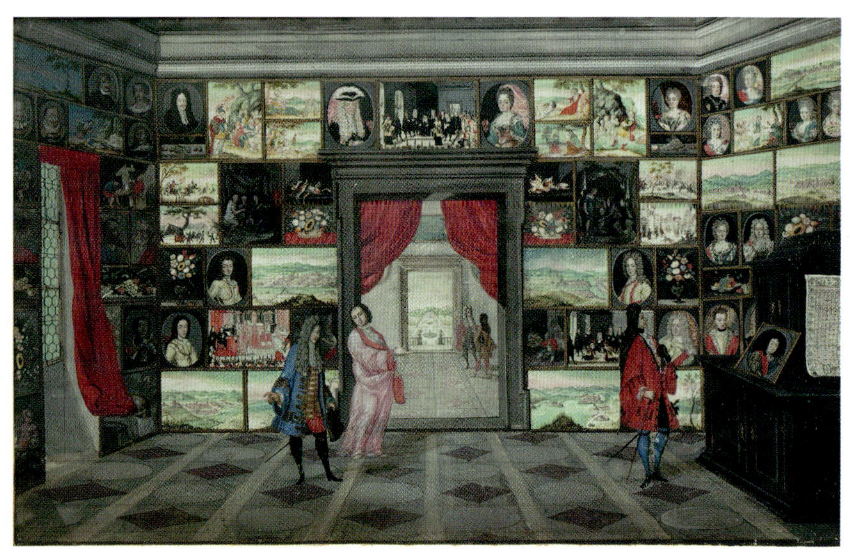

15 Anonymous, *Aristocratic Visitors in the Gallery of Prince Eugene in Belvedere Palace, Vienna*, 18th century, gouache on parchment, mounted on wood panel.

# 6

# ENJOYMENT, EDUCATION AND ENLIGHTENMENT

Elements of the increasing pressure in the wake of the Enlightenment in the eighteenth century to open princely collections to a wider public than just the nobility and academic world are known.[1] A panel from Vienna (illus. 15) illustrates the exclusive access to a gallery. In the first room, the host welcomes an elegantly dressed visitor while a second visitor admires the paintings. As was usual at the time, the paintings are arranged symmetrically on the wall by genre in line with the curtained entrance. The portraits are genealogical documents, and the city views have commercial, courtly or military themes. From the entrance room, where there are two further visitors of rank, the expansive grounds can be seen. The inscription on the back of the panel says: 'Watercolour, purchased in Berlin 1859 (G. Fr. d'a) showing a picture gallery in the Belvedere (palace of Prince Eugene of Savoy) during his lifetime'.[2] It is thus supposed to be showing part of the collection of the renowned Prince Eugene of Savoy, but it could well be an imaginary princely collection with noble visitors, to whom the owner wishes to reveal his treasures so as to be admired for his wealth and expertise.[3] Under Maria Theresa, the hitherto private imperial art collections in the palace of the prince, who died in 1736, were gradually opened to the public.[4] In spite of the wealth of literature on museums in Vienna, little is known about the access to them and their opening hours.[5] The opening of private art collections and cabinets of curiosities while retaining property rights and title was presented to subjects as an act of gracious condescension and lauded by them. In 1787, a catalogue was published of the works in the Munich Hofgartengalerie, written by the first director, the 'wirklicher churfürstlicher Hofkammerrath etc.' [the real electoral court chamber councillor], Joseph Nepomuk Edler von Weizenfeld, who in the foreword addressed to his 'most venerable friends' expressed his most humble gratitude to the prince:

> Never can we express our gratitude worthily to our most serene prince for his noble and truly paternal nobility of spirit, sparing no costs to collect these most precious examples, offering free access to anyone who wishes to learn about the first masters and to enable his children to benefit from the good deeds that our fathers never enjoyed.[6]

The supporters of the Enlightenment in France and Germany exerted pressure by denouncing the privatization of works in princely collections as a violation of the common good and the human right to share art.

*Tempel der Kunst*, published in 2015, a collection of essays on the early period of public museums in Germany, discusses the conditions for access to the newly opened galleries. In the eighteenth century, access to galleries and collections was still restricted everywhere, so that talk of public museums may at best be seen as an intention and a requirement. For example, wealthy travellers, artists and prominent personalities, from Denis Diderot and Joshua Reynolds to the Humboldt brothers, were able to visit the picture gallery in Dusseldorf.[7] Access was a favour by the prince and not a public right. The opening hours were limited everywhere, and in the winter months a picture gallery like the one in Dresden, for example, remained closed. The visitor regulations for the Königl. Gallerie der Wissenschaft [Royal Gallery of Science] in Dresden in 1718 are among the first of their type, but there were still none for the picture gallery, although it received visitors, who paid an admission fee and took part in the guided tour, which was subject to a charge, by the gallery inspector.[8] Artists were offered free admission practically everywhere to study or copy the works, but the young Johann Joachim Winckelmann was also granted unimpeded access through the gallery inspector's secret entrance.

In 1699 the general intendant and protector of the Académie royale in Paris wrote that he had expressed to the king the desire of the members to reintroduce the old tradition of exhibiting their works so as to determine the opinion of the public and to cultivate among the artists themselves the commendable competition so necessary for the advancement of the fine arts. At the same time, the members of the Académie listened only to the opinion of selected *amateurs honoraires*, and they bowed only to the *public éclairé*.[9] Louis XIV graciously allowed the exhibition of works in the Grande Gallerie of the Louvre and gave instructions for its decoration with precious tapestries and other ornamentations, with the inclusion of François Girardon's bust of Alexander the Great. Fréart de Chambray's suspicion, mentioned earlier, that artists expected only praise and flattery as thanks for their attention to the public is confirmed by a report on the Salon in *Mercure galant* which stressed the advantages compared with the earlier presentation of works for one day in the courtyard of the Louvre and at the same time also highlighted the superiority of the French nation. The *peuple* were not the common people, but those members of the public privileged by being ennobled or educated: 'The people have shown through their support the pleasure afforded by the exhibition of so many masterpieces, which are admired by foreigners, and they are all agreed that only France is capable of producing such marvels.'[10]

The *Livrets du Salon* in Paris around the middle of the eighteenth century show how the Académie royale de peinture et de sculpture flattered the educated public and complied with its demands. The 1742 *Livret* stresses first the advantages of noble competition among artists and then the importance of *le public éclairé*: 'Just as the approval of an enlightened public confirms the true value of all genres of work, the [artist's] reputation is formed by this collective approval.'[11] It goes on to say that there is no better way of enabling the public to form a fair opinion than the exhibition of works permitting a comparison. For the Salon of 1751, the public waited with extreme impatience for the publication of the *Livret* with the descriptions and explanations of the works. A new hanging arrangement was planned, the works were numbered, and the *Livret* with the numbered paintings published in time for the opening.

The Grand Tour of the Continent was designed to refine the artistic taste of the offspring of the English nobility and wealthy citizens. The young men usually had companions of their own rank, and from the seventeenth century onwards they also had printed travel guides at their disposal. The English were followed by the Dutch, French, German and Swiss, who undertook such educational tours until the nineteenth century.[12] The Grand Tourists, who required horses, servants, food and lodging, and guides, became an important special artistic public in Italy.

Among the printed travel guides used by the English for orientation, the two-volume *Voyage of Italy* published posthumously in 1670 in London and Paris by the priest Richard Lassels was particularly popular. It provided information on the character of the Italian people and a guided tour of the cities and their architectural sites and offered practical travel information.[13] The second volume had detailed descriptions of the buildings in Rome. For Villa Borghese, the author notes its location outside the city, the grounds with the trees, grottos and statues, and then the villa itself, with a description of the exterior and the great hall with its statues and paintings. He wrote detailed comments on the works of Gian Lorenzo Bernini and described his sculpture *Apollo and Daphne* (see illus. 9) as follows: 'The statue also of Daphne, and Apollo in alabaster; Apollo running after Daphne, and she stiffening into a tree being overtaken: her fingers shooting into branches, and her toes into roots, are admirably well done. It must be Bernini's work.'[14]

The brief description, which is wrong about the material, gives the names and the subject and emphasizes the artist's great skill. This information guides the visitor's perception, helps to form a consensus and enriches the conversation of the returning travellers. The author writes about Santa Maria del Popolo and the buildings on the Corso and dwells at length on the church and convent of penitent prostitutes. He points out that women enter the convent voluntarily and find happiness through true repentance, in contrast to Amsterdam, where they are locked up and undergo physical punishment. He also quotes the reaction of one Dutchman: 'O but, said a Hollander to me, the pope allows whores in Rome.'[15] The justifications and accusations go on for pages. He says that the pope no more allows prostitution than the Dutch drunkenness, which is a greater sin than whoring, because it encourages lust and debauchery. Moreover, lies have been recounted about those who declaim against the pope, claiming that he levies taxes on both vices. In truth, the pope has young girls brought up by the Dominicans of Santa Maria sopra Minerva until they are married or enter a nunnery so that they do not fall victim out of poverty to the desires of rich men. Lassels devotes ten pages to a discussion of prostitution in Rome and papal measures so as to warn the young English Grand

Tourists against sexual adventures, but also provides useful information on that subject.

He apparently encountered no difficulties in visiting the palazzi. He describes how he simply entered the courtyard of Palazzo Farnese, went up to the *piano nobile*, admired the statues, the Sala dei Fasti Farnesiani, the Galleria of Annibale Carracci and the painting collection, and then came back down to the small rear courtyard that contained the famous *Farnese Bull*. The author also entered Palazzo Spada without difficulty and viewed the exquisite paintings there.[16] The Grand Tourists normally had letters of introduction and were offered guided tours, which they had to pay for, by a *cicerone* – an antiquarian, expert or artist – of the palaces and collections.[17] After Rome, Lassels's guide takes visitors to Naples and then back via Rimini and Padua to Venice, where they are informed that they are not allowed to take their weapons into the Arsenal.[18]

The illustrated guide in English and French by François Maximilien Misson, a Huguenot who had emigrated from France, was also widely distributed and reprinted several times. It was used in 1687 and 1688 by the brothers James and Charles Ormond, grandsons of James Butler, 1st Duke of Ormond, on their Grand Tour of Holland, Germany and Italy. With reference to his comments on Italy and its inhabitants, the author advises the reader in the foreword to the French version of the need to distinguish between serious statements and *on dit*, rumours that are often incorrect.[19] He recommends that travellers stay clear in Italy particularly of politics, intrigues and corruption. He states that libraries are more accessible in general than princely collections, but that visitors will not have access to rare items without a serious recommendation and a *teston* or obolus. As an example, he describes how he was refused access in the Biblioteca Ambrosiana in Milan to study documents about Pope Joan because of the fear that as a Huguenot his intention was to harm the Catholic Church.[20]

Misson believes that most of the young people sent by their parents on a tour of Italy are children without taste and discernment who want only to eat, sleep and have a good time. But there are some who seek actively to educate themselves and devour all books providing precise information about the cities they visit. These are the readers for whom his guide is intended.[21] In the fourth volume, the author fills several pages with practical hints for the journey, information about the costs of travel and negotiations with the wagoners.[22] For an acceptable coach with two good horses the author pays 14 pistoles (gold coins), not without noting that in a different season he would have managed with 12 or 10 pistoles. The monthly rent for a palazzo in Rome comes to 20 piasters, around £6. In Rome, where many servants are available, the tourist should prefer locals, who know their way around, but it is even better to follow the recommendations of friends. Misson gives the normal remuneration for servants (*valets*) and grooms (*stafieri*). For a short visit of two or three months in Rome, the author recommends: 'It is important above all to spend time with a good antiquarian so as to visit the major sights in this famous city.'[23]

Misson recommends teaming up with other foreigners to visit the sights together, which is also more enjoyable, because together they will see more than as individuals. He gives the important tip to take a measuring cup with markings for the different dimensions and a long waxed and knotted rope to measure the amounts, lengths and heights of the towers and the diameters of the columns. He also recommends obtaining a dispensation to eat meat during Lent and warns of cheats when travelling to Naples. He suggests taking several pairs of binoculars (*lunettes d'approche*) for greater distances or for viewing paintings, statues, inscriptions and architectural decor. The author does not give precise details of the cost of travel to Italy but the amount can be guessed at, because he advises the parents of travellers in particular not to begrudge a few thousand kronen (*ecus*) for this once-in-a-lifetime tour.[24]

The sights and artworks that the travellers should visit or see are only recommendations. He says, for example, of Bernini's works in Villa Borghese: 'David with the sling against Goliath, Aeneas carrying off Anchises and the transformation of Daphne are three modern pieces by Cavaliere Bernini that deserve to be considered alongside the former [that is, the antiquities].'[25] Bernini's work, he stresses, bears comparison with the previously mentioned antique statues. Note (a) praises *Apollo and Daphne* as one of the most accomplished works in Italy, pointing to the natural beauty of Apollo at his most vigorous age, neither feminine nor muscular. In Villa Ludovisi there are a fossilized human bone, fossilized fruits, flowers and animals of all kinds, and a child turned to stone in its mother's womb, to which the author adds: 'believe it if you will.'[26] Following a sermon on St Mary Magdalene, Misson compares the prostitutes in Rome and Venice and the unsuccessful attempts to reduce their number.[27]

Johann Zoffany, commissioned by Queen Charlotte, the wife of George III, completed an informative painting from 1772 to 1777, *Tribuna of the Uffizi*, showing the English Grand Tourists as an imaginary public in the famous Uffizi Gallery of Grand Duke Leopold II of Habsburg-Lorraine (illus. 16).[28] He was given the exceptional sum of £300 and letters of introduction from the queen to the grand duke for the painting in Florence.[29] The group of English gentlemen is imaginary to the extent that they took part in the Grand Tour but were never all in the Tribuna at the same time. There are only two young men, one of whom, the painter Charles Loraine Smith, is drawing the group *Amor and Psyche*, while the other, Richard Edgcumbe, future 2nd Earl of Mount Edgcumbe, observes him attentively. Zoffany squeezes 22 Grand Tourists, companions and Uffizi personnel in four groups between the

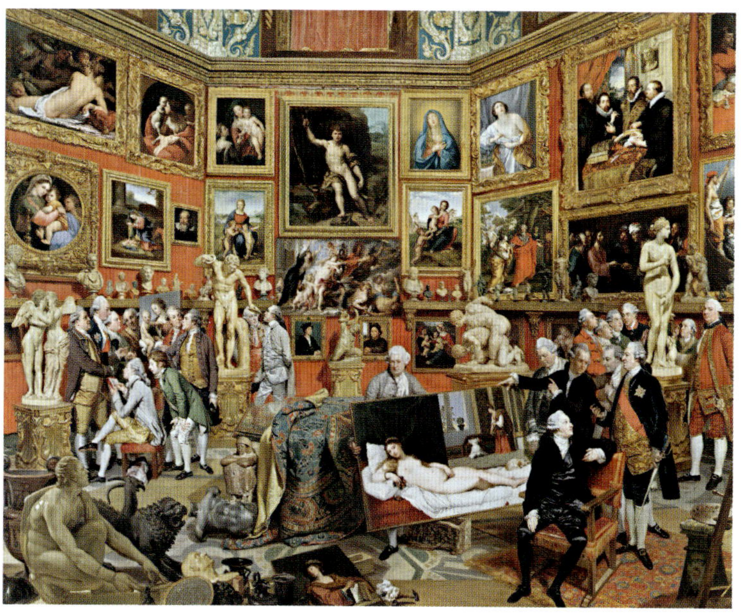

16 Johann Joseph Zoffany, *The Tribuna of the Uffizi*, 1772–7, oil on canvas.

masterpieces from the archduke's collection.[30] He also includes people living in Florence, such as the British consul Sir Horace Mann (standing in the right foreground), the curator of the Gallery Pietro Bastianelli (presenting Titian's *Venus of Urbino*) and Thomas Patch (with his hand on Titian's painting).[31] There is also a half-hidden portrait of himself lifting Raphael's *Madonna* in the group on the far left.[32] On the right in front are George Legge (Lord Lewisham) and his half-hidden companion Mr Stevenson.

The crowded assembly of Grand Tourists with masterpieces from the grand duke's collection in Florence gave rise to smug criticism. Horace Mann complained at the impropriety of including people of unknown status in the room, while the royal family objected to the presence of Horace Mann and Thomas Patch, for which reason the queen refused to accept the painting in her apartments, as the painter Joseph Farington noted in his diary in December 1804.[33]

Zoffany's painting is a classic example of the popular 'conversation piece' genre, which included depictions of noble families, dinner parties and select gatherings.[34] Zoffany gives British high society in the Uffizi Gallery the veneer of connoisseurship. As with his portrait of the academics in the Royal Academy in 1772, he brings together an imagined group and presents them so that they can be easily distinguished from the visitors in front of the painting. The artworks are enhanced by the noble visitors, and the gentlemen are conceited enough to believe that their presence increases the significance of the paintings. The Honourable Felton Hervey, former equerry of the queen, sitting on a velvet sofa in the foreground in front of the Titian, and the decorated Horace Mann are depicted with an arrogant bearing, in contrast to the painter Thomas Patch and Sir John Taylor who stand side by side. Some of the gentlemen, one of whom is using a *lunette d'approche*, admire the *Medici Venus*, while the famous Nile explorer James Bruce turns his back on it.

Zoffany transformed the Medici cabinet of curiosities, which is packed with paintings, sculptures and interested observers, into a warehouse, as can be seen from the jumble of objects and antiquities in the left foreground: an urn, a Grecian sculpture, the Chimera of Arezzo, oil lamps, vases and jars, a Greek bronze torso and the bust of Julius Caesar, and finally the painting *Sibyl* by Guercino next to a hammer and a pair of pliers. The grand duke is not present to witness his chamber of curiosities transformed in this way. Zoffany places the antique sculptures and most prominent Italian pictures practically at the disposal of the English gentlemen, who examine them or turn away in boredom. The artist portrays them as customers, and they did in fact seek to acquire the works available to them – statues and paintings – since the trip to Italy was also a shopping expedition for works of art. The English Grand Tourists, in particular, bought everything offered to them and therefore required a certain amount of expertise to avoid being cheated. All of this served to furnish the English stately homes and collections and to encourage the interest of the upper social classes in antiquity and Italian art.[35]

The pre-eminent public took advantage of the commission to present themselves full figure in both elegant attire and the right society. At almost the same time as the depiction of the Grand Tourists in the Tribuna of the Uffizi, one of the most remarkable representations of the highest princes of Europe was also completed. The French painter Bénigne Gagneraux shows Pope Pius VI welcoming the Swedish king Gustav III in 1782 to the classical collection of the Museo Pio-Clementino (illus. 17).[36] The Swedish king had been in Rome since Christmas Eve under the name Count of Haga, visiting the Vatican on several occasions. He attended the papal mass on New Year's Day in the Sistine Chapel and then proceeded with his retinue to the Museo Pio-Clementino. The pope arranged a coincidental meeting with the Lutheran monarch in the gallery, as reported by the Roman press.[37]

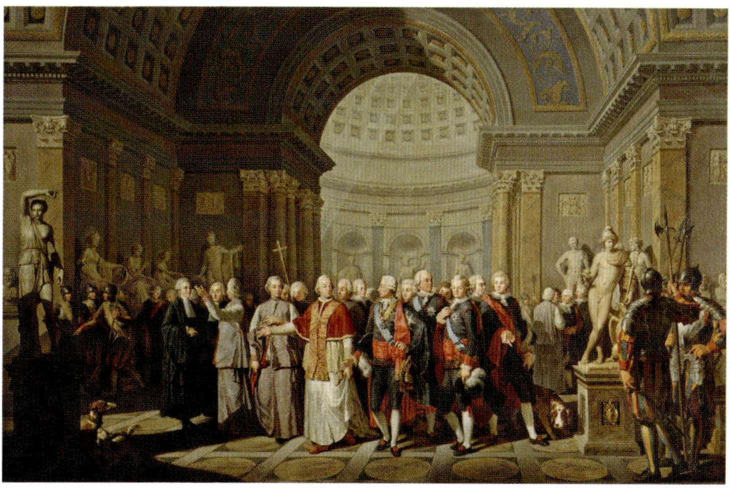

17 Bénigne Gagneraux, *Pius VI Showing King Gustav III the Vatican Galleries*, 1785, oil on canvas.

The most prominent persons are shown recognizably in full view in the first row, choreographed in a line formation. Behind them, the room opens into the Sala Rotonda, built on the model of the Pantheon. Gagneraux faithfully fulfils the obligation to present the persons in the front row in a worthy manner, and he also depicts the statues in the papal collection in great detail, even if some of them are moved from their original positions. He occasionally changes the dimensions, as is the case with the *Apollo Belvedere* in the niche on the left, but the statue of *Ganymede* on the right is true to the original. Gagneraux avoids creating parallels between the persons and the statues, with one small exception. The prelate underneath *Apollo* mirrors the latter's arm position, although he is fully dressed and wigged, while the god is presented casually in his classical naturalness. The prelate is talking to the two Visconti brothers in black cassocks, sons of Giovanni Battista Visconti, the superintendent of antiquities, who were destined to occupy important functions in the Vatican. The king of Sweden is looking towards the pope, resplendent in purple, white and gold, who is inviting him to view the collection, and the officially dressed Swedish courtiers look around interestedly. In the right centre ground a prelate can be seen from behind talking with Swedish visitors. It is interesting to note the presence of armoured guards on both sides of the group of prominent personalities.

Gagneraux based his representation of the pope and king with retinue among the sculptures on Raphael's *School of Athens*, the imaginary assembly of classical philosophers, but changed the composition. In Raphael's painting, the philosophers Plato and Aristotle are in the centre background, while Gagneraux puts the prominent figures in the foreground to heighten their significance and visibility. At the same time, the reference to Raphael serves to give the meeting between the pope and the king more prominence. Gagneraux does this by presenting them frontally and in full figure in a line formation, with clothing to demonstrate rank and subordination of the retinue in the background.

At the end of January 1785, Gagneraux showed the painting for fourteen days in his studio to great acclaim, after which it was presented in the Vatican in March and then to the inhabitants of Rome at the seat of Cardinal de Bernis, the French envoy. Before it went to Stockholm, Gagneraux made a copy for the pope with the identical format but minor changes in the figures; this was stolen in 1798 by the French.

A further example of a conversation piece is the painting *A Private View at the Royal Academy, 1881*, by William Powell Frith. It shows an opening at the Royal Academy in London with select guests from high society. In the left foreground is a full-figure portrait of the writer Anthony Trollope; in the second row behind a group of women is the long-serving prime minister William Gladstone; and in front of the seated group of prominent ladies is the painter Sir Frederic Leighton, some years later to become the first painter to be appointed a baron, shown here near the archbishop. The following group is dominated by the enraptured dandy Oscar Wilde, to whom ironically a lady is presenting her child. Frith creates a vivid depiction of this opening at the Royal Academy, the significance of the figures being enhanced by their being presented together. The paintings are of secondary importance, because the only visitors looking at a work are Oscar Wilde with an upward gaze and an anonymous bald-headed man with a magnifying glass being observed by the top-hatted painter John Everett Millais. Before it became an accessory of Sherlock Holmes, the magnifying glass was a requisite of the meticulous critic and an object of derision by artists.

In 1885, Henry Graves and Company made a 47.5 × 90.8 centimetre (18 × 36 in.) photogravure of Frith's painting and offered a

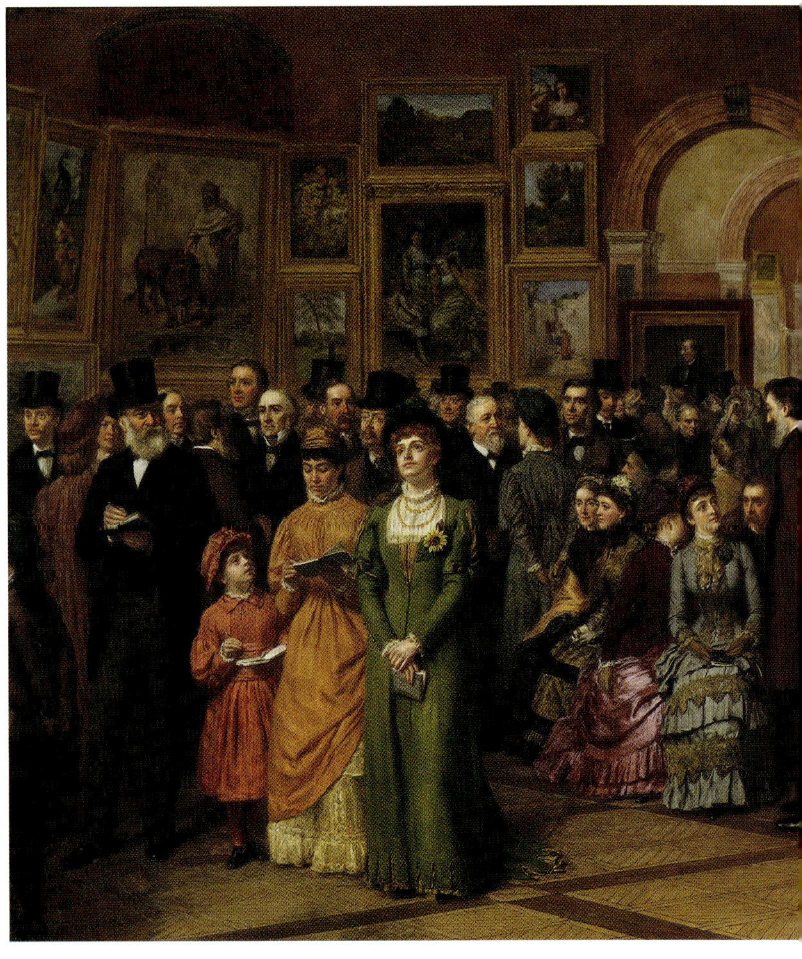

lithographed key plate in which 32 of the personages are identified by name but without a single painting being indicated. The anonymous figures are referred to succinctly: 'The other persons are symbols of aestheticism and hero-worship, not of special persons.'[38] In his autobiography in 1888, Frith named the eminent persons and described the idea behind his composition: 'I therefore planned a group, consisting of a well-known apostle of the beautiful, with eager worshippers surrounding him. He is supposed to be explaining

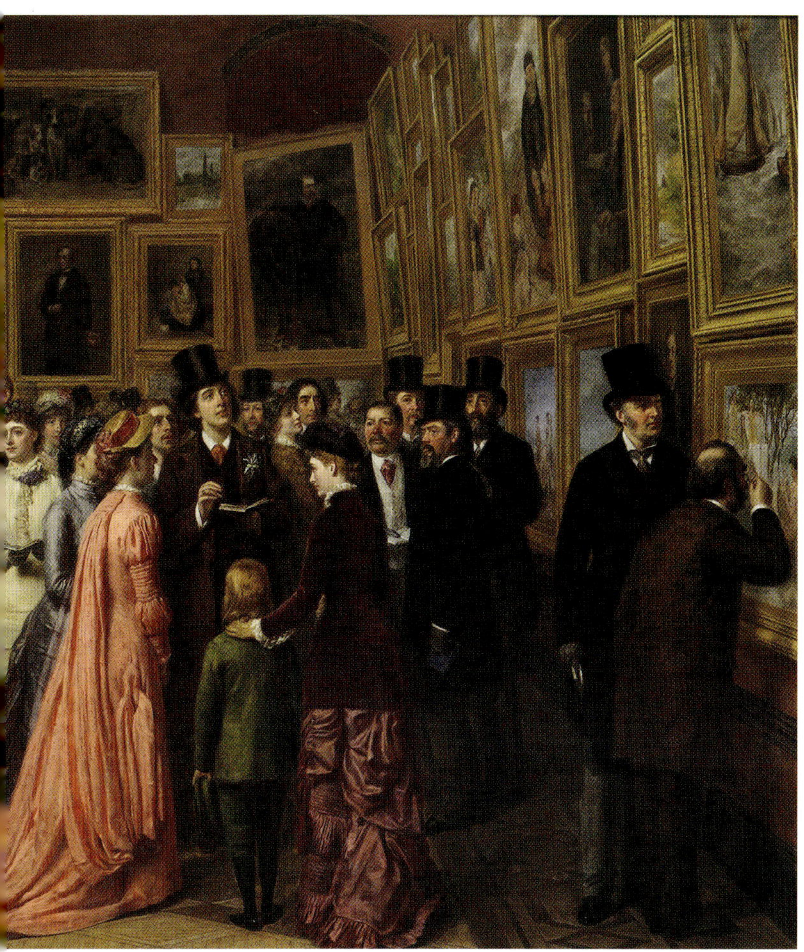

18 William Powell Frith, *A Private View at the Royal Academy, 1881*, 1883, oil on canvas.

his theories to willing ears, taking some picture on the Academy walls for his text.'[39] Frith thus refers briefly to Oscar Wilde and talks at length about the willingness of 'all these eminent persons' to have their portraits painted in the studio, leading to lengthy discussions of individuals and patriotism. It is important to Frith to speak of a picture 'that obtained a large share of popular approval'.[40]

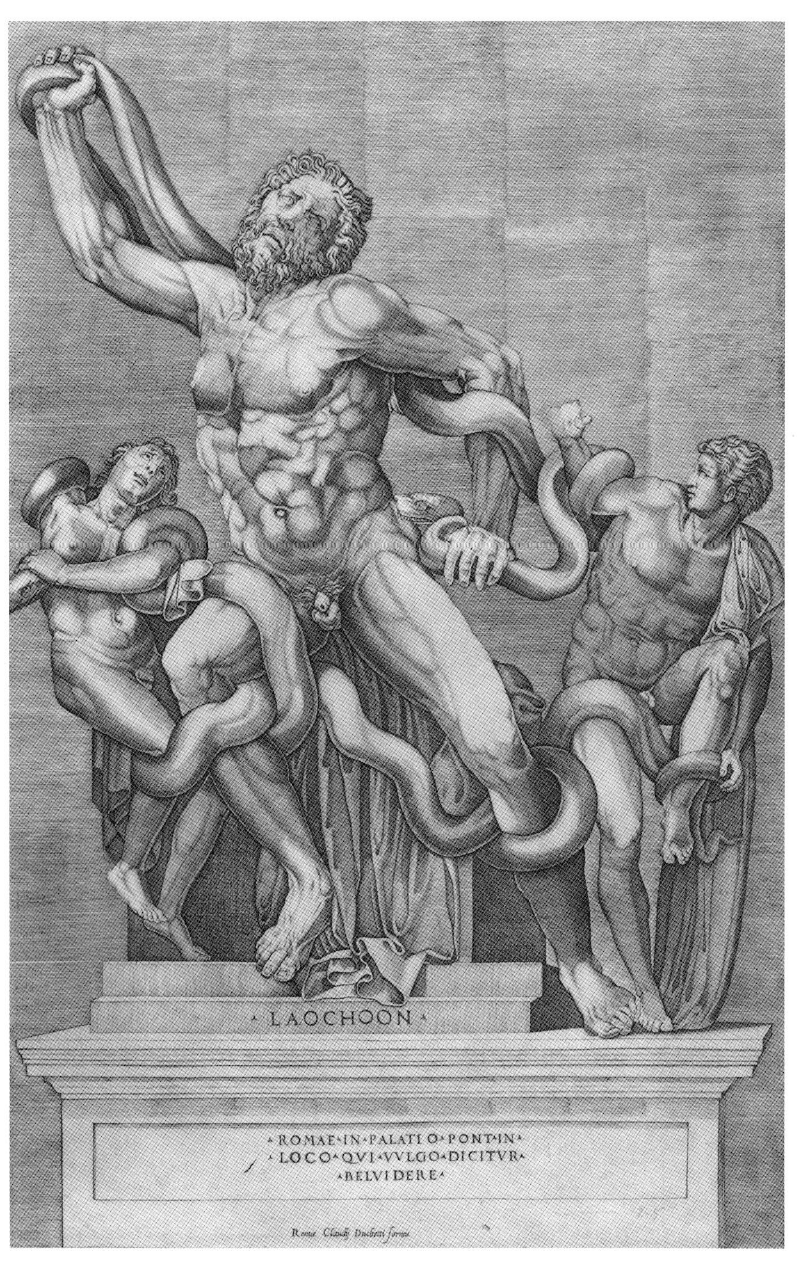


19 Nicolas Beatrizet, *Speculum Romanae Magnificentiae: Laocoon*, 16th century, engraving.

# 7

# THE FRUITFUL PUBLIC

In the second half of the eighteenth century, Enlightenment figures supported the public demand for greater consideration and active participation in art. Gotthold Ephraim Lessing did not maintain the separation of the public from the masses that Dubos and Klopstock advocated. In his famous essay *Laocoon* of 1766, he talks of the 'fruitful moment', in fact a plea for a 'fruitful public', which was not acknowledged, the discussion focusing on a less relevant matter, the association of the body with the fine arts and actions with the literary arts.[1] After the discovery of the Laocoön group on 14 January 1506 and its attribution by Giuliano da Sangallo and Michelangelo Buonarroti to Pliny the Elder, copies and graphic reproductions, guides to Rome and antiquarian literature helped to steadily increase its renown in a culture dominated by a reverence for antiquity.[2] The group of statues was regarded as a technical wonder, Laocoön's head becoming the model for the expression of pain, and the three figures defining the ideal proportions. Johann Joachim Winckelmann praised Laocoön as a stoic example of 'noble simplicity' and 'silent greatness', which remained a preferred study and research object for artists, art schools and art historians for centuries, while *Laocoon* was inflicted on secondary school pupils until they rejected this 'scholastic delusion', as Paul Klee wrote in 1920: 'Movement is the source of all change. In Lessing's *Laocoon*, on which we squandered study time when we were young, much fuss is made about the difference between temporal and spatial art. Yet looking into the matter more closely, we find that all this is but a scholastic delusion. For space, too, is a temporal concept.'[3]

The 'scholastic delusion' concealed Lessing's revaluation of the public from a passive recipient to an active or 'fruitful' one. Lessing's new assessment was prompted by his theatre experience and the behaviour of the public at exhibitions. In 1765, he left the service of Prussian General Friedrich Bogislav von Tauentzien in Breslau (Wrocław) and returned as a writer to Berlin. As a playwright he had already to consider the audience, even before he became theatrical director at the National Theatre in Hamburg in 1767, a position he held for three years. It was there that he formed his idea of an active art public. In Chapter Sixteen of *Laocoon*, Lessing claimed that bodies existing near one another are 'the particular object of painting', while action, with its 'articulated sounds in time', is the object of poetry.[4] Lessing infers from this that painting can and may only represent a single moment of an action: 'In coexisting compositions, painting can only make use of a single instant of action, and must therefore choose the one which is most pregnant and from which what has already taken place and what is about to follow can be most easily gathered.'[5]

According to the interpretation by Alexander Gottlieb, author of the *Metaphysica* of 1739, the pregnant moment contains a number of features.[6] The limitation of painting to the representation of a single moment of action, derived from the classical rules of time and place in drama, was known through the fault found in the Académie royale de peinture et de sculpture in Paris in 1667 with Nicolas Poussin's *Gathering of Manna*.[7] Poussin's painting was criticized for not showing the sequence as it was related in the Bible. Charles Le Brun attempted spontaneously to designate the differences between the narration and the pictorial depiction of an action:

> Monsieur Le Brun replied that painting is not the same as history. A historian makes himself understood through a framework of words and a sequence of discourses. These form an image of the things he wishes to communicate and represent a sequence of actions as he sees it. The painter, however, has only *one* moment in which he has to pack what he wants to convey. In order to depict what is happening in this moment, however, he has to include many prior events so that the subject on which the depiction is based can be understood. Because without this, the viewer of the painting would be just as uninformed as if the historian were to relate not the entire story but just the ending.[8]

Le Brun uses the argument of the viewer's understanding again in the discussion on the means available to painting for pictorial expression. One of the academicians recalled the licence of poets to join several events in a single credible action and claimed that painters had even more reasons than poets to make use of this licence. For that reason, Poussin should not be criticized for having ignored the unity of action.[9] Instead of revoking an apparently arbitrary rule, the Académie presumes to allow painters to break it.

Lessing is even more insistent than Le Brun on the need for public understanding. The 'pregnant' instant the painter should choose is one that enables the public to understand what precedes and what follows the depicted action and, in this way, to make the moment 'fruitful' for its understanding. Lessing refers explicitly to the public in the discussion on the publication by Anne-Claude-Philippe, Comte de Caylus, titled *Nouveaux Sujets de peintre et de sculpture* (1755), in which he usurps the authority of the Académie royale in Paris to suggest new subjects for artists taken from authors less well known than Homer and Virgil.[10] For example, he recommends the story of the brothers Kleobis and Biton, who sacrificed themselves for their mother and the goddess Hera, as an example of filial love: 'The observer knows that the two boys will die after their action, which is so full of devotion and whose most beautiful moments are captured by the painter.'[11] To these suggestions by the lover of antiquity, which he repeated incessantly in different forms, Lessing replied that in hundreds of years an interpreter would be needed to explain such scenes: 'Or do we desire that the public be as learned as the expert with his books, that it should be well acquainted and familiar with every scene of history and of fable which can yield materials for a beautiful picture?'[12]

Lessing refers explicitly to the public in his argument against the scholarly search for new subjects. He claims earlier that the reaction to pictures and sculptures is fruitful if the 'pregnant' instant is chosen such that the imagination is stimulated:

> If the artist, out of the ever-varying nature, can only make use of a single moment, and the painter especially can only use this moment from one point of view, whilst their works are intended to stand the test not only of a passing glance but of long and repeated contemplation, it is clear that this moment and the point from which this moment is viewed cannot be chosen too happily. Now that only is a happy moment which allows the imagination free scope.[13]

The moment is pregnant if it enables the fruitful mental activity of the public. If the selection of the 'most pregnant' moment is up to the painter or sculptor, its transformation into something 'fruitful' is a matter for the recipient public.

Lessing speaks explicitly of the public, in contrast to Johann Joachim Winckelmann, who, in 'Beschreibung des *Torso im Belvedere*

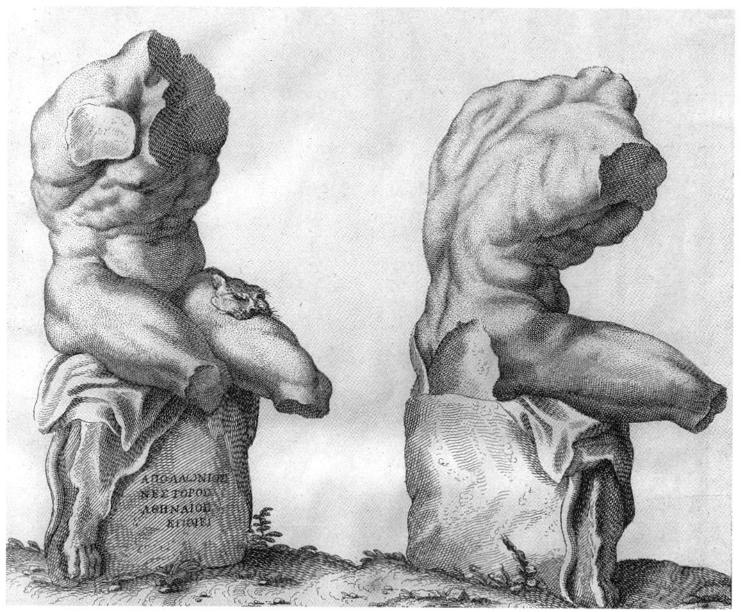

20 *Belvedere Torso*, 1430s, engraving in Domenico de Rossi and Paolo Alessandro Maffei, *Raccolta di statue antiche e moderne* (1704).

zu Rom' in 1759, focuses on the erotic reaction of a single viewer to the work. The author describes the sensations experienced by him, from the first view of the almost unrecognizable figure (illus. 20) and the erotic stimulation and imaginations engendered by the material to his departure from it. Winckelmann envisions the parts of the world travelled by Hercules, and the delightful view of his back conjures up the spirituality of the material and brings the mutilated marble to life:

> On top of the back, which on close observation appears bent, I imagine a head full of happy memories of his astounding feats; and as a head full of majesty and wisdom appears before my eyes, my thoughts also begin to imagine the other missing limbs: an emanation from the present forms and immediately completes the picture.[14]

The ecstatic autosuggestion creates a Pygmalion effect, animation through enthusiastic admiration, combined with erotic fantasies and desires. Pygmalion, the mythological sculptor who fell in love with his statue and asked Venus to bring it to life, became a model for the perception of art in the second half of the eighteenth century.[15] As with Winckelmann, it refers to the intimate reaction to sculptures by a single male observer. Lessing opposes this with the intellectual perception of an artwork by a fruitful public. Already in his criticism of Caylus, he stated explicitly that art should be understandable for the public. In Chapter Three of *Laocoon*, after the 'fruitful instant' has been determined, he uses the plural pronoun 'we' to describe more intensive perception and thought: 'The longer we gaze, the more our imagination must add; and the more our imagination adds, the more we must believe we see.'[16] Lessing is referring here to Leon Battista Alberti, who wrote in *On Painting* that the painter should paint things that stimulate the public's mind. He uses the word *excogitare*, 'to invent', and compares it to artistic invention.[17] Alberti's demand for mental stimulation forms the basis for Lessing's demand for inciting the public in the 'fruitful instant'.

In 1798 Johann Wolfgang Goethe's essay 'Upon the Laocoön' proposed a different idea of a fruitful public, which he called 'millions of spectators'.[18] Goethe advocated the representation of a transitory moment in art, giving the public the opportunity to create and re-create the illusions of a work in movement:

> In order to conceive rightly the intention of the Laocoön, let a man place himself before it at a proper distance, with his eyes shut; then let him open his eyes and shut them again instantly. By this means, he will see the whole marble in motion; he will fear lest he find the whole group changed.

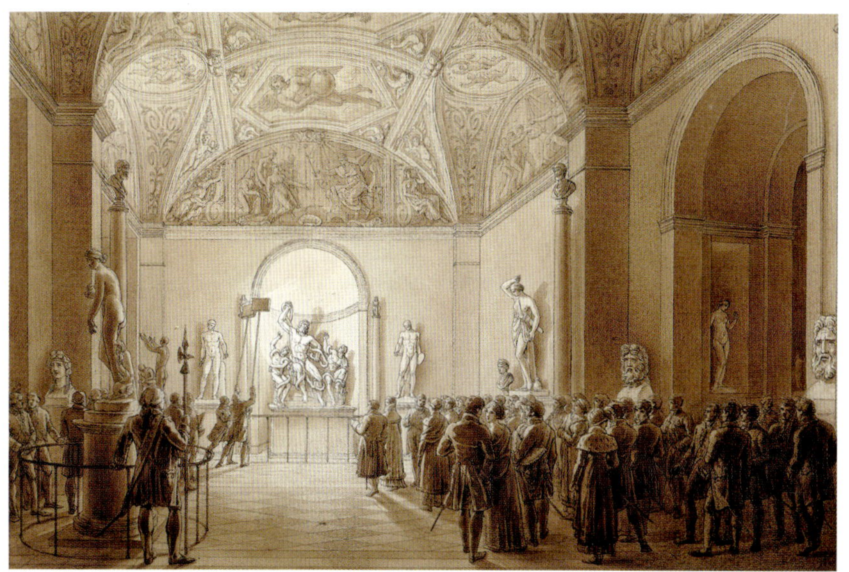

21 Benjamin Zix, *Napoleon and Empress Marie-Louise Visit the Laocoön Room at Night*, c. 1810–11, pen and ink and brown wash on paper.

This exercise is recommended to a society desirous in its leisure time of experiencing everything pictorial, and particularly the dead stone statues, as being alive. This can be achieved by means of two different entertainments: nocturnal torchlit visits and *tableaux vivants*, living pictures. Male and female art lovers were keen on bringing the statues in museums eerily to life through the flickering torches.[19] Around 1810, Benjamin Zix drew an illustrious group with Napoleon I and Marie-Louise admiring the Laocoön group stolen from Rome by torchlight. This amusement supplemented other contemporary attempts by the public to bring artworks to life, be it through erotic associations (Pygmalion) or the reproduction in *tableaux vivants* by live participants.[20]

For a *tableau vivant*, a society divides itself into audience and performers for its entertainment. Once the roles have been allocated and the costumes found, the participants imitate the figures in a work of art. The audience observes the pantomime closely, attempts to identify the work of art and evaluates the performance. Then the roles are exchanged and the next work chosen. The paradox of this amusement – that the living become dead for a minute in order to portray a living picture – was soon noted.[21] It is interesting that a company was split into performers, who were frozen motionless, and spectators, who applauded and provided commentaries. The most detailed analysis of this entertainment, which originated in France around 1770 and came to Germany in the early nineteenth century, is provided by Goethe in his 1809 novel *Elective Affinities*.[22] The public thus also participate actively in the appropriation of art.

The precursors of this transformation of pictures into pantomime scenes were the *tableaux* with extras arranged for the ceremonial entrance of princes. The structures for the entrance of Archduke Ernest of Austria into Brussels in 1596, for example, included a large pyramid. At the foot the Muses sat with their musical instruments, in the middle was a winged Pegasus, and perched at the top was Apollo with his lyre as the sun god.[23] In contrast to the *tableaux vivants* in the eighteenth and nineteenth centuries, public participation was confined to admiration, as in the representation of agriculture, which shows a rider surrounded by men and women seen from the rear looking up at a large platform.[24]

The most significant achievement of the active art public in the late eighteenth and early nineteenth centuries was the founding of art associations and societies, usually in collaboration with artists. The aim was to close the gap between life and art. One of the oldest and still extant art associations is the Zürcher Kunstgesellschaft, founded in 1787 by artists and art lovers.[25] In 1815 the banker and merchant Johann Friedrich Städel bequeathed the decorative Städelsches Kunstinstitut on Rossmarkt in Frankfurt am Main for repurposing as a museum and art school for the inhabitants of the city. He stated in his will: 'As a basis for the Städelsches Kunstinstitut donated by me for the benefit of the city and its inhabitants, I hereby bequeath my collection of paintings, drawings, engravings and art objects and associated books.'[26] Together with his art collection, Städel donated his vast fortune of 1.3 million florins to the inhabitants of Frankfurt, creating one of the first civic museums in this way.[27]

The Kunstverein in Munich was established in 1823 as a joint-stock company (Aktiengesellschaft), a model that was copied by many other cities. In the article on art associations in the *Real-Encyklopädie*, Jacob Burckhardt wrote in 1845: 'Art associations today are undeniably the main material support for painting; they have once again attracted a larger public and, for all the one-sidedness, have made a bold and successful start to the difficult task of attempting to reconcile art and life.'[28]

Wilhelm Schlink described the efforts between the 1820s and the March revolution of 1848 in the German art world as the 'expectation of art' (Kunsterwartung), which covered both the attitude of the public to artists and the demand by artists for acknowledgement.[29] The reconciliation of art and life was not enough for the pre-revolutionary society, which demanded a close connection between art and public life.[30] Schlink believed that the problem with contemporary art was that although it was meant to move people like a natural force, it only reached the 'educated art association public', maintaining the fiction that 'the interests of the educated classes' had priority over the general public interest.[31] The real task in working towards this goal was to enlarge the informed public through education and cultural awareness.

# 8

# SENSITIVE AND MOVED

Towards the end of the eighteenth century, depictions of dying or dead artists gave rise to respectful mourning by the public, similar to its reaction to dead rulers and heroes. There were pictures of famous artists such as Raphael, Dürer, Titian and above all Leonardo da Vinci, who allegedly died in the arms of the French king Francis I. Through the reciprocal devotion of rulers and artists, Leonardo's dying moments became highly popular between 1781 and 1886.[1] This popularity started with the official commission of François-Guillaume Ménageot's *Death of Leonardo da Vinci in the Arms of Francis I* for the 1781 Salon and as a model for tapestries. Leonardo is lying on the bed; a doctor is taking his pulse and holding back a servant girl. On the other side the king, accompanied by courtiers and pages, consoles the artist, who is looking up to him reverently. In the 1824 Salon, Jean-Auguste-Dominique Ingres, who had to find a new public after the fall of Napoleon I, presented his version of the king sitting at the artist's deathbed, which is reminiscent of the powerful sitting figure in the Laocoön.[2]

In his work on the pictorial arts in France, the writer and art critic Pierre-Jean-Baptiste Chaussard touches briefly on the painting *Honours Paid to Raphael after His Death* by Pierre-Nolasque Bergeret, which was shown in the 1806 Salon.[3] He quotes the text from the *Livret* and describes the emotion, despair and melancholy engendered by the painting:

> This is a painting that ideally fulfils the aims of painting. The theme is moving and interesting; it effortlessly exercises all the seductiveness of a drama taken from nature and great memories. The most sublime genius expiring before his middle years; the homage paid to the supreme talent by the all-powerful; the tears of his rivals; his last wonderful painting [*Transfiguration*] hanging over his deathbed like a trophy; such great hopes suddenly extinguished in the grief at an irreparable loss, this sign of bereavement by the Church over the skilful and now icy hands that once adorned the building; this pious, delicate assembly of nobles, scholars, artists, students, common people, smitten by a diverse but deeply powerful and desolate feeling as with a public disaster, everything carrying an irresistible melancholy of the soul, because it is not necessary to be an artist or a savant to experience this – it is sufficient to be sensitive.[4]

Chaussard stresses that, thanks to their sentience, ordinary people can appreciate the scene without literary training. Artists have always used displays of emotion to communicate with the public. According to Pliny, in his painting of the sacrifice of Iphigenia, the highly gifted Timanthes gradually built up the expression of grief to its culmination in the father's inexpressible pain.[5] Dubos still asked in 1733 whether the public was capable of empathy, but in 1806 Chaussard acknowledged that the 'common people' could also appreciate the sentiments inspired by the works, which could provoke tears, delight or shivers. At the same time, he criticized artists for exaggerating or corrupting art in the interests of public approval.[6]

In the 1820s, paintings were directed at public empathy in much the same way as theatre from the second half of the seventeenth century.[7] There was a mutual relationship between the two in terms of composition, colour, gestures and facial expressions. Jacques-Louis

David's painting *The Lictors Bring to Brutus the Bodies of His Sons* of 1789 is in the form of a theatrical scene and was reproduced in the theatre as a *tableau vivant*.[8] The production of Giacomo Rossini's *William Tell* at the Paris Opéra in 1829 is based on the painting *Oath of Three Swiss Rütli* by Charles Steuben, which had been acclaimed five years earlier in the Salon.[9] In the 1824 Salon, Eugène Delacroix presented the large-format painting *The Massacre at Chios* (Musée du Louvre, Paris), with its wretched and dead Greek victims and the battle scene in the middle distance.[10] Stendhal (Marie-Henri Beyle), who did not like the painting, criticized 'l'exagération du triste et du sombre' (the exaggeration of the sad and dark), but noted that the public, bored by the Académie genre, paused before the 'pale, half-painted cadavers'.[11] For the many Philhellenes in France, Delacroix's *Massacre* was a disturbing work, but for Stendhal it was nothing more than pale cadavers.[12] The author's senses were delightfully and ecstatically inspired by the brilliant colours of an artist like Correggio or a statue of Venus. The quasi-erotic rapture and sensory overload that pictures apparently provoked in tourists in Florence was known as Stendhal syndrome.[13]

The three-day July Revolution in 1830 in France led to the overthrow of Charles X, the last king of France and Navarre. The revolution saw an alliance of citizens, royal guards, workers and street urchins.[14] On 15 August 1830, the parliament elected Louis-Philippe, Duke of Orleans, as constitutional monarch, 'roi des Français'. When the 1831 Salon opened in May, the revolutionary unrest had not yet died down, and the noise from the street could be heard in the rooms of the Louvre. Reports on the Salon acknowledge the loud power of the street but do not remove the prejudice against the 'mob'.

Impressed by the revolution, Ingres, who had enjoyed favour under Charles X, created a mythological exaltation of the people in the form of a monument showing Hercules, armed with a club, being crowned by Victoria, who is floating above him. In the top right is the inscription 'peuple jeune fort et beau' (young, strong and beautiful people); around the head of the largest figure are the July dates and 'honneur au peuple' (honour to the people); and to the right below the statue is 'le trône cassé' (the broken throne). Is Ingres really celebrating the victory of the people? Under Charles X in 1825, Ingres received the Cross of the Legion of Honour and became a member of the Académie des Beaux-Arts, and in 1829 he was appointed a professor at the École des Beaux-Arts. Together with Eugène Delacroix, Paul Delaroche and others, he is said to have protected the artworks in the Louvre from destruction by the 'populace' during the July Revolution.

In contrast to Ingres' exaltation of the people, Delacroix's large picture of the Revolution, *Liberty Leading the People*, shows the

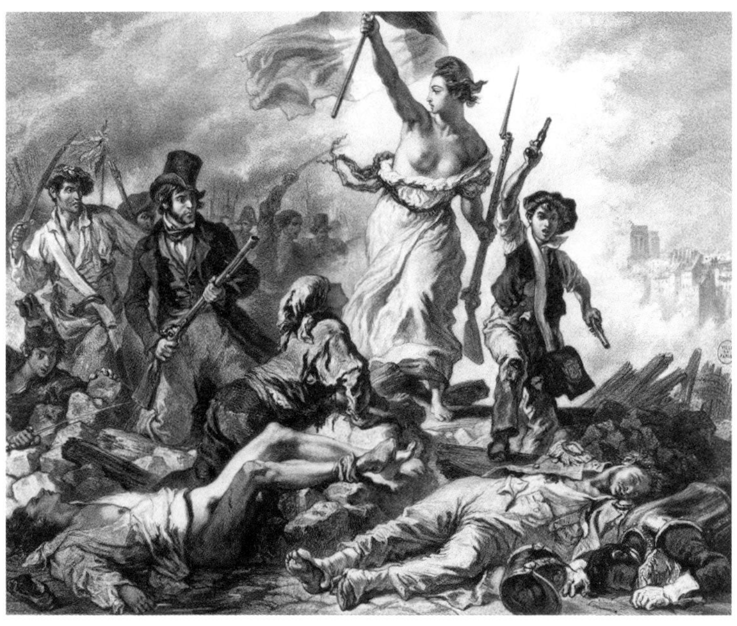

22 Adolphe Mouilleron, after Eugène Delacroix, *Liberty Leading the People, 28 July 1830*, 1831, lithograph.

concerted action of the inhabitants of Paris – from street urchins and workers to top-hatted citizens – led by the figure of Liberty, both in admiration and indignation at the 'populace'.[15] The writer, poet and journalist Heinrich Heine, who had just arrived in Paris, wrote an important critique of the first Salon after the July Revolution, which attracted visitors through its contemporary political representations, calling it 'the most significant manifestation' in the realm of art.[16] Heine noted that Delacroix's picture of the Revolution was one of the paintings to attract most attention, and that there was 'always a large crowd' standing in front of it in the Salon. He celebrated the work with the exclamation: 'Holy July days! How beautiful was the sun and how great were the people!' He describes the triumphant woman with her rifle as 'the wild people's power' and notes that 'a great idea ennobled and sanctified this common people, the *crapule*'.[17] Whereas the term *populace* means 'mob', the term *crapule* refers to criminal rogues, whom Heine nevertheless sanctifies.

The savage forcefulness of this picture gave it an overwhelming power unmatched by any other depiction of the July Revolution in the 1831 Salon. Delacroix boldly placed this revolutionary *peuple* before the public standing in front of the painting. The authorities realized the danger of this revolutionary depiction of Liberty on the barricades, acquired the picture and put it out of sight.[18] Reproductions kept its memory alive, and when the painting re-emerged in 1855, it once again exerted a powerful effect on the public. Théophile Gautier wrote that this Liberty 'astonishes and surprises with her fantastic aspect among persons of rough and brutal reality'.[19] Heine listened in the 1831 Salon to the comments by the public, many of whom he suspected had been involved in the fighting and praised the painting:

> 'Matin!' cried a grocer, 'these urchins fought like giants!' He quotes a family discussion verbatim: 'Papa!' cried a little Karlistinn [*sic*], 'who is the dirty woman with the red cap?' – 'Clearly,' said the noble papa sarcastically with a sweet half-smile, 'clearly, dear child, she has nothing to do with the purity of lilies. She is the goddess of liberty.' – 'Papa, she's not even wearing a blouse.' – 'A true goddess of liberty, dear child, doesn't normally wear a blouse and is therefore very bitter about all the people who wear white linen.'[20]

Apart from this scornful conversation, Heine also repeats the cynical words exchanged between a noble and a cardinal disguised, out of fear, in civilian clothes. The marquis was afraid that the new popular insurrection could have been provoked by atrocities, while the cleric would like to see such terrible acts committed in order to put down the revolution.

In 1831 Heine admitted that because of the political situation and the mass agitation, he could not find the peace and quiet necessary to deal with art.[21] For his essay, he chose the eight artists whom he had heard talked about most by the public.[22] He claimed that their comments were sufficient for him to talk of 'public opinion': 'I may thus confine myself to talking about public opinion. It does not differ much from my own.'[23] Stendhal took a different view in his discussion of the 1824 Salon. Although he noted which works attracted most public attention, he took it upon himself to inform them on the basis of his own personal feelings. He claimed that art was on the threshold of a revolution, the elimination of the Classicist taste and its replacement by *bonne peinture moderne*: 'Ignoring the clamour of the opposing party, I will tell the public frankly and simply what I feel about each of the pictures it deigns to give its attention to.'[24]

In 1830 an anonymous contributor to Ludwig Schorn's *Kunstblatt* sought to define the 'art-loving public', which was held up as an example by some and vilified by others. The author describes the public as a 'chaotic being' with many voices: 'It is not unimportant to consider this chaotic being because it confronts the entire world of art as a chorus of voices, opinions, judgements and decisions and has a most decisive influence on existing and future art.'[25] The author recommends discarding any 'premature, incompetent, sneering' judgement and attending only to the 'publicly stated opinion' given by 'a really informed art-loving public' about important works belonging to the nation. But, he claims, this public is so small and isolated that its members cannot talk to one another or to artists. The only option for the artist is therefore to deliver works that please everyone: 'Then he won't have to seek out his public or to listen to praise and criticism. If he is successful, all hearts will be cheered and all hands will applaud him.'[26]

Among the masses, there are also more people who find materiality and earthiness beautiful in both life and art than there are among those 'educated to real beauty', who are, however, the only true judges as far as artists are concerned:

> The public is the soul of art and the wish and need of the artist; his work is for the world, as it has been taken from the world as it is; he wants it to be looked at, enjoyed and appreciated by the world, to be accessible to the largest possible sector he can reach; . . . A genuine artist, like every hardworking person, wants the well-being of the world and its beneficial progress.[27]

The only way, therefore, is to educate people to judge correctly, and those who are not yet able to do so should exercise restraint and listen to those who are already competent to judge. The author considers this 'moral aesthetic attention' to be necessary for the creation of a 'good public', but he is nevertheless sceptical since the directors of public art institutions encourage the distortion of public taste by submissively giving in to its demand for 'sensory material': 'The public used to apply itself to art, but now art applies itself to the public; the greater rivalry by donors makes talent a commodity for sale and yields to the consumers and arbitrary demand.'[28] The author believes indubitably that 'higher, classical art' has always been only for the 'most educated minds'. This is another way of saying that art should be for all mankind, but not everyone can understand it, either because they are not interested or because they do not have the necessary competence. The anonymous author ends his short essay by distinguishing between the 'over-educated public', which always seeks underlying meanings, the 'average public', which praises everything but cannot recognize the best, and the iconoclastic public, which attacks art.

In the 1834 Salon, Paul Delaroche presented a major work attacking public sentiments, the dramatic *Execution of Lady Jane Grey*.[29] The young Jane Grey was drawn by her uncle John Dudley, Duke of Northumberland, into a Machiavellian plot that was to end badly for all concerned. Jane was married to Dudley's son Guildford and was persuaded after the death of Edward VI to allow herself to be proclaimed Queen of England, abdicating just nine days later. The conspirators were all charged with treason and executed. In the *Livret* to the 1834 Salon, Delaroche quotes a Protestant martyrology by way of explanation.[30] The painter positions the victim left of centre, her white satin undergarment glowing innocently in the dark prison. She is blindfolded and is assisted by Sir John Brydges, lieutenant of the Tower, in feeling for the block on which she will lay her head. To the right is the executioner, standing in elegant contrapposto with his axe, rope and dagger, while to the left in front of a massive pillar is one of the ladies-in-waiting, grieving and holding Jane's dress in her lap, while the other places her head and hands on the cold stone in despair.[31] Delaroche's painting and the many reproductions popularized Jane Grey's tragic end in France and recalled the executions of the king of France and the queen during the Revolution.[32] In 1840 Heine drew attention to the picture, coining the expression *Rührungswerk* (emotive work): 'One of the main "Rührungswerke" by Delaroche shows the queen Jeanne Grey about to lay her blonde head on the block.'[33]

Heine ironically lists the painter's preference for tragic *Rührstücke* with crowned heads and concludes from the high-born persons condemned or executed in his pictures: 'Mr Delaroche is the court

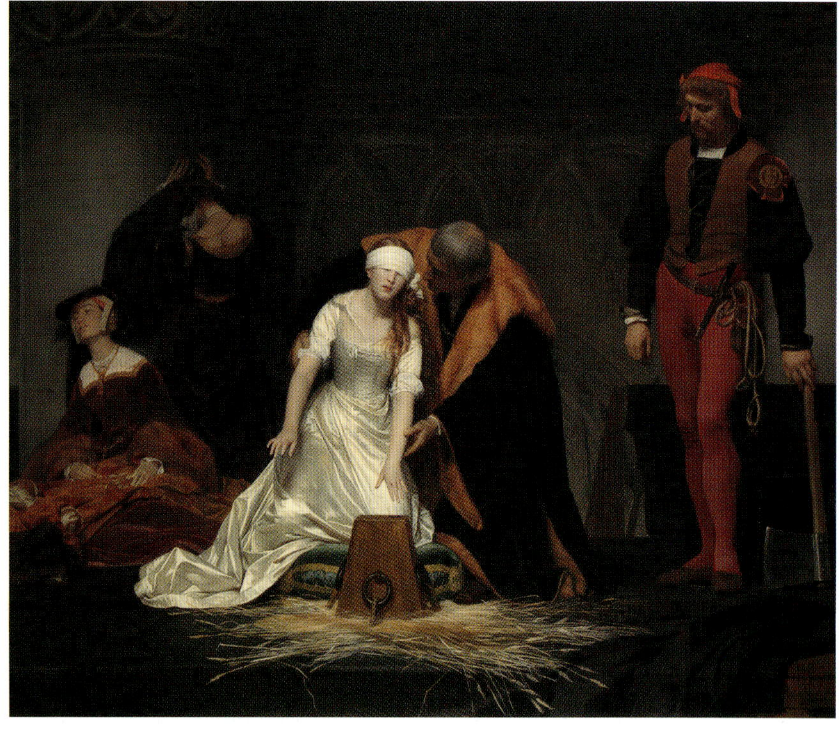

23 Paul Delaroche, *The Execution of Lady Jane Grey*, 1833, oil on canvas.

painter of all decapitated majesties.' He claims that Delaroche uses similar emotive methods in his *Rührungswerke* as those employed in the theatre, hence the adaptation of the word *Rührstück* (melodrama) used for plays and musical dramas to painting.

The figures in the highly sentimental composition with Jane Grey were changed by Auguste Bouquet even before the presentation of the painting in the Salon and used for a satire in *La Caricature*.[34] It shows Louis-Philippe himself as the executioner of Désirée Françoise Liberté, the freedom fought for by the French in July 1830. There were several attempts on the life of Louis-Philippe, who within a short time was transformed from a constitutional monarch to a despot, and he was attacked above all in the satirical magazines *La Caricature* and *Le Charivari*, which presented him as the destroyer of freedom and as being hand-in-glove with high finance.[35]

Around 1830, the direct approach to the public as a collective through an emotional theme and theatrical presentation was criticized, although there had long been interaction between painting and theatre.[36] Eduard Collow from Berlin, the *Kunstblatt* correspondent, selected only *The Execution of Lady Jane Grey* and François-Marius Granet's *The Death of Poussin* for praise in the 1834 Salon.[37] He reproduced the random descriptions of Delaroche's painting – 'charming, superb, admirable, astonishing, capital' – and the empty criteria – 'finesse, delicacy, elegance, clarity, harmony, truth'.[38] He provided a wholesale critique of the age, in which art was declining and artists were either descending into cheap reality or drifting in airless space. There were hardly any traces left, he said, of 'genuine art', but rather more and more 'contrivance and artistic dalliance', and the 'so-called artists' merely followed the opinion of the masses or served the demands of the 'Croesuses'. Moreover, modern painting and sculpture were a lamentable rehash of past eras, and the arts and sciences were in any case inaccessible to 'the mass of people' as they had 'no vital and meaningful relationship' to the 'educated half' and did not exist for the 'crude uneducated half'.[39] Collow's criticism could not be more comprehensive: decadence, corruption, disinterest, meaninglessness for all, educated and uneducated alike.

In 1831 the literary critic Gustave Planche discussed the different relationships to the public of Eugène Delacroix and Paul Delaroche. Delacroix had discovered a new form of presentation and was only gradually being understood by the public, whereas Delaroche had popularized and refined the form of representation. As an original talent, Delacroix had chosen the difficult path to the public, whereas Delaroche had lowered himself and was rewarded with immediate admiration.[40] *Faire son public* (attracting his own public), the legitimate aim of artists, can be achieved in different ways. Either the artist, who is assumed or required to stand above the public, stoops down, or the public raises its standards to the artist. Kandinsky wrote precisely this in 1912, thus repeating, like countless others, the topos of poor public taste.

A typical *Rührungswerk* as defined by Heine is the painting *The Execution of Major Davel* by Charles Gleyre, commissioned by the canton Waadt.[41] The patriotic painting of the execution of the hero, who fought in vain in 1723 for the freedom of the subject country Waadt (Vaud), was an outstanding public success when it was shown in Lausanne in 1850. Gleyre paints the hero in a white frock coat and shirt facing the viewer. In front of the wall are the half-figures of two grieving soldiers. To the left of Davel are two pastors dressed in black, one holding Davel's hand and the other wringing his hands in anguish. On the right is the executioner dressed in red and holding a sword, along with his assistant. Davel is looking calmly upwards and waving his hand to the beyond, while the sky begins to darken. Between the execution site and the poplars on the banks of the lake

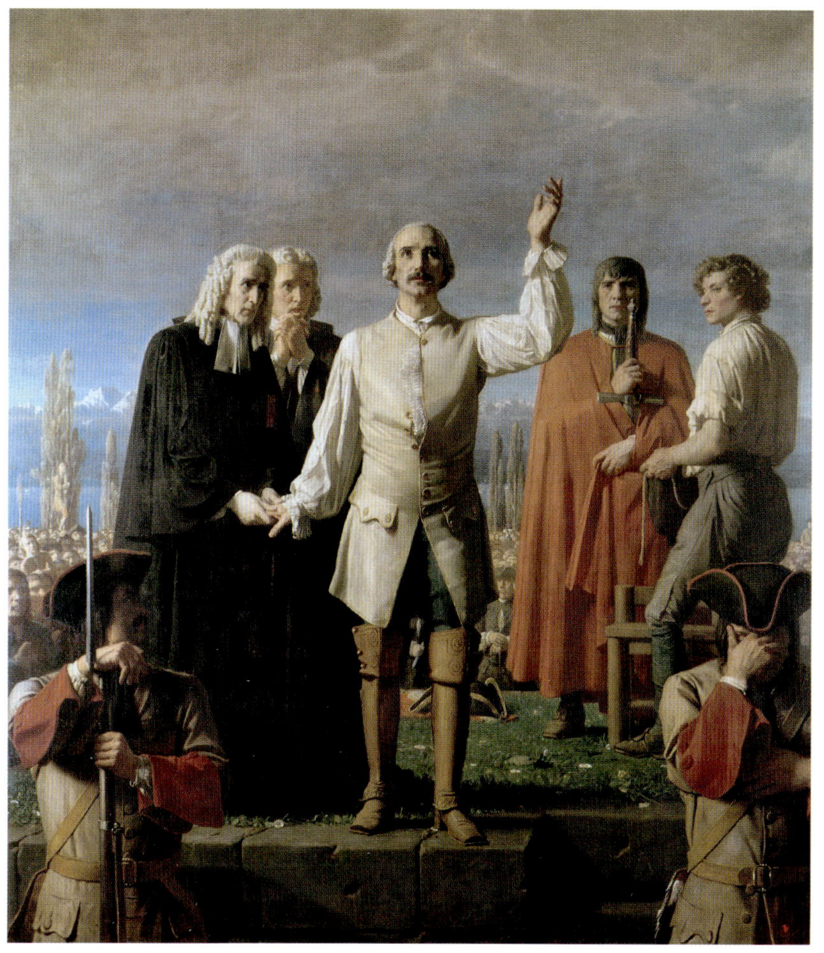

24 Charles Gleyre, *The Execution of Major Davel*, 1850, oil on canvas (now destroyed).

can be seen the tightly packed crowd, or at least their heads, and in the background, beyond the lake, are the Savoy Alps. The crowd in the picture mirrors the public standing in front of it.

The grieving soldiers, the mourning black pastors, the threatening red executioner and his indifferent assistant, and the calm hero of the failed liberation waving to the sky are all designed to touch the emotions of the people of the Waadtland in the middle of the nineteenth century. In September 1851 Gleyre drew a portrait of the ailing Heinrich Heine for the *Revue des Deux-Mondes*.[42] There is no indication that he had met the writer earlier on. Gleyre's depiction of Major Davel keeps alive the memory of Bern's violent reign over the Waadt, which did not end until 1798. In August 1980 the painting was set on fire and almost completely destroyed. The perpetrator or perpetrators are not known, and it is therefore uncertain whether it was a statement about the oppressor Bern or the hero of Waadt. This painting, a perfect *Rührungswerk* in Heine's definition, offers a surfeit of emotional communication, dictating or strengthening the outrage and grief felt by the patriotic public.

# 9

# GRINNING, LAUGHING, MOCKING

Mockery of the public in drawings and prints inevitably took on a new form when the institutionalization of exhibitions meant that the Church, the court and the wealthy were replaced as arbiters of taste by the public. Some artists saw this as liberating, while others were disconcerted by it. Artists could once again be accused of exploiting the inferior public taste for their own purposes. Valentine Green, one of the best print publishers of the eighteenth century, did precisely this when he compared the state of the arts in France and Britain with Benjamin West and John Singleton Copley, unpopular rivals from the American colonies, whose exhibitions fascinated the London public. Green called their art 'works of speculation' that attracted the public, while painters themselves had their eyes on the admission charges and marketed the reproductions.[1]

Green pointed to a work such as Copley's *The Death of the Earl of Chatham*, which showed the tragic collapse of William Pitt, Lord Chatham, during a session of Parliament in 1778. Copley presented his painting in 1781 exclusively in the House of Lords, the upper house, before the public were allowed to view it. An etching by William Angus based on a drawing by Daniel Dodd documents the presentation of the painting in a frame decorated with the British lion and a large curtain, and the visit by peers with their spouses (illus. 25).[2] A key plate hangs on the wall to the left with the names of those depicted. Angus shows three women and three men from the back. One of the men is standing stiffly, a fat man assumes a ridiculous contrapposto, and the third man is bent forward holding tightly to a child. The three women in front of the painting are fashionably dressed and wearing similar hats. The couple approaching from the right are attired according to the latest French fashions, as are the couple leaving the scene on the left. Dodd and Angus satirize the fat, modishly dressed public in front of the painting, in which Copley presents the peers in their ceremonial red robes.

This mocking poke at the exclusive public attending exhibitions by eighteenth-century English artists achieves its satirical effect through the anonymous back views. Frontal views of the public serving to highlight and distinguish the site and the exhibition had satirical elements incorporated in them. The 1787 etching (illus. 27) by Pierre Antoine Martini shows the large Royal Academy exhibition

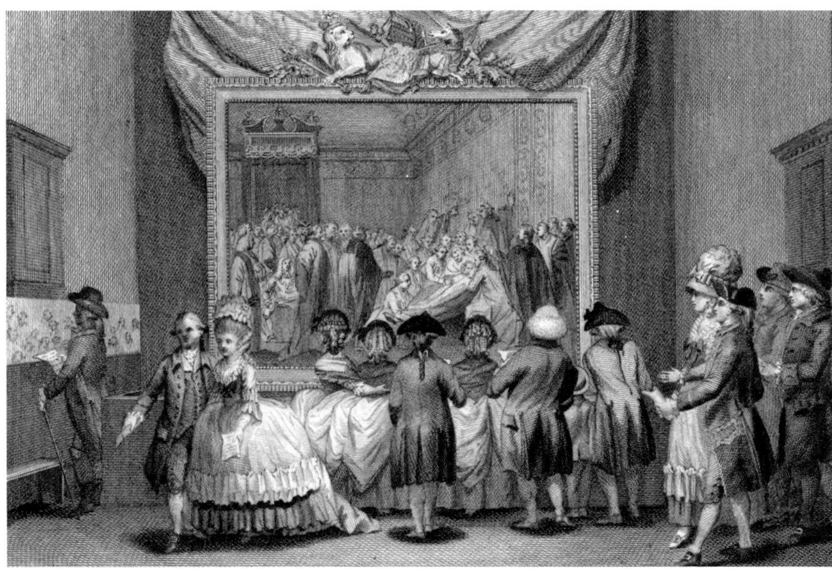

25 William Angus, after Daniel Dodd, *The Death of Lord Chatham in the House of Peers,* 1781, engraving.

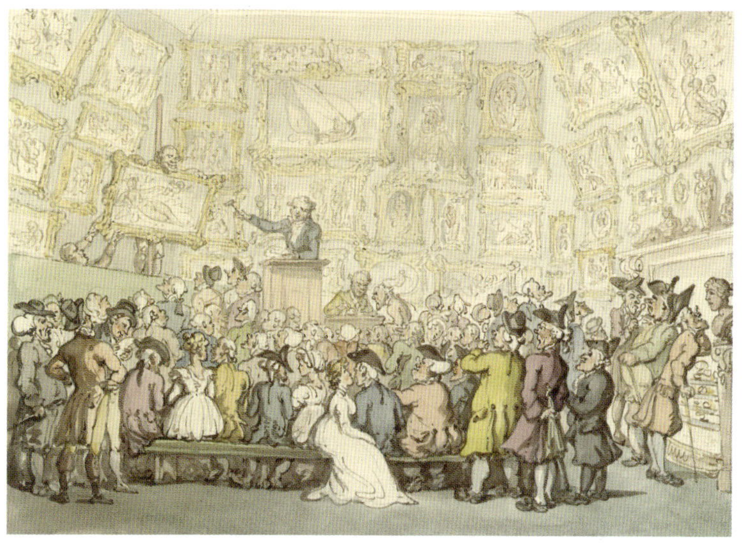

26 Thomas Rowlandson, *An Auction at Christie's*, c. 1808, pen and grey and brown ink and watercolour.

room in Somerset House with its walls packed with paintings and a crowd of visitors. In the foreground in elegant contrapposto is the scandal-ridden Prince of Wales (later George IV), highlighted in red and yellow in the colour version. Next to him, Joshua Reynolds is holding his ear trumpet and giving explanations to the prince. The postures and clothing of some of the elegant audience mirror the paintings on the walls. The dogs, the importunate seducer, the corpulent bishop, the elegant connoisseur with his magnifying glasses, the fat man with his wife and her lover – in other words, English high society in all its diversity – are present.

One of the first prints showing the public in the Royal Academy in London, by Richard Earlom from a drawing by Michel Charles Brandoin, puts the illustrious public, particularly the experts and critics, through the wringer. Thomas Rowlandson's satire on the public at an auction at Christie's in London was published in 1808. The auctioneer calls up the painting of a reclining female nude,

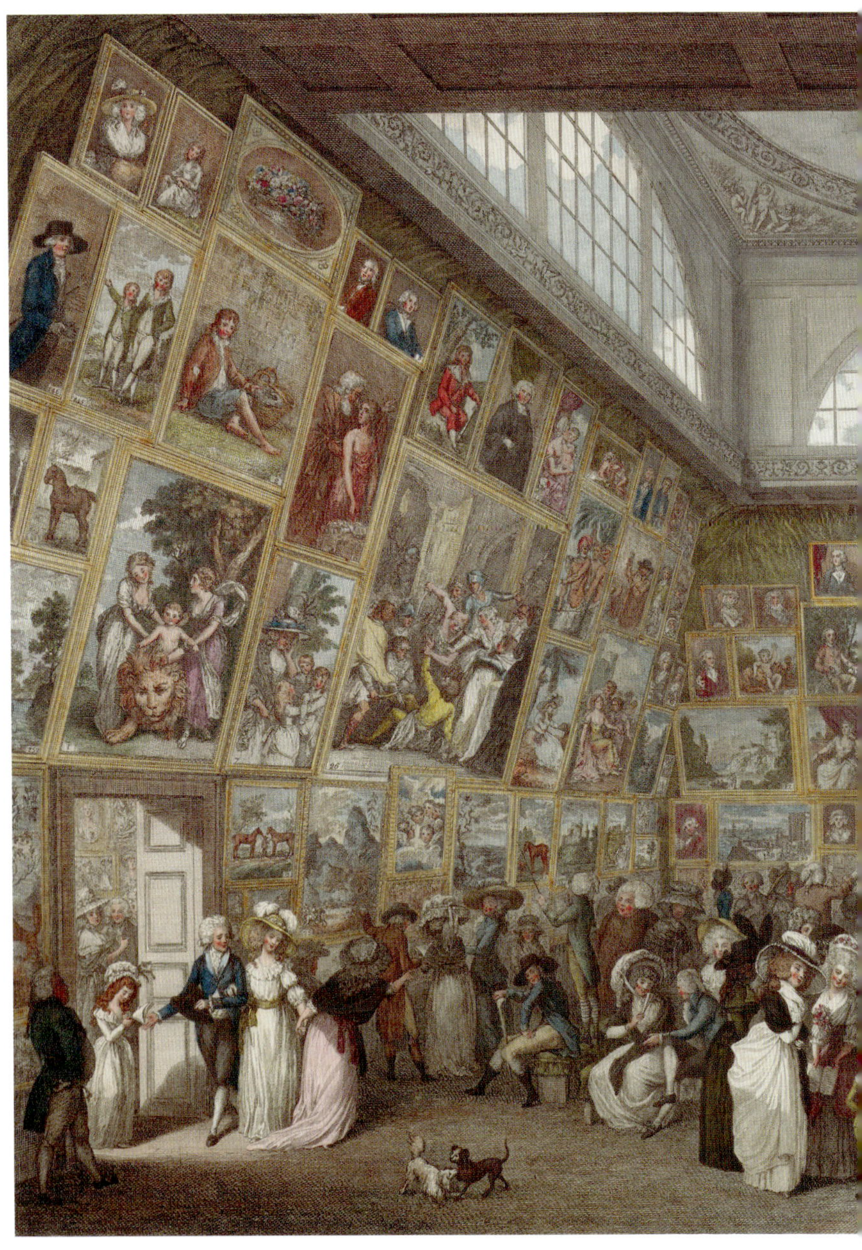

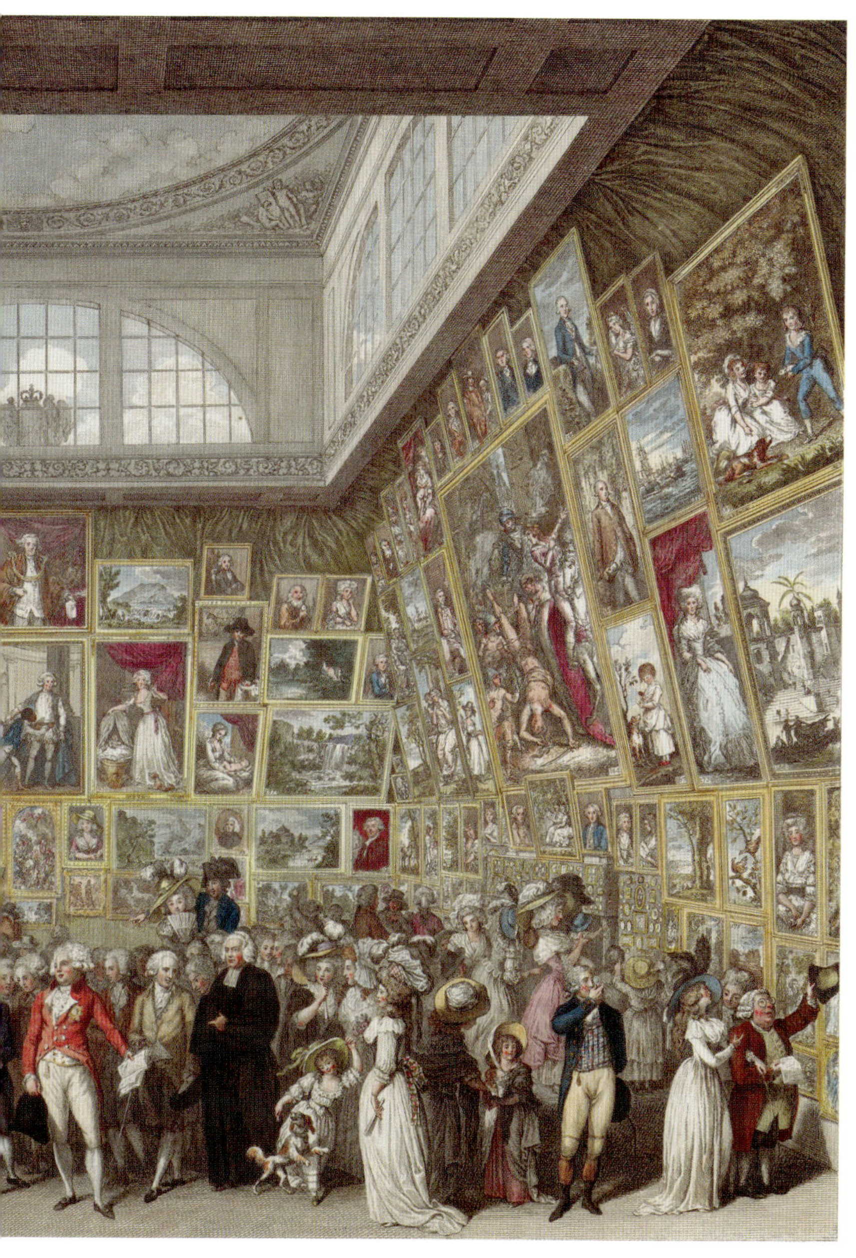

27 Pietro Antonio Martini, after Johann Heinrich Ramberg, *The Exhibition of the Royal Academy*, 1787, hand-coloured etching.

which is held for inspection by lascivious men by an attendant with the face of a satyr. Rowlandson portrays the public as grotesque, from the pompous man on the left to the couples billing and cooing and the old man on the right admiring a portrait bust and the fat connoisseur with a magnifying glass. All of the men have grotesquely distorted faces and ridiculous hats, but the women are generally spared.

As soon as a large audience forms, artists and museum officials fear that the unpredictable mass will turn into a mob. Caricaturists like Thomas Rowlandson or George Cruikshank transform the mob into an object of amusement for those who feel superior to the vulgar masses. Rowlandson places the boorish John Bull, the personification of Great Britain invented by the Scot John Arbuthnot, in the midst of the mob, to whom he devotes the highly amusing depiction of Napoleon's travelling coach, the greatest attraction ever seen in

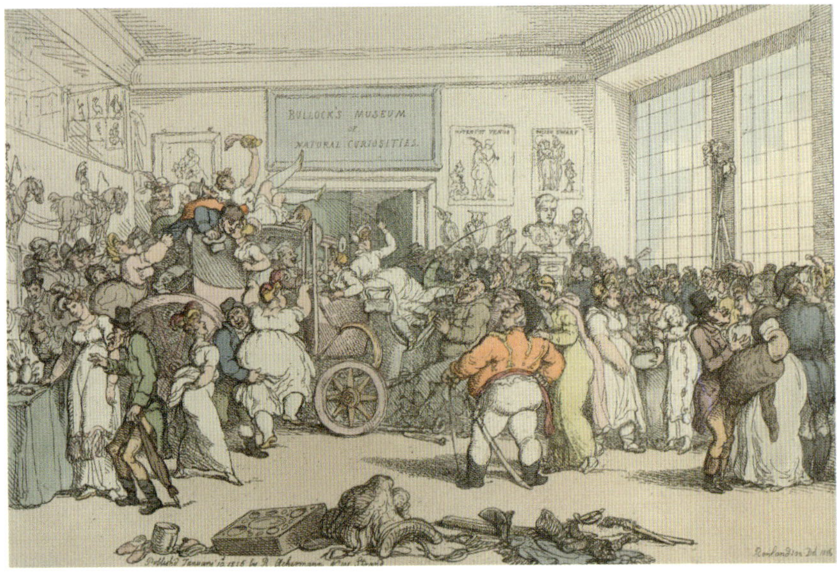


28 Thomas Rowlandson, *Exhibition at Bullock's Museum of Bonaparte's Carriage Taken at Waterloo*, 1816, hand-coloured etching.

William Bullock's Museum of Natural Curiosities. It was captured by the Prussians at Waterloo in 1815 and given by General Blücher to the Prince of Wales.[3] Bullock bought it from the prince for £2,500 and exhibited it in his Egyptian Hall in Piccadilly from January to August 1816. It attracted 220,000 visitors and earned him an incredible £35,000. Then the coach went on tour in England with other Napoleonic relics, returning to London in April 1817. After the tour, the coach was in such poor condition that it was sold for only £168 to a coachmaker and ended up in Madame Tussaud & Sons. In 1816, Rowlandson depicted the shabby citizens marvelling at the coach. It is surrounded by other Napoleonic relics such as the bust of the overthrown emperor, and in the foreground the contents of the coach are laid out on display. The back view of the corpulent John Bull, the plump ladies, the gouty, lecherous men, the young woman lying on her back with her legs obscenely in the air, the grabbed bosoms and behinds show the vulgar behaviour of the visitors to Bullock's Museum. A further contemporary satirical portrayal of Napoleon's coach comes from George Cruikshank, who has the members of high society mixing with the common people.[4] In this caricature, Rowlandson makes clear that vulgar behaviour is not a matter of class.

Georg Wilhelm Friedrich Hegel, since 1818 a well-known philosopher in Berlin, described the development of the mob based on events taking place in England. In *Elements of the Philosophy of Right* (1821), he wrote of the emergence of a 'pauper class' that occurs when the masses are debased and lose 'the sense of right, rectitude and honour'. They can no longer survive through activity or work and descend into poverty. At the same time, this process means that 'wealth accumulates disproportionately in the hands of a few.'[5] However, the seeming paradox then arises that the 'civic community' is excessively wealthy, but not rich enough 'to stem the excess of poverty and the creation of paupers'.[6]

The growing poverty accompanying the Industrial Revolution is reflected in the societal processes in England. Théodore Géricault in 1821, James Mahony in 1840 and Gustave Doré in 1872 drew illustrations of ragged and hungry poor people, and newspapers such as the *Illustrated London News* contained woodcuts showing this situation, but none of the illustrators made fun of the wretched existences that were no longer self-sufficient.[7] In 1837 and 1838, in a serial in a London magazine, Charles Dickens published the socially critical story of the orphan Oliver Twist, who fell into the clutches of villains, thieves and criminals, but after suffering various vicissitudes was ultimately identified through a portrait of his mother and acquired wealth and social status as a reward for his unfailingly noble spirit.[8] George Cruikshank illustrated the first edition of *Oliver Twist* in 1838. In *Les Misérables* in 1862, Victor Hugo told the story of Jean Valjean, who is imprisoned for stealing a piece of bread and remains in prison for nineteen years, all the time maintaining noble sentiments and receiving his reward on his deathbed. Hugo's novel was published in 1862 in Neuchâtel and Brussels, and was reprinted many times and translated into several languages. An edition by Gustave Brion with two hundred woodcut illustrations was published in Paris in 1867 by Hetzel and Lacroix.[9]

In 1730, William Hogarth, the most acute social critic in England, issued a subscription ticket for his graphic series *A Rake's Progress*, which he called *The Laughing Audience*.[10] At the bottom are three musicians and behind the spiked barrier are the grotesque heads of the laughing audience. In the box above them two gentlemen are importuning two young women, while a third woman with a basket of oranges tugs at the sleeve of one of the gentlemen to distract him from her competitor – all nicely matching the title. The spectators at plays and the opera were pilloried more mercilessly than art exhibition visitors. In 1796 Isaac Cruikshank published a satire in London on opera audiences visibly enjoying looking up the skirt of the dancer Rose Parisot as she performs a *grand battement jeté*.[11] The dancer is balanced on her right leg, lifts her left leg towards the audience and stretches out her arms. Two men in the open door look up at the enticing dancer. Political rivals are united in their lasciviousness and some of them are identified: the Duke of Queensbury with telescope is at the far left of the first row, and William Pitt the Younger is at the far right.[12]

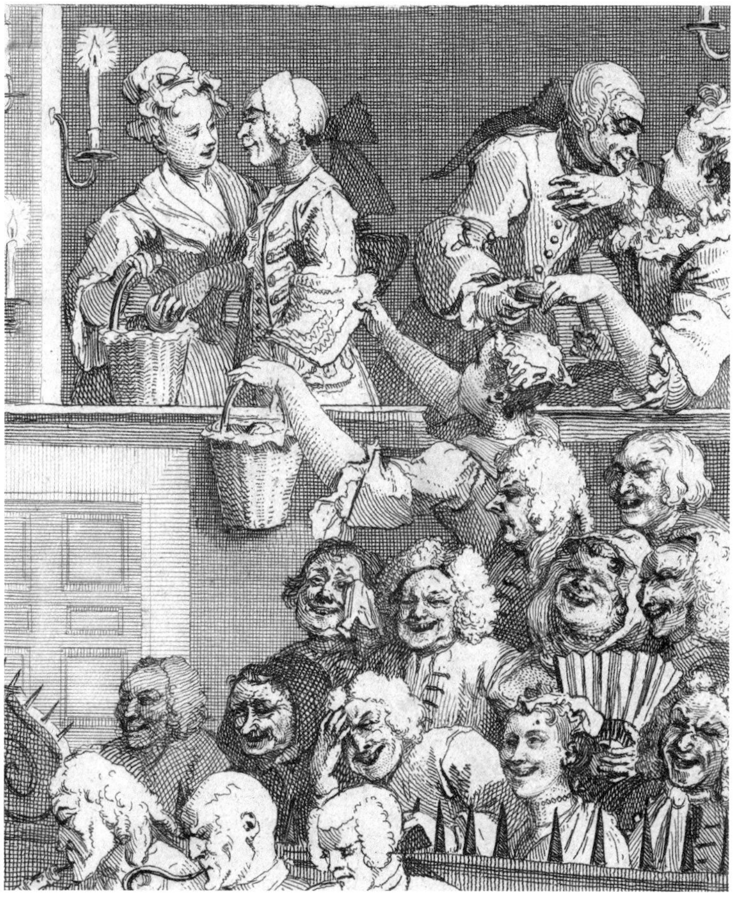

29 William Hogarth, *The Laughing Audience*, 1733, etching.

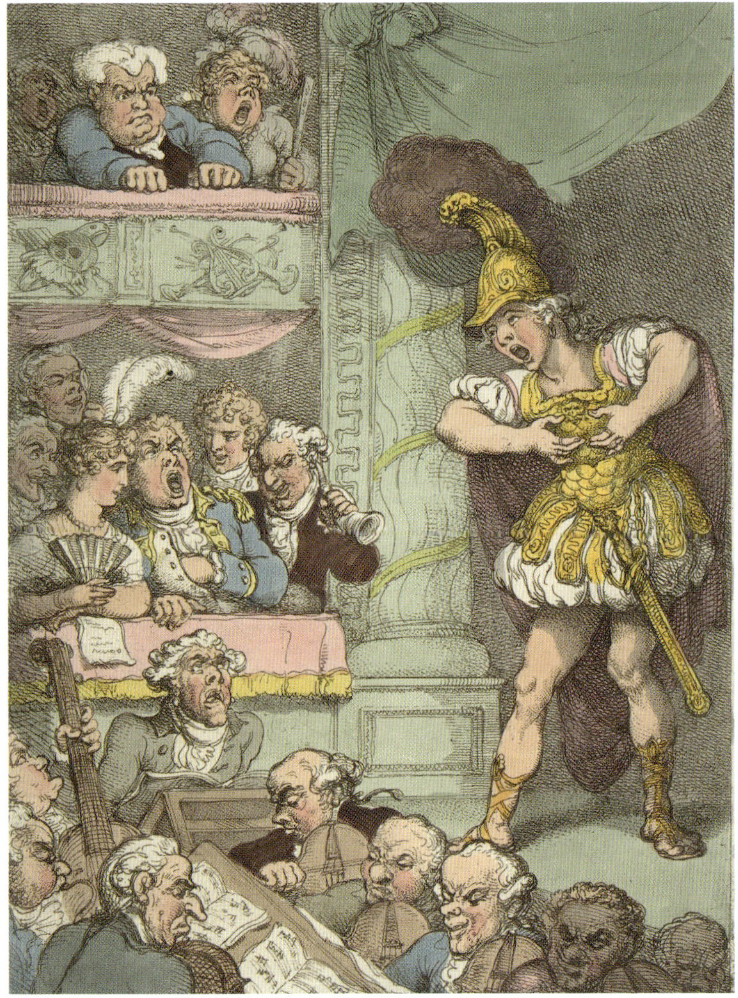

30 Thomas Rowlandson, *John Bull at the Italian Opera*, 1811, hand-coloured etching.

In 1811 Thomas Rowlandson published an etching entitled *John Bull at the Italian Opera*.[13] John Bull is sitting with a grim expression in the upper box between two yawning female figures. On the stage, a singer in Roman garb is giving his best while a spectator in a blue coat yawns widely, another is holding an ear trumpet, and the other spectators are seen to be enjoying themselves. The conductor and musicians in the orchestra pit are all caricatured in the style of Hogarth. Rowlandson shows the vulgar behaviour of opera audiences but also the ridiculous musicians and the grimacing singer, whose open mouth is mirrored by the yawning spectators.

Artists often use donkey's ears to mock the public and critics. This ploy had already been used with the legendary King Midas, who foolishly decided in favour of the flute-playing Pan in a competition with the god Apollo playing the lyre.[14] Apelles painted a picture, *The Calumny of Apelles*, which had been reconstructed several times since the end of the fifteenth century as a warning to customers and the public.[15] In his *Satire on Art Criticism* in 1644, Rembrandt gave a critic donkey's ears. On the ground in front of the critic is a picture, evidently the object of his criticism. Three people are listening to the critic. On the right are two men with tall hats representing the public. Through scatological humour, Rembrandt elevates derision to wicked mockery.[16]

François Boucher in France and Nicolai Abildgaard in Denmark took a radical approach by placing a braying donkey in the audience. In Boucher's drawing, used twice as a frontispiece, the melancholy gagged figure of Painting sits inactive before the easel, while the carefree putti at his feet draw to their heart's content. Behind Painting, a figure representing Envy, accompanied by a drunkard, points at the picture, and a donkey brays over the art critics and the crowd.[17] In Nicolai Abildgaard's *Le Sort des Artistes* (illus. 31) the painter hides behind the canvas as a modern Apelles and plugs his ears while the old man with donkey's ears in the centre of the picture, accompanied by a turkey and a goose, points to the painting of two philosophers. A child gestures at a fold in the robe, and two women admire the picture. A ram's head and a pig's head are visible in the public behind. Finally, the large figure of Athena with winged helmet places her

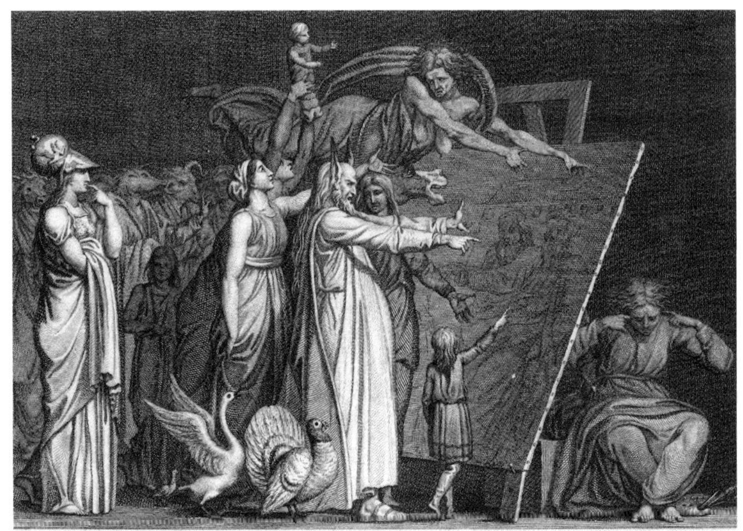

31 Johan Frederik Clemens, after Nicolai Abildgaard, *Le Sort des Artistes*, 1786, etching.

finger to her lips vainly asking for silence. Abildgaard's satire expresses mistrust and disdain for critics and spares only the 'naive' public.

In an etching of 1817, Wolfgang-Adam Töpffer shows the people of Geneva in front of Wessel's stationery shop.[18] Passers-by and art lovers are standing on the street in front of the entrance as a short-sighted student adjusts his glasses and then four fashionably dressed women come out. An elderly man is holding a magnifying glass in front of his nose, while a funny hat almost completely hides a little girl on the left of the group. On the right is an egg seller on a donkey carrying a fat boy in front of him, just as the she-ass protects the foal underneath her. On the left a corpulent peasant-looking man stands prominently with an old military cap and a rucksack, from which a piece of cloth protrudes. Between him and the girl holding a loaf of bread are two thin male figures seen from behind, identified through their pre-revolutionary knee breeches as being members of the upper class. Some members of the public are looking at the framed pictures covering the wall. Several of these drawings or prints are satirical pictures – for example, one of three heads on jugs entitled *Les Grands Hommes*. To the right of it, Töpffer shows the basic inventory of the caricaturist: the diverse heads distorted in various ways. To the left of the shop sign is a comic figure and to the right a fat man seen from behind, the stereotype of a ridiculous figure drawn by Giovanni Battista Tiepolo around 1760.[19] The only drawing that is not a caricature is one in the top right corner of a mother with her child. This etching reflects Töpffer's hope for a public as an audience discussing and admiring his work.

A few years earlier, Pierre-Nolasque Bergeret had set the pattern for caricatures of the mixed art public in a lithograph of Aaron Martinet's bookshop at 15, rue du Coq in Paris (illus. 33).[20] Bergeret gathers in front of the shop a comical kaleidoscope of urban types: the fat saleswoman with a tray, the spindly scholar with glasses and a lorgnon, the fashionably dressed ladies, the mistrustful husband

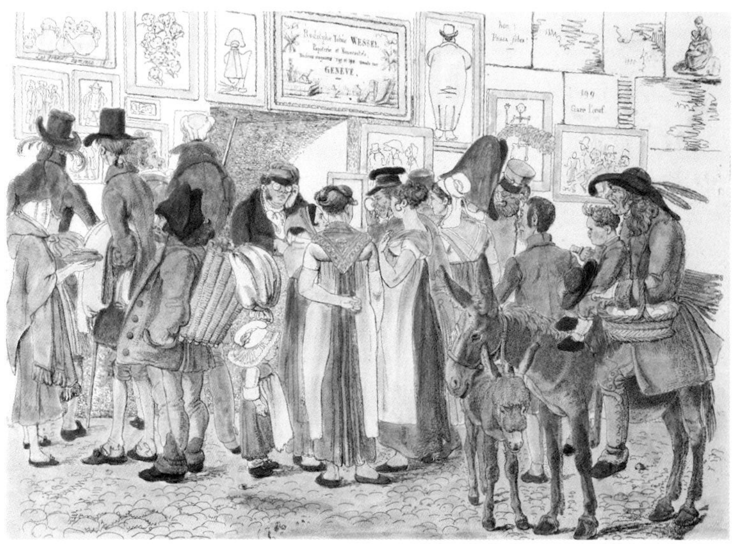

32 Wolfgang-Adam Töpffer, *People in Front of Rodolphe Tobie Wessel's Shop in Geneva*, c. 1817, etching with watercolour.

with the delicate young woman, the back view in contrapposto, the comical back view of the fat man, and finally a daintily made-up lady. The most ridiculous character is the pompous know-all in the centre of the picture with his legs wide apart, bicorn, monkey's face and magnifying glass.

The theatre, music hall, concert and salon audiences offered caricaturists and satirists an inexhaustible supply of material. In France in the mid-nineteenth century, Honoré Daumier's subjects included all facets of society: the common people, petty bourgeoisie, artists, lawyers, swindlers and profiteers, ministers and the king. He accused Salon audiences of stupidity, complacency and narrow-mindedness and published lithographs in the satirical magazine *Le Charivari*. One lithograph in the series *Le Public du Salon* in 1852 shows the public crowding into the Salon on a day when no admission was charged. A very corpulent women is visibly suffering from the heat, the expression in the noble physiognomy of the man next to her is one of indignation, and behind are top-hatted citizens who put up

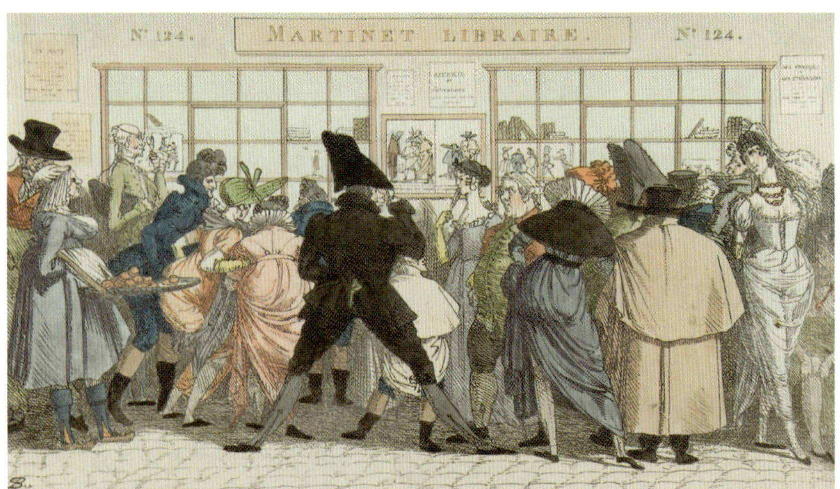


33 Pierre-Nolasque Bergeret, *Dawdlers of the Rue du Coq*, 1805, hand-coloured lithograph.

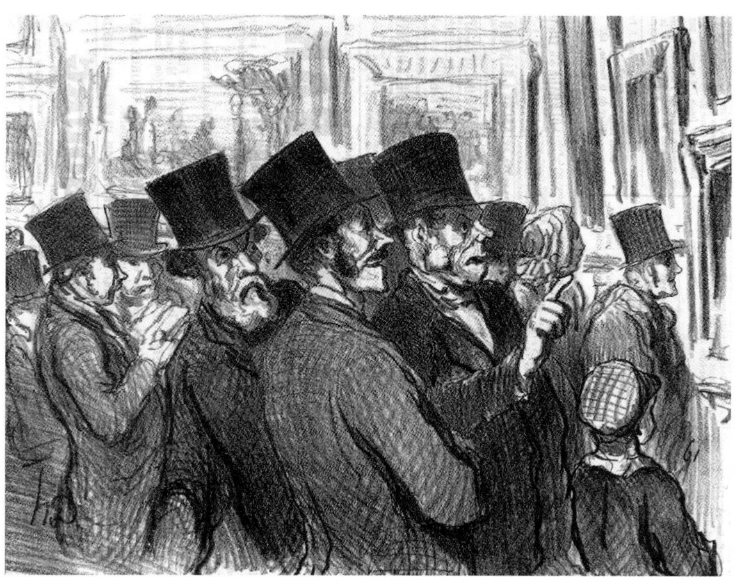

34 Honoré Daumier, 'Aspect du salon le jour de l'ouverture . . .', lithograph, published in *Le Charivari*, 22 June 1857.

with the masses for the sake of the free admission. Two urchins push their way through the crowds in search of money and watches in the citizens' waistcoat pockets. A lithograph from the series *Le Salon de 1857* is even more vicious and aggressive than usual. It shows a group of citizens in top hats with a woman and child in the corner of the exhibition room. The three gentlemen in the middle look particularly evil. The foremost figure raises his bony index finger in criticism of the picture, the second grins, and the third looks on in the most furious disgust. These three, who imagine they are being insulted by the artist, are not merely critics or appalled visitors. Daumier creates a new aggressive species: the enemies of art.

Laughing at artists and their works is the most spontaneous and clear expression of public hostility. The journalist Adolphe Tabarant quotes a report by the painter Charles Cazin, whose submission was rejected by the jury, on the visitors to the Salon des Refusés in

1863, who at the turnstile listened impatiently and enviously to the bursts of laughter at the paintings: 'They laughed so loud that the people waiting to be admitted complained about the slowness of the turnstile. "It was like entering the Chamber of Horrors in Madame Tussaud's in London. People started laughing as soon as they entered," wrote the rejected painter Charles Cazin.'[21]

The main targets of the public's laughter at the first Salon of Rejected Paintings was Édouard Manet's *Déjeuner sur l'herbe* (Paris, Musée d'Orsay) and the American James McNeill Whistler's *Symphony in White, No. 1: The White Girl* (Washington, DC, National Gallery

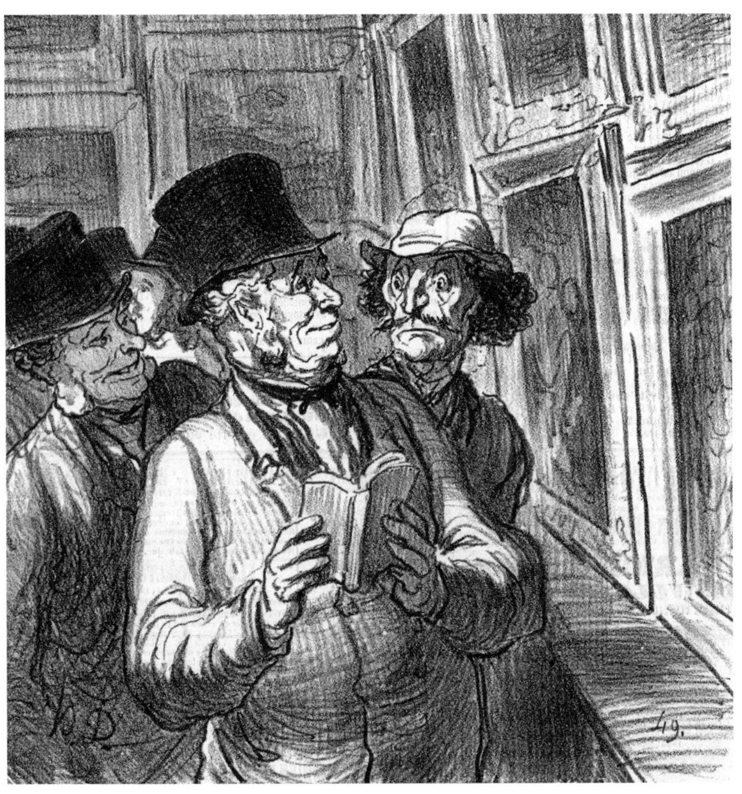

35 Honoré Daumier, 'The Visitor and the Artist', lithograph, published in *Le Charivari*, 30 May 1864.

of Art). Daumier exposed the aggressive maliciousness of those who laugh at a picture to humiliate the painter. Among the sketches of the Salon published in *Le Charivari* in 1864 was a lithograph showing a grinning, top-hatted man in the foreground and another man with the same expression to his left (illus. 35). The artist reacts fiercely to the aggression, and the caption reproduces the mockery and insults: 'The Visitor: Just look at this senseless arrangement . . . and these colours! . . . hideous! The Artist: Cretin bourgeois!'[22]

In his essay on the essence of laughter in 1855, Charles Baudelaire quoted Jacques-Bénigne Bossuet, Louis XIV's court preacher: 'The wise man trembles when he laughs.' Baudelaire corrects those who assume that laughter comes from superiority and claims that to laugh at others' misfortune is a sign of weakness, which can be seen in the nervous twitching and contorted facial expression.[23] In the summary he repeats, 'Laughing is satanic and profoundly human' and is therefore also profoundly contradictory, as a sign of 'infinite misery' in comparison with the absolute entity and of 'infinite greatness' in comparison with animals: 'Laughter occurs through the constant collision of these two infinities.' Baudelaire went on to separate laughter from the person laughing: 'The humour and power of laughter is in the person laughing and not at all in what he is laughing at.'[24] He makes no mention of the effect of laughter on the person being laughed at. Daumier replied to this omission with a caricature of a bourgeois couple who burst into laughter at a painting while the artist, evidently from a much lower class, looks on grimly: 'The idiots . . . A picture with a religious subject is painted for them and they laugh . . . they don't even believe in art.'[25] For Daumier in the 1860s, the relationship between artists and the public was one of aggression and insult.

In his defence of Édouard Manet, the young journalist and writer Émile Zola suggested that there was a conspiracy by the public against the artist. In 1866, the ambitious Zola, a youthful friend of Paul Cézanne, came out in support of Manet, who had seen two of his paintings rejected. In his essay, he insulted almost all the members of the jury. He signed his essays, which appeared in seven instalments in the short-lived magazine *L'Évènement*, with the pseudonym 'Claude', appointing himself 'Moi, public' and complaining about the violation of freedom of opinion by the jury. On behalf of the public, he showed his outrage at the censorship of an art movement and demanded imperiously that the corrupt jury be exposed.[26] Zola criticized the arbitrary voting right restricted to established artists, who could show their works without judgement and blocked young artists. For Zola, the rejection of Manet's paintings was confirmation that the jury allowed itself to be swayed by cliques, and he declared himself militantly to be a 'défenseur de la réalité'.[27] He attacked the established artists and compared them with Manet, who was at the start of his career. In the last article, he announced his retirement as an art critic and admitted ironically that all of the enormities he was accused of had been committed deliberately.[28]

In January of the following year, Zola published an essay on Manet entitled 'Édouard Manet, étude biographique et critique'. The third and last section is devoted to the public. He starts by criticizing the antics of jokers and freeloaders, who turn Manet into a villain and *enfant terrible* with the shabby aim of making the public laugh.[29] Zola said that Manet the artist and his works were known but there was something else that needed to be known: the masses, *la foule*, who laughed offensively at Manet, whom they regarded as a pariah, rejected by society.

Did claqueurs appear in the nineteenth century at exhibitions as they did from the 1820s onwards in Paris theatres, led by a *chef de claque*, who ensured success through their organized applause?[30] There are few reports of such devices in the visual arts, and artists sought favour through good reviews by friendly critics or journalists. Were there secret arrangements to humiliate a rival through public laughter? Zola's text, some of which is fictional, suggests an arrangement between the public and the critics to attack Manet. Zola invents the harassment of the painter on the street by a gang of 'gamins' who throw stones, while the critics, who are meant to protect him, themselves pick up cobblestones and add to the tumult. To prevent further harm, Zola speaks with the urchins, the critics and Manet, and in view of the public rage at the crime by this pariah, he can only be acting to calm the situation.[31] He attempts to persuade the public, who feel insulted by the painter, of his decency, the fact that he goes to work every day like other citizens and spends his evenings with his friends and family.

In the last chapter, entitled 'Le Public', Zola presents his observations on the behaviour of the masses. The first reproach aimed at artist colleagues is of the cowardly way they laugh with the mob instead of attempting to calm them. He believes that the behaviour of the mob, which will burst out laughing for little reason, much as they might mock an actor in the theatre who repeatedly stumbles over his lines, to be childish. He writes of the reaction of an intelligent group to something new and its infectious effect on the masses: 'Place ten people of sufficient intelligence in front of a new and original painting and they will all behave like children; they will nudge one another and joke about the work. Onlookers will come and join the group, and soon there will be mayhem, an outbreak of stupid madness.'[32]

Zola knew that such outbreaks of stupidity and madness passed, but also that the public reacted the same way to every innovation in art – before Manet there was the same reaction to Delacroix – and that it would be the same for any original artist. The greatest curse is originality, as it disturbs our habitual way of thinking. At the same time, the fury is still dangerous: 'There is a whole army interested in keeping the crowd entertained, which it does well. The caricaturists attack the man and the work. The journalists laugh even louder than the disinterested mockers. Ultimately it is nothing but laughter, just wind.'[33]

Zola shows contempt for the childish and mean behaviour of the mob. But what should they do, when in the din of contemporary opinions no one listens to or guides them? And what do the artists do? The great realm of art is divided into many artist republics, each with its own partisan supporters: 'Every artist has attracted his own crowd, who flatter him, give him the toys he likes, gilded and decorated with pink favours. Art here has become a huge sweet shop with bonbons for all tastes.'[34]

Apart from aggression, public laughter is an expression of powerlessness and puzzlement at new art. One example of the bouts of laughter in exhibitions comes from a cultural backwater in 1911. The journalist Hans Bloesch starts his review of the exhibition of his boyhood friend Paul Klee in Bern with a comment on the public which might or might not be invented. Bloesch writes of the bourgeois public of a small town:

> The result was always cautious silence by the critics and the helpless puzzlement of the public, who after the initial shock laughed in mockery or turned in revulsion to the more accustomed pastures of their aesthetic judgement. Some made it easier for themselves to turn away from such temerity with cheap jokes, others with indignant complaints. Only a few took the time to find their way in this new world.[35]

# 10

# THE MASSES

In 1835 the Belgian statistician Adolphe Quetelet undertook the first statistical survey of mankind, creating 'social physics' by defining the average development and the 'average man'.[1] The perception of a collection of people as a mass began to form later, after Quetelet's statistical survey. The attitude to the masses has always been ambivalent: they are welcome for statistical purposes, for the revenue they produce and for the acclaim and applause they provide, but on the other hand they are the object of social disdain, typically expressed in terms such as 'plebs' used in reference to large uneducated groups.

Events speculating on a mass public included the world's fairs from 1851, which from 1855 also had sections for the arts. Attendance rose from 6 million (1851, London) to 32 million (1889, Paris) and 28 million (1893, Chicago), peaking in 1900 in Paris with 48 million. The highest attendance to date (64.2 million) was registered in Osaka in 1970.[2] In 1878, 36 countries took part in the World's Fair in Paris, which attracted 16.2 million visitors, almost twice the number as the 1867 event in the same city. Interestingly, a colour view of the exhibition site in front of the Palais du Champ-de-Mars in 1878 shows neither masses nor 'plebs', but rather elegantly arranged groups of wealthy visitors. The German Empire initially declined to participate for political reasons and attempted to persuade other countries to boycott the Paris World's Fair, but then decided to

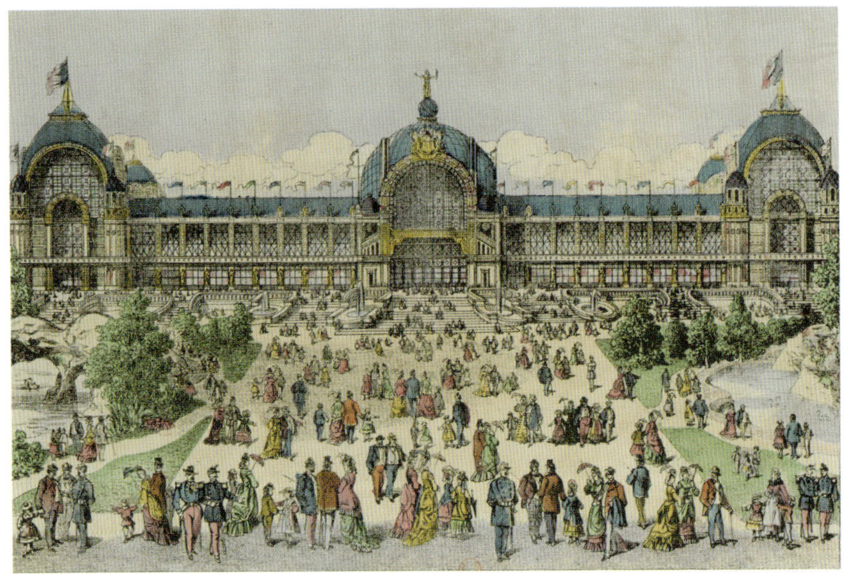

36 View of Palais du Champ-de-Mars, Exposition Universelle, 1878, coloured woodcut.

attempt a reconciliation with France with the help of contemporary German art.[3] A lithograph in the *Illustrirte Zeitung* of 7 September 1878 shows the success of the German section with interested visitors in the salon, whose furnishing was even praised by the French press, which naturally pleased the Germans.[4]

The rapidly growing number of visitors after 1851 to major events like the world's fairs correlates with the increase in population in European cities between 1850 and 1900, the period of importance for the perception of the masses. The population of cities such as London, Paris, Rome and Milan grew in this time by an average of 2.5 times per decade – from 2.37 times for Milan to 2.6 for Rome. In Zurich, a smaller city, the population increased by a factor of 8.88, from 17,000 to 151,000. Budapest and Vienna also grew by above-average amounts, from 178,000 (1850) to 732,000 (1900) in the former and from 444,000 to 1,675,000, or 3.77 times, in the latter.[5]

In the album *London: A Pilgrimage*, published in 1872 by the English writer Blanchard Jerrold, the illustrations by Gustave Doré of the wretched life of the masses clash with the pleasures of the upper classes, but it also shows that at the Epsom Derby, the legendary horse race, the crowds came from all social classes.[6] Doré's bird's-eye view depicts the spectators with a decreasing degree of detail, from close-ups of persons with different physiognomies, poses and clothing to the indistinguishable mass of people extending into the distance. The Epsom Derby was one of the few days in the year in which 'the excitement in the clubs; the vivacity of the mob; and the abnormal mixture of classes and of strangers' were evident, as Jerrold wrote.[7] Doré puts the horses, which are just crossing the finishing line, at the right-hand edge, along with a bird casting its shadow as it flies across the racetrack. The main focus is the immense crowd of spectators in the grandstand, forming a wedge that tapers between the cordon and the edge of the picture. At the narrow end of the wedge women's clothes, men's heads and

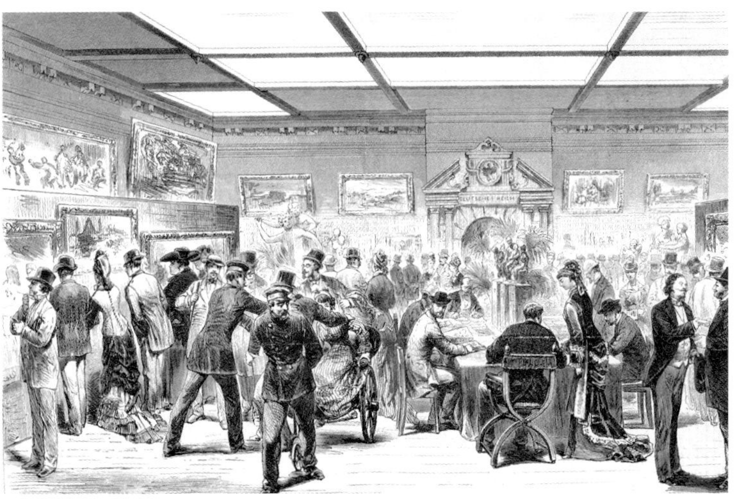

37 Leo von Elliot, 'At the German Art Exhibition', lithograph, published in *Illustrirte Zeitung*, 7 September 1878.

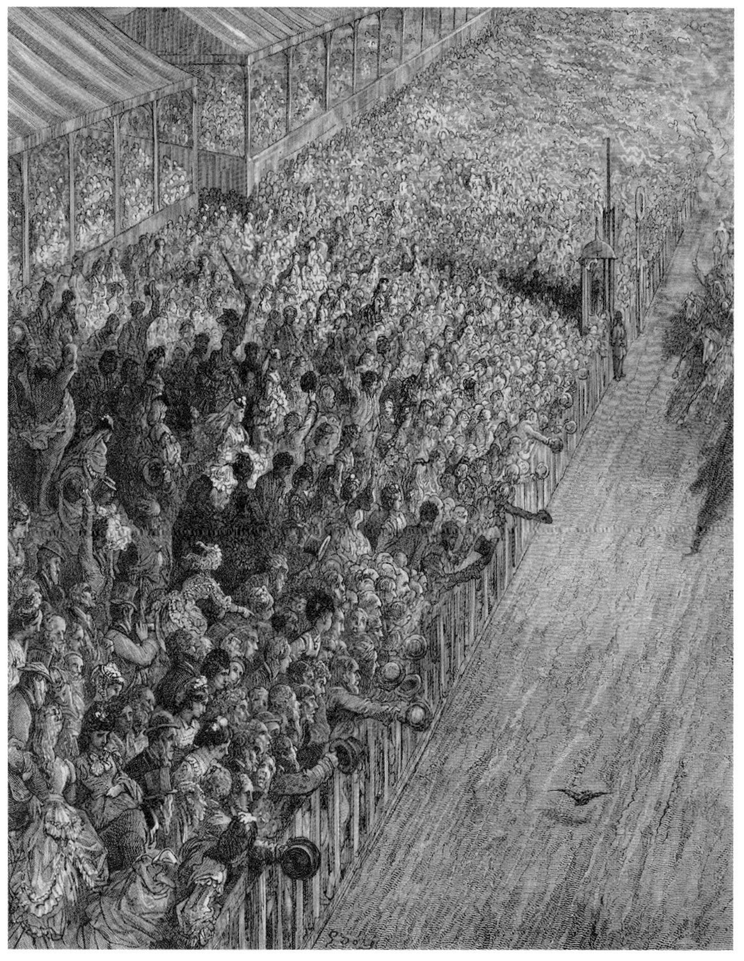

38 Gustave Doré, 'The Epsom Derby', wood engraving, published in Gustave Doré and Blanchard Jerrold, *London: A Pilgrimage* (1872).

hats – mainly the top hats of the upper classes required according to the Epsom dress code, but also some middle-class bowlers – are piled up. Some of the spectators hold their hats and stretch out their arms over the cordon to greet the passing riders. The crowd is packed closely together at the cordon. As the wedge widens, a row of dark figures cuts through the crowd, spreading out into a formless cluster in front of the grandstand. Above the dark row and in the gallery is a swarm of circles that become smaller and end in wavy lines, the mass of heads transforming into an indistinct sea.

In his comments on Doré's pictures, Jerrold makes frequent use of a wave metaphor to describe the movement of the crowds: 'A flutter goes through the sea of heads on the Grand Stand.'[8] Or:

> But the most curious spectacle is the human tide which, instantaneously and in a body, pours forth and rolls over the course behind the runners, like a wave of ink; the black and motionless crowd has suddenly melted and become molten; in a moment it spreads itself abroad in vast proportions till the eye cannot follow it, and appears in front of the stand.[9]

In his short story 'The Man of the Crowd', written in 1840, Edgar Allan Poe describes the mass of people as a 'tumultuous sea of human heads'. After a long illness, the narrator sits in the D coffee house on one of the busiest streets in London, smokes a cigar and is transformed from reader to observer, watching the people passing the window with a heightened sensitivity.[10] He attempts first to guess their social status and then their profession from their facial expressions and behaviour. He assumes that those who behave decently are engaged in private affairs. Wearers of outdated fashions are most likely junior clerks, while upper clerks are identifiable by their black suits. He discerns pickpockets and gamblers, dandies and soldiers on the basis of their clothing and hairstyles. Then follows the observation of the lower and most wretched classes: pedlars, beggars, drunkards, prostitutes, hopeless young girls, then the colliers, organ grinders, street singers, ragged artists and exhausted labourers. As darkness falls, the more orderly citizens disappear, to be replaced increasingly by underworld characters. The flickering gaslight

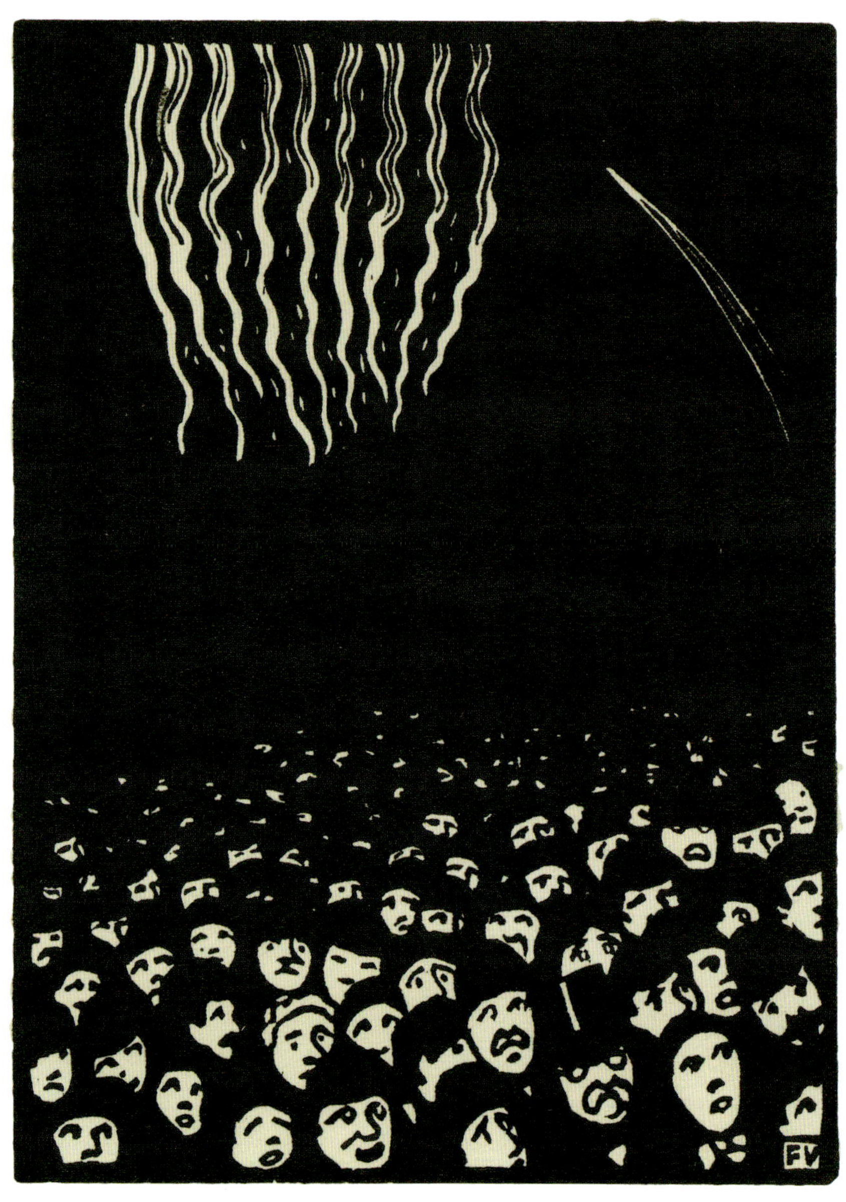


39 Félix Vallotton, *Fireworks*, plate VI from *The World's Fair* (*L'exposition universelle*), 1901, woodcut.

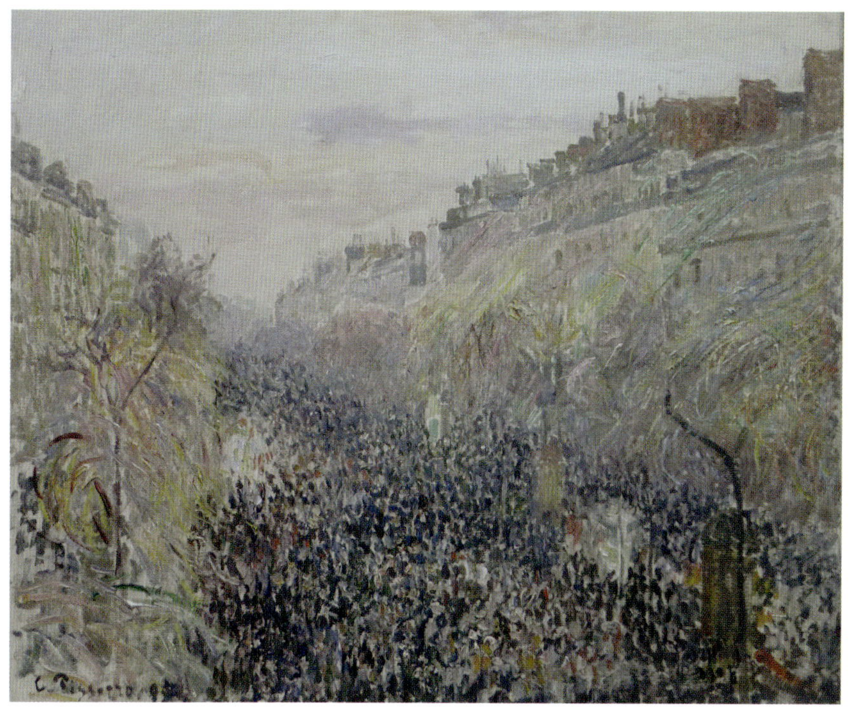

40 Camille Pissarro, *Boulevard Montmartre, Mardi Gras, Sunset*, 1897, oil on canvas.

forces the observer to switch from studying the mob to looking closely at individuals. He is suddenly struck by the facial expression of an elderly man who seems to resemble Mephisto, and he surmises that 'Retzsch' might well have used him as a model for the Devil.[11] Poe is referring to the illustrations by Moritz Retzsch for Goethe's *Faust*, published in Germany in 1816 and reprinted on 6 May 1837 by the British *Saturday Magazine* with the caption 'Satan playing at chess with man, for his soul'.

In 1895 Gustave Le Bon, doctor and founder of mass psychology, published his major and unexpectedly popular opus, *Psychologie des foules*. Le Bon suggests that under certain circumstances a collection of people develops a 'collective soul': the conscious personality disappears, and feelings and thoughts are turned in a specific direction. The 'organized crowd . . . forms a single being and is subject to the law of the mental unity of crowds.'[12] Le Bon fears that the recent emergence of the masses will signify a return to 'periods of confused anarchy' and the 'last stages of Western civilization'. He claims that civilizations have always been created by a 'small intellectual aristocracy' and that crowds are only powerful for destruction.[13] As a doctor, Le Bon asserts that in a crowd of people, 'contagion' unifies individuals and turns them into a mass capable of violent acts that the individual would not commit:

> An isolated individual knows well enough that alone he cannot set fire to a palace or loot a shop, and should he be tempted to do so, he will easily resist the temptation. Making part of a crowd, he is conscious of the power given him by numbers, and it is sufficient to suggest to him ideas of murder or pillage for him to yield immediately to temptation.[14]

In a lecture on tuberculosis in Berlin in 1882, Robert Koch described the process of contagion with diseases.[15] Le Bon applies the virologist's discovery to social psychology in his description of crowd phenomena. Like most of his contemporaries, he based his arguments on racial theory, making a distinction between Latin and Anglo-Saxon crowds and comparing their crowd behaviour with that of primitive beings. Crowds can be manipulated not only to destroy and commit crimes, which Le Bon emphasizes, but also to heroism, religious feeling and fanaticism. In fact, he claims, all crowd convictions have a religious form: 'The hero acclaimed by a crowd is a veritable god for that crowd. Napoleon was such a god for fifteen years, and a divinity never had more frequent worshippers or sent men to their death with greater ease.'[16]

At the same time as Gustave Le Bon, Félix Vallotton in Paris also analysed crowd behaviour. He produced his perfect pictorial representations of the masses in the early 1890s. One of his woodcuts, *La Foule à Paris*, shows a number of male and female heads being herded together in a confined space by a policeman. In *Le Couplet patriotique* of 1893, men clap and sing a patriotic song in the balcony of a theatre. For the graphic art dealer Edmond Sagot, Vallotton made a woodcut in 1892 showing a dense crowd of men in top hats and bowlers in front of a shop. In the woodcut *La Manifestation* of 1893 people are running in all kinds of grotesque contortions for a street demonstration. *Feu d'artifice* from the 1901 series *L'Exposition universelle* shows a crowd of faces looking upward at the streams of light descending from the sky and a single rocket ascending.

In 1897, Camille Pissarro painted two pictures of the crowd during Mardi Gras in Paris, calling it *faire la foule* (doing the crowd). He rented a room in Hôtel de Russie at 1, rue Drouot and in a short time painted two versions of the crowd streaming down boulevard Montmartre during Mardi Gras. The larger version is in the Hammer Museum in Los Angeles and the somewhat smaller one is in the Kunst Museum, Winterthur.[17] It shows the boulevard lined by green trees between two rows of tall buildings, its entire length and breadth filled, except for two small areas, with black dots suggesting the uniform movement of the crowd.

11

# MOURNING CROWDS

There has been little study of the funeral services for artists in the nineteenth and twentieth centuries, although they frequently aroused considerable public interest.[1] The largest turnout was achieved for the burial of Bertel Thorvaldsen in Copenhagen in 1844.[2] This Danish sculptor, who worked mostly in Rome and was renowned throughout Europe in the first half of the nineteenth century alongside Antonio Canova, had a monographic museum erected in Copenhagen, where he was born. Interestingly, he was supported not only by the king and the authorities, but by the public. The poet Hans Christian Andersen wrote in his monograph on Thorvaldsen: 'A committee of his Danish admirers and friends sent out a requisition for the people, that every one might give their mite; many a poor servant-girl and many a peasant gave theirs, so that a good sum was soon collected.'[3]

This significant event is the first example of the sponsoring of a one-person museum by the public. From that point of view, Andersen's statement that Thorvaldsen's life was a triumphal procession since fortune accompanied him and 'men have in him acknowledged and paid homage to art' is understandable.[4] One illustration is the enthusiasm with which Copenhagen greeted the artist on 17 September 1838 after a long absence.[5] Denmark, a former great nation, had been punished by the victorious powers for having supported Napoleon and had been forced in 1814 to cede Heligoland to Great Britain and Norway to Sweden. Thorvaldsen's European celebrity therefore appeared to the Danes as a consolation and moral atonement. In his 1867 monograph, Eugène Plon described Thorvaldsen's reception in Copenhagen: 'The extraordinary festivities occasioned by the artist's return to his country find a natural explanation in the just admiration of compatriots for a fame which flattered their national pride.'[6]

The unique solidarity of the entire population with their famous artist is evident at his funeral. Thorvaldsen died unexpectedly during a theatre performance, and Andersen describes how the news spread in Copenhagen: 'The news spread through the town like an electric current. His rooms in Charlottenborg were filled with people. The most distraught was Baroness Stampe, who had lost a dear sister only a few days before; a child's heart mourned the great artist.'[7] In a note, Andersen provided information about Thorvaldsen's will, in which he bequeathed his artworks and 25,000 reichstaler to the city of Copenhagen for a museum in his name. The unfinished works were to be completed by Herman Wilhelm Bissen, professor at the Copenhagen Academy of Art, against payment from the museum fund.

The interesting point of this major funeral is not the public viewing of the corpse, the funeral orations or the Italian opera singers, but rather the immense funeral procession to the church, led by two artists and a few sailors, followed by almost eight hundred students, then Icelanders and artists of all classes, then the pallbearers, the crown prince and members of the Academy, and finally the citizenry. Andersen continues: 'At the end of the long line are the people, even ragged boys, holding hands and forming a chain, a peace chain; next to the Church of Our Lady a line of students began. All windows, walls, trees and many roofs are filled with people.'[8]

In spite of the huge crowds, absolute silence reigned. Two wreaths lay on the coffin, one from the queen and the other from schoolchildren, who had all made a 'modest contribution'; flowers and bouquets were thrown on to the coffin, then all the church bells rang. Once again Andersen highlights the role of the people: 'It is a festive procession, the people led by the king of artists.' At the entrance to the church, the king of Denmark received the coffin of the king of artists.[9] And even more: the heavens sent the most beautiful Northern Lights to mark Thorvaldsen's return from Italy, a rainbow appeared in greeting, and higher powers rewarded the sailors who had correctly entered the deceased's age and the date of birth and death in the lottery with a substantial prize.

The three-part lithograph based on a drawing by Joel Ballin of the funeral has at the top a profile of Thorvaldsen in a laurel wreath above the lying-in-state in the Academy, then the coffin carried by members of the Academy, and also the crown prince and flagbearers, the dense rows of citizens in top hats and above them the women and children looking out of the windows. Between the statues of Martin Luther and Philipp Melanchthon, the bottom section shows the funeral service in the Church of Our Lady. On the outside of the Thorvaldsen Museum, the painter Jørgen Sonne recalls the triumphant reception of the artist and his works by the public.

After Antonio Canova, Thorvaldsen was the second European star artist celebrated by all segments of the population, royal houses and monarchies. Thorvaldsen had an incredible career, going from success to success and being acclaimed wherever he went. Like Canova, he had prominent patrons, and both stimulated and made use of the public interest in statues, tombs and monuments. They heightened the interest in 'statuomania', which they were able to satisfy with their outstanding works. Their clients – popes, emperors, kings and princes, governments and cities – participated in their

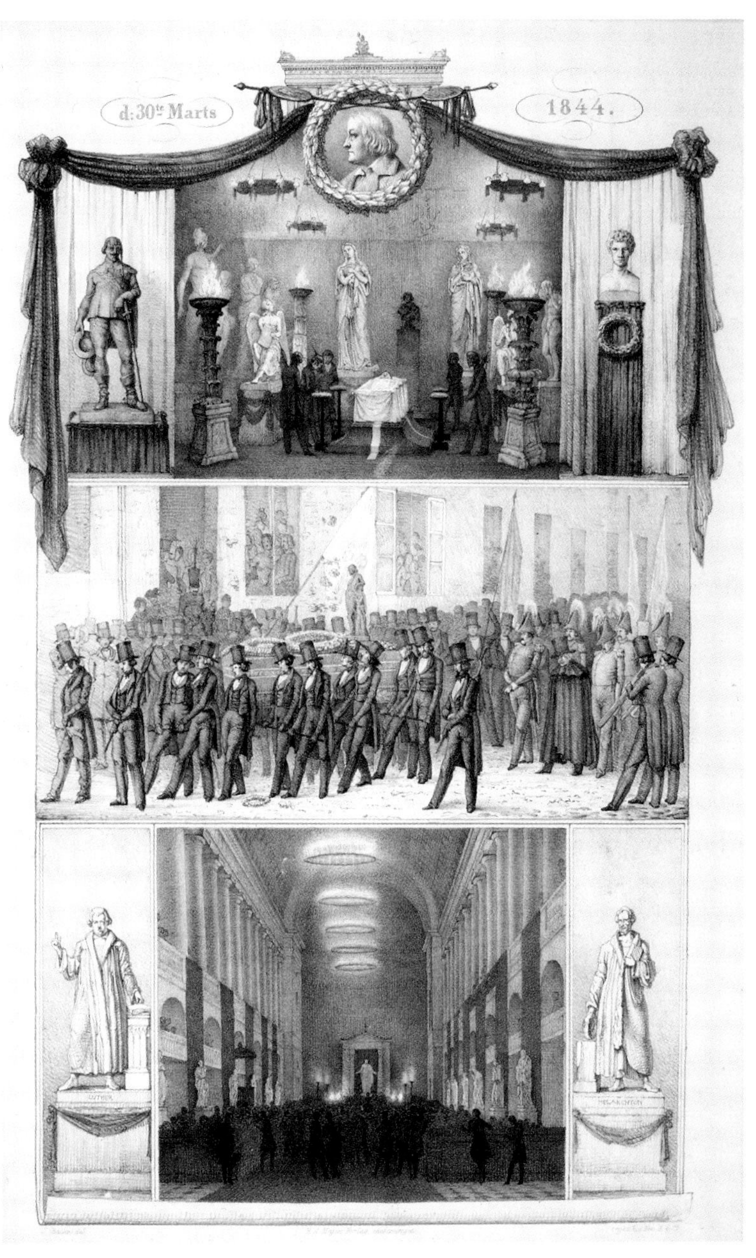


41 Joel Ballin, *Memorial of Thorvaldsen on the Occasion of His Funeral*, 1844, lithograph.

art and competed for their attention. The boundless approval of both artists by both the bourgeoisie and the aristocracy, whom they supplied with flawless beauties in marble or plaster, is remarkable.[10]

There are but a few other examples of similarly large public funerals of popular artists. One was Richard Wagner, who died of a heart attack in Venice on 13 February 1883.[11] Three days later, the embalmed body was laid in a stately sarcophagus with bronze lid and transported to Bayreuth by train. On 17 February the mayor made a 'respectful' appeal in the *Oberfränkische Zeitung* to the population to take part in the funeral reception at the train station and to accompany the body to Villa Wahnfried. At 4 p.m. on 18 February, the family and dignitaries led the sarcophagus through the densely lined and black-flagged streets. Illustrations bear witness to the huge public turnout for the funeral of this famous but not uncontroversial composer.

A large public funeral also marked the death in Vienna in 1884 of Hans Makart, who was popular in artists' circles with a reputation for being a man of good character.[12] The mayor wrote a letter of condolence to his widow, attended the burial, laid a wreath on the coffin and read an obituary at a council meeting, where there was also discussion of naming a street after him and approving a special grave for him in the section for prominent figures in the Central Cemetery. The artist community made great preparations for the funeral, recruiting soloists and the chorus of the court opera. The Academy of Arts also considered taking part, while Professor Tilgner asked the widow for permission to make a death mask. In its issue of 5 October 1884, the *Morgen-Post* published a full-page portrait of the painter on the front page and an obituary stating that Vienna was in deep mourning and the entire civilized world was shattered by the 'severe blow to the world of beauty delivered by Makart's death'. Mention was made of Makart's greatest achievement, the procession on the Ringstrasse in Vienna in 1879 at the end of the week-long celebration of the 25th anniversary of the marriage of Emperor Franz Joseph and Empress Elisabeth. The inhabitants set off as early as 4 a.m. on their way to the Ringstrasse. Makart appeared at 9 a.m. dressed as Peter Paul Rubens on a magnificent white horse, leading a procession of diverse groups – from the clergy, aristocracy and military to artisans, industries and associations.[13]

Makart's body was laid out in his studio, his head turned towards his unfinished last work, *The Spring*, in obvious imitation of Raphael's legendary laying out under his unfinished last work.[14] Thousands of people demanded admission to view the body, and at around 11 a.m. the crowd attempted to force its way in. In the afternoon, Prince Konstantin of Hohenlohe, Lord High Steward of His Majesty the Emperor, came to express the emperor's condolences and to regretfully announce his inability to attend the funeral. It was not until the evening that the grief-stricken widow and her two children approached the coffin again to take leave of the deceased: 'She threw herself over the open coffin and repeatedly kissed the eyes, mouth and hands of the body.' The next day, the artist community gathered in the black-draped Künstlerhaus and carried torches for the funeral procession to the Karlskirche, where the body was blessed. At the last moment it was decided that the funeral procession should not set off for the Central Cemetery until after the president's address. There was an absence of official pomp, but the scene was notable for the crowds of people who lined the route and the 'profound sentiments that gripped the heart of the entire city'.[15]

The *Algemeen Handelsblad* reported at length on the funeral of Sir Lawrence Alma-Tadema in London on Saturday, 6 July 1912, noting the rise of the artist from a village in Frisia to become a recipient of the highest social and academic honours in the United Kingdom.[16] The reporter emphasized the fact that the funeral took place in the imposing St Paul's Cathedral and was attended by the most noteworthy personalities, from members of the royal family and the Dutch ambassador to prominent municipal figures and the Nederlandsche Vereeniging. The funeral in St Paul's was the highpoint in the career of a man of the people.

In 1991 the city of Fribourg in Switzerland took leave of its native son, the artist Jean Tinguely, with a noisy funeral celebration broadcast on television. The *Neue Zürcher Zeitung* wrote: 'Many people, including young ones, marched in procession through Fribourg town centre on this hot afternoon, on which schools were closed.'[17] In the cortège from the university to the cathedral, the musicians of the Fribourg Landwehr marched slowly and solemnly to funeral music, followed by federal and government councillors, religious and political dignitaries, and finally the *Klamauk*, a rattling kinetic machine made by the artist. 'Kuttleputzer', the notorious Basel Fasnacht clique, followed with vanguard, drummers and pipers. The requiem was celebrated by the bishop, who welcomed the honoured funeral guests at the main entrance, while the common people had to wait outside. The address was given by the federal president, who to the astonishment of all praised the patriotic commitment of the formerly scandal-ridden artist. This was followed by an exuberant public celebration with food and drink, as Tinguely had requested, on place Notre-Dame. The celebrations were reported in the evening news, coming before an item on the devastating damage caused by the greatest financial fraud ever committed in Switzerland.[18]

It is impossible from these few examples to make generalizations about public funerals for artists. High public acceptance of a male artist is probably a condition, and an unlikely rise from an underprivileged class to the highest society is no doubt helpful. It is also useful if the artist and his art were valuable in financial terms, and a tragic or at least sudden death appears necessary to provoke public mourning.

# 12

# ESTEEMED PUBLIC

The widespread derision of the art public contrasts with the few professions of esteem for it. Praise and appreciation for theatre and concert audiences are probably more frequent than for the art public, because the former are able to express their enthusiasm. One of the first instances of praise for the art public was by the Paris critic Hilaire Sazerac in his discussion of the 1834 Salon. Because of an error in the press regarding the opening, he found himself in the uncomfortable position of being practically alone in the exhibition. He felt much more comfortable among the *gens du monde*, the cultured audience of painters, journalists and art lovers. He wrote of the different feelings in the exhibition room, which he compared with a well-attended opera: 'Yesterday the room was full, as for *Don Juan*. The museum looked quite different, and it felt more comfortable to be surrounded by men and women of such diverse intellect and taste passing judgement.'[1]

Sazerac believed that the public brought art exhibitions to life, much like theatre and opera audiences: 'In terms of formality, a painting exhibition is like a theatre performance: it is the public that brings them both to life. Without a public, everything is dead! If a play is performed in front of an empty house, even the best drama will receive no applause.'[2] Sazarac also trusted the crowd to be able to judge art: 'The assembled crowd almost always produce the most unbiased judgements.'[3] An appreciation of the public of this type was rare in the nineteenth century, but like everyone when speaking about the public, Sazerac meant the educated visitors to the Salon, not the ignorant masses.

In September 1855, the painter and illustrator Adolph Menzel from Berlin spent two weeks in Paris. He had come for the World's Fair to view the display of one of his pictures of Frederick the Great of Prussia.[4] During his visit Menzel attended the Théâtre du Gymnase, a vaudeville theatre on boulevard Bonne-Nouvelle that attracted a wide public with its comedies and musical sketches.[5] The souvenir picture *Théâtre du Gymnase* was completed a year after the visit. Menzel chose a composition with a dominant diagonal for the stage, the orchestra pit and the audience seated in rows in the auditorium so that the boxes on the side are viewed straight on, while the stage, orchestra and spectators are seen from an angle. On the stage is a man flanked by two women. The spectators in the auditorium are all male, and there are just two women sitting in the box.

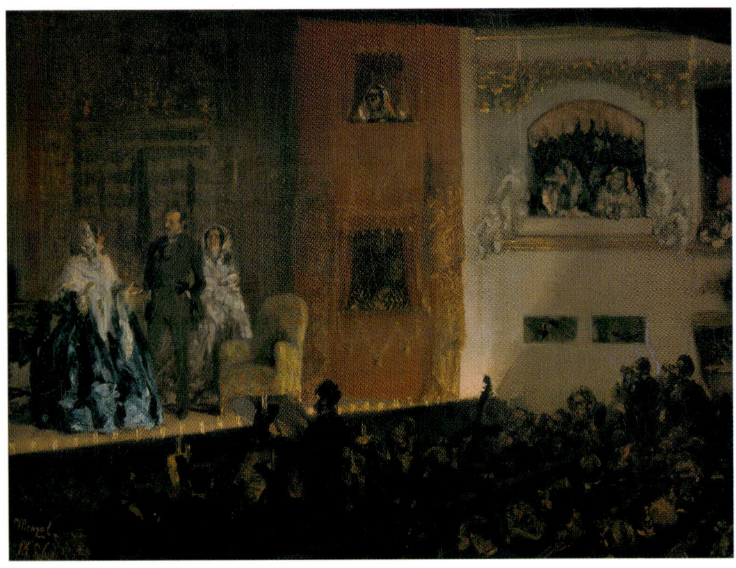

42 Adolph Menzel, *Théâtre du Gymnase*, 1856, oil on canvas.

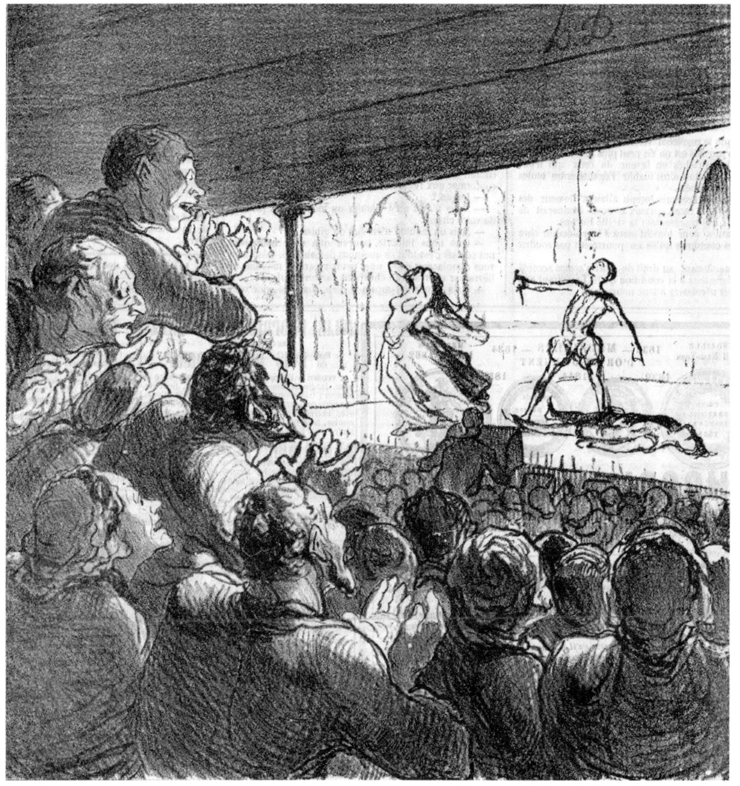

43 Honoré Daumier, 'The Actor and a Street Urchin', lithograph, published in *Le Charivari*, 18 April 1864.

One is looking through binoculars to get a closer view, as are two men standing downstairs below her.

Honoré Daumier also drew several illustrations of the view from the auditorium on to the stage, the audience in the parterre or spectators. In the lithograph 'The Actor and a Street Urchin' in the series *Croquis dramatiques*, published in 1864 in *Le Charivari* (illus. 43), Daumier shows the audience from the side and behind, so that their expressions of horror, puzzlement and enjoyment can be seen. On the bright stage is the fatal end of a play about jealousy, as is evident from the caption, which includes not only the cheers by the

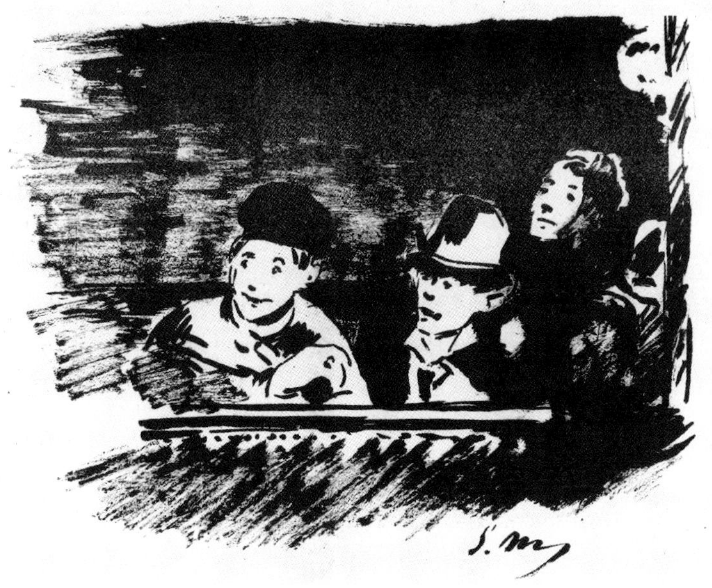

44 Édouard Manet, *Au Paradis* (*In the Balcony*), 1877, lithograph.

audience but the husband threatening to kill both his wife and himself, as well as the protests of a street urchin among the spectators.[6]

Édouard Manet's sketch of a few spectators in 'the gods', the highest and cheapest seats in the theatre, also demonstrates an indubitable sympathy for the public. Two urchins are peering intently over the balcony at the stage, while a woman is sitting unmoved behind them and a boy is sleeping. This rapid sketch suggests a spontaneous observation of the theatre audience by the illustrator, who on a number of occasions confirmed his appreciation of the public. In the brochure accompanying his exhibition in 1867 organized during the World's Fair in Paris, Manet wrote of the need for contact with the public. After being obstructed several times by the jury, he decided to address the public directly through the exhibition and to discuss his art with them. If an artist did not have the possibility to exhibit, he would be trapped, since he could no longer practise his art without a public.[7] Manet attacks the system and the hypocritical jury:

> It is said that official recognition, encouragement and rewards are actually a guarantee of talent in the eyes of a certain part of the public; they are thereby forewarned on behalf of or against the accepted or rejected works. But, on the other hand, the painter is assured that it is the spontaneous impression of this same public which motivates the chilly welcome the various juries give his canvas.[8]

Contact with the public is vital for Manet as an artist and necessary for his creativity: 'To exhibit is for the artist the vital concern, the sine qua non,' which also involves finding friends and allies for the struggle. Manet notes that he has been shown great sympathy, and the expert judgements have become more and more favourable. He concludes by saying: 'Therefore it is now only a question for the painter of gaining the good will of the public which has been turned into a would-be enemy.'[9]

Too little attention has been paid to the degree to which Manet's painting is directed at the public. After his rejection by the jury, Manet presented himself to exhibition visitors as the martyred and dead Christ.[10] He repeatedly involved the public in his paintings. In *Lola from Valencia* (illus. 45) of 1862, showing the star dancer of Spanish ballet at the Teatro Real in Madrid, which visited Paris to great acclaim in summer and autumn 1862, he offered the full performance spectrum. He showed the group and Lola individually in an aquatint etching, about which Charles Baudelaire composed an obscene four-line verse. The painter depicts the celebrated dancer behind the scenes in a non-public part of the theatre, and Lola poses

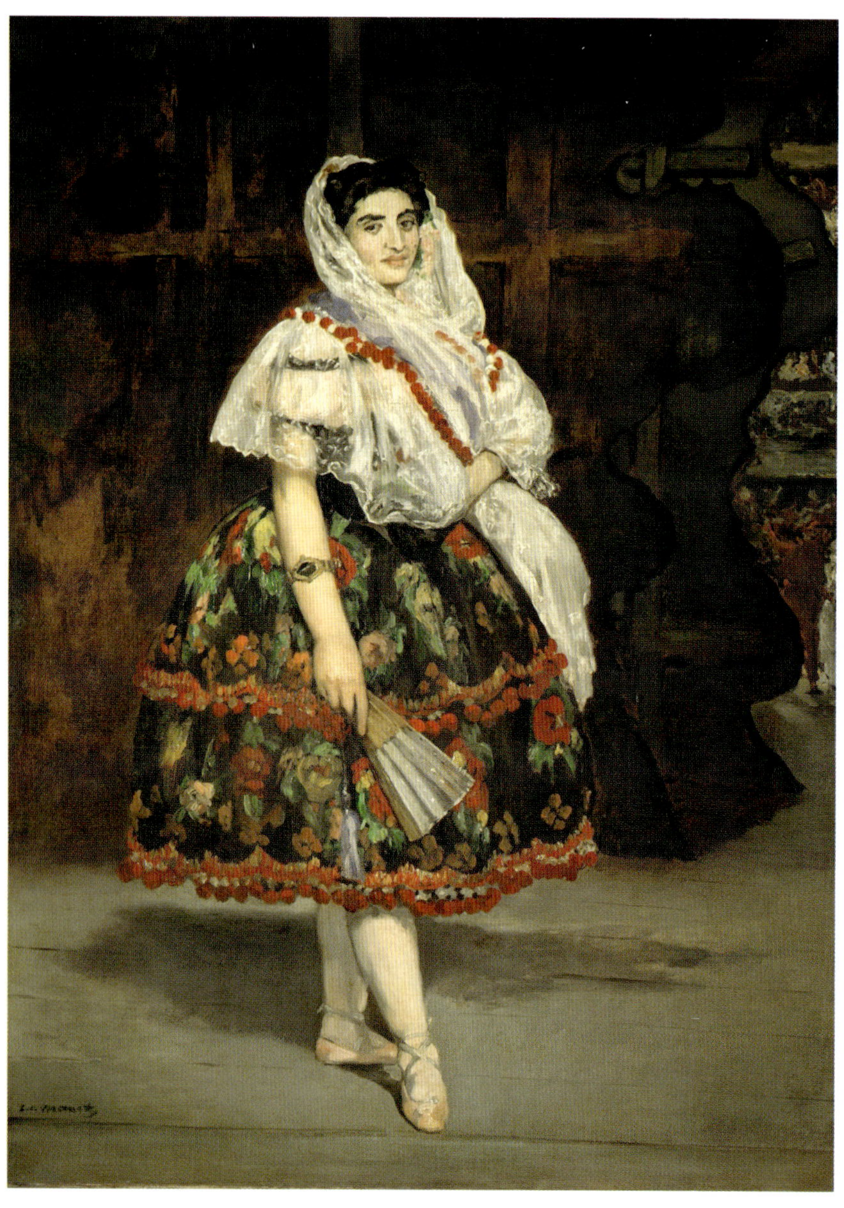

45 Édouard Manet, *Lola from Valencia*, 1862, oil on canvas.

in a colourful Spanish costume with her right leg stretched forward, her arm resting on her hip, a fan in her right hand and her head turned half-right. The pose is aimed at male observers. Behind the dancer are the grey-brown backs of two stage sets, and next to them is a glimpse of the stage with an actor performing and the auditorium with the spectators sitting in rows. The simultaneous presentation of actors and spectators is a frequent theme in Manet's work, culminating in his inscrutable last work on solitude in the crowd, *A Bar at the Folies-Bergère*, painted in 1881–2.[11]

The 1867 painting *Peasants at the Museum* by genre painter Benjamin Vautier from Morges on Lake Geneva, which was exhibited in Dusseldorf, shows a genuine sympathy for simple people in a location usually reserved for the 'educated classes'. A family from the country in their Sunday best are admiring the paintings, particularly

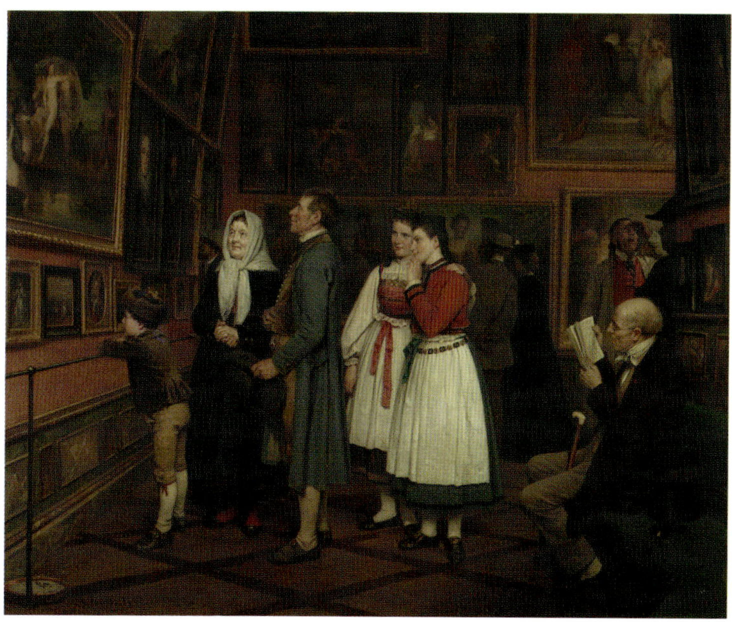

46 Benjamin Vautier, *Peasants at the Museum*, 1867, oil on canvas.

*Diana and Actaeon*, while on the right a burgher is sitting on a bench engrossed in the catalogue but ignoring the pictures. Vautier accuses the educated people of preferring reading to the direct sensation, while the common people show their amazement at the pictures.

At almost the same time as Vautier's peasants in the museum, Edgar Degas drew a portrait of two representatives of the educated art public (illus. 47). His etching from around 1876 shows a very well-dressed woman from behind, leaning on an umbrella and

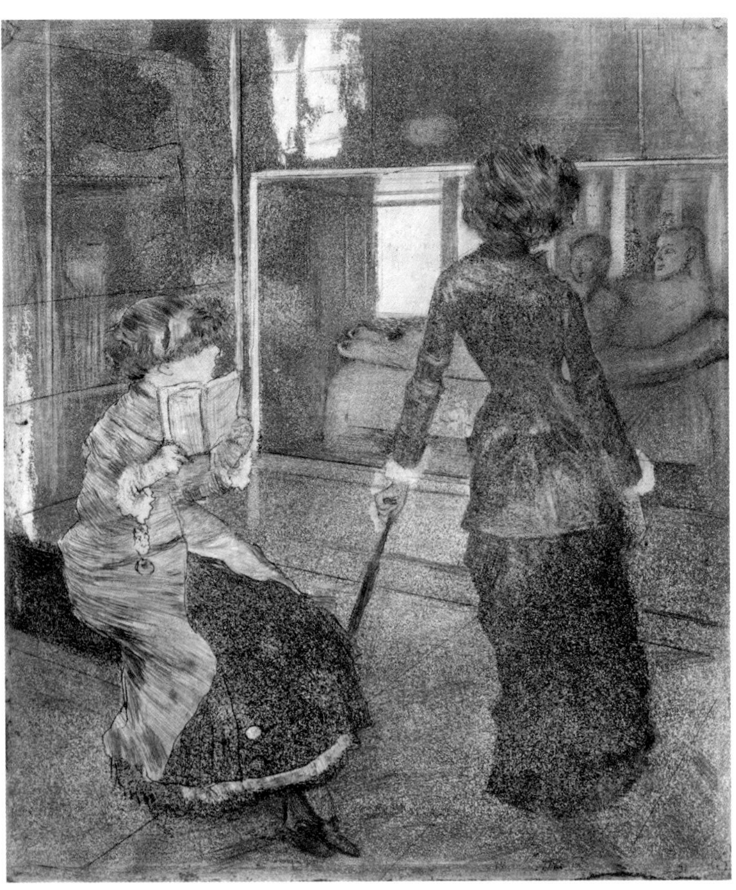

47 Edgar Degas, *Mary Cassatt in the Louvre: The Etruscan Gallery*, c. 1879, etching and aquatint on laid paper.

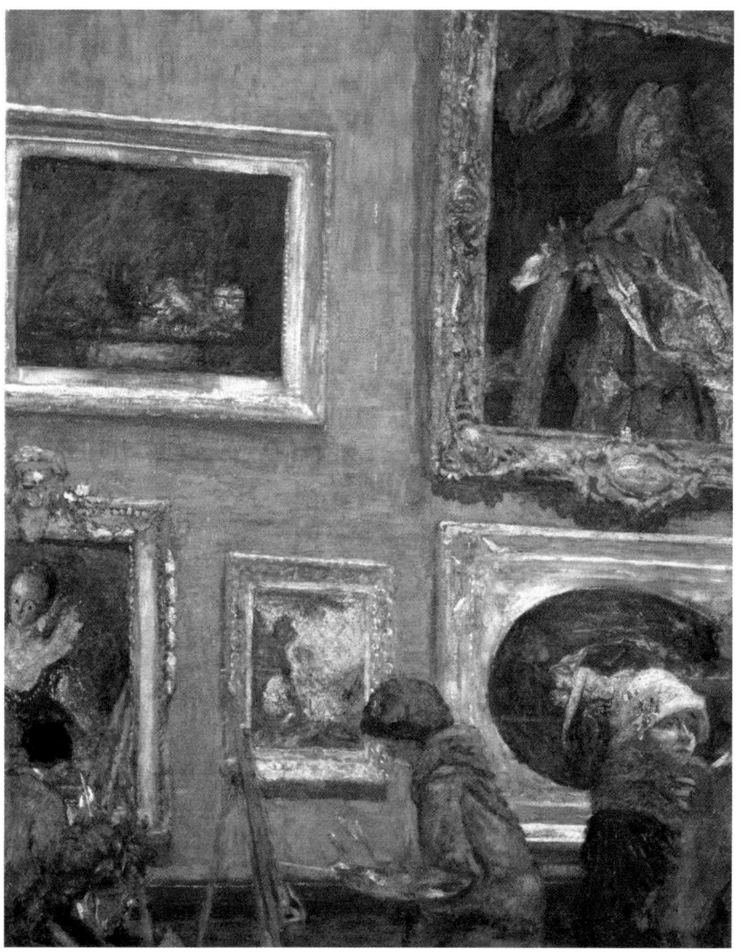

48 Édouard Vuillard, *At the Louvre, la Salle La Caze*, 1921, distemper on canvas.

standing in elegant contrapposto in front of a case containing an Etruscan sarcophagus. Her companion is sitting to her left, looking up from the catalogue at the sculpture. The subjects are thought to be Degas' American friend the painter Mary Cassatt and her sister Lydia. The painted clay sarcophagus with the reclining couple was found in Cerveteri in 1845–6 and arrived in the Louvre in 1863.[12]

In 1921–2, Édouard Vuillard offered a personal selection from the large collection of works intended for the Louvre and its public in the form of four paintings and two overdoors commissioned by the entrepreneur Camille Bauer and his wife, Maria Bauer-Judlin, to furnish their villa at Aeschengraben in Basel.[13] The painting *At the Louvre, la Salle La Caze* shows a part of five works bequeathed to the Louvre from the collection of the Paris doctor Louis La Caze.[14] It features a still-life by Jean-Baptiste Siméon Chardin, a work by Jean-Antoine Watteau and another painting ascribed to him, which the copyist is working on. To the left is a section of a portrait by Jean-Honoré Fragonard. By placing his mother to the left in front of the Fragonard and his niece Annette to the right in front of the Watteau, he establishes a family relationship to the paintings in the public museum, enhanced through Vuillard's own early artistic relationship to Chardin.

13

# THE 1871 SURVEY IN DRESDEN

In 1871 the Leipzig physicist and psychologist Gustav Theodor Fechner organized the first recorded public survey of an exhibition. Little is known about the first survey of sculptors and painters by the scholar Benedetto Varchi in Florence. Varchi presented the artists' arguments in the Accademia Fiorentina in 1546.[1] Fechner, professor of physics at the University of Leipzig since 1834, was forced by illness to retire in 1843 but continued his study of natural philosophy, psychophysics and psychological aesthetics. At the major Holbein exhibition in Dresden in 1871, he asked the public which of the heads in the two versions of the Meyer Madonna made a 'more favourable, more attractive and more precious impression'.[2]

The occasion for the exhibition in Dresden, which showed around four hundred works by Hans Holbein the Elder, Ambrosius and Hans Holbein the Younger, was to clarify the status of the two versions of the Meyer Madonna. The aim was to determine which of the versions, in Darmstadt and Dresden, might be the original and how the less valuable version should be judged: as a replica, copy or forgery. The inhabitants of Dresden particularly favoured their own version, not least as it was profiled in the gallery as the German counterpart to Raphael's *Sistine Madonna*. Full of local patriotism, Fechner wrote in 1871: 'A new version threatens to put paid to the pride of the Dresden gallery, the German rival to Raphael's

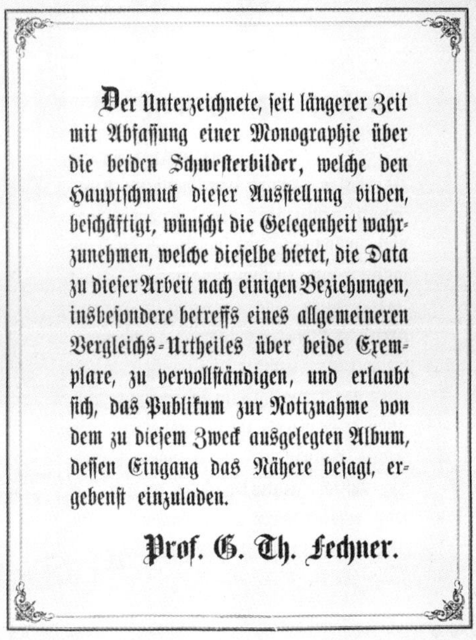

Der Unterzeichnete, seit längerer Zeit mit Abfassung einer Monographie über die beiden Schwesterbilder, welche den Hauptschmuck dieser Ausstellung bilden, beschäftigt, wünscht die Gelegenheit wahrzunehmen, welche dieselbe bietet, die Data zu dieser Arbeit nach einigen Beziehungen, insbesondere betreffs eines allgemeineren Vergleichs-Urtheiles über beide Exemplare, zu vervollständigen, und erlaubt sich, das Publikum zur Notiznahme von dem zu diesem Zweck ausgelegten Album, dessen Eingang das Nähere besagt, ergebenst einzuladen.

**Prof. G. Th. Fechner.**

49 Gustav Theodor Fechner, notice for poll in Dresden, 1871.

*Sistine Madonna*.'[3] The dispute on the status of the two versions of the Meyer Madonna also spread to Switzerland, England and France.

The Dresden Holbein exhibition is of great significance in terms of the history of science but also of the history of the art public, because it was the first time that a controversial art history question was presented to the public, together with the organization by art historians of the first committee to reach a joint decision. The Munich curator Adolf Bayersdorfer wrote in 1872 that it was not about the status of the Darmstadt version but merely about whether the Dresden version was the original.[4] At the end of their council, however, the art historians came out in favour of the Darmstadt version, calling the Dresden version a copy and publishing their results as an 'explanation'.[5] There was much criticism of a decision on a scientific question by a committee of fourteen experts, and the artists felt obliged to issue a statement opposing the art historians' declaration.[6]

The idea of a public comparison of the two Meyer Madonnas during an exhibition of paintings, drawings and prints by the Holbein family was proposed by the Dresden councillor Albert von Zahn. It gave the art public a hitherto unknown significance, much to the annoyance of the exhibition organizers, who were not in favour of the active involvement of the public. Although a large number of visitors were expected, they were meant to admire the exhibits but not to interfere. The outsider Fechner alone took the opportunity of inviting the exhibition visitors to express their opinion (illus. 49).

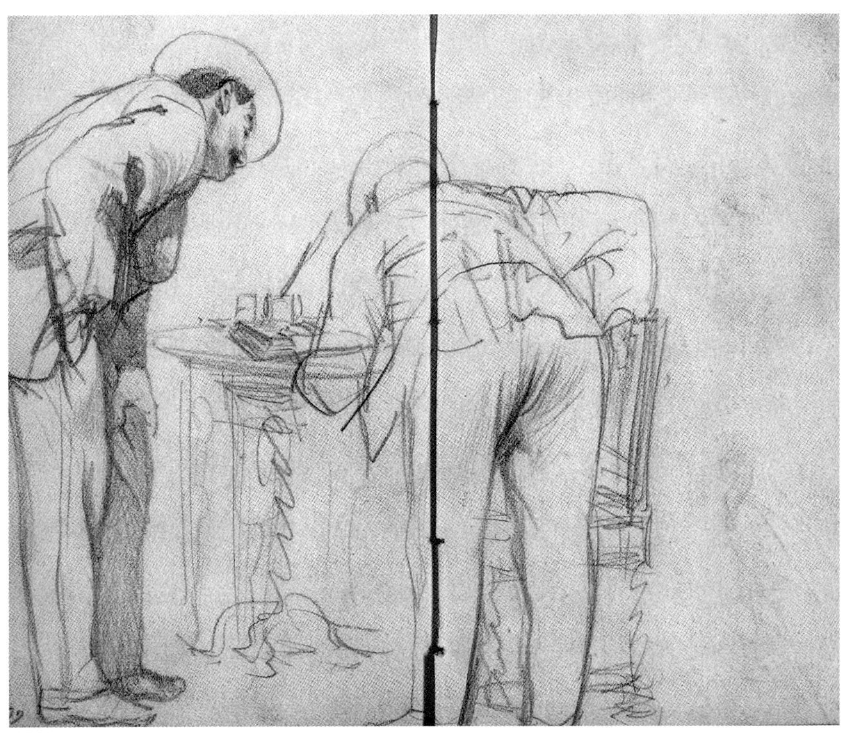

50 Adolph Menzel, 'Holbein Exhibition, plebiscite table', 1871, pencil.

The idea had already been introduced in Fechner's book, published in 1871, on the Holbein Madonnas, in which he cited and compared in detail the opinions of experts and laypersons. With the approval of the committee, Fechner posted a notice in the exhibition inviting the public to compare the two versions of the Meyer Madonna and to write their comments in the book provided for that purpose and giving notice of a planned publication on the subject.[7] During his visit to Dresden, Adolph Menzel, who always had an eye open for the unusual, sketched the table for the plebiscite and two visitors signing their names (illus. 50).[8] The exhibition visitors were also given recognition by the painter Alfred Richard Diethe, born in Dresden in 1836, who on a tiny piece of paper drew five people studying the two Meyer Madonnas (illus. 51). The binoculars used by the seated woman suggest a close examination and an exceptional expert knowledge by the four women and one man.

Fechner, who saw the survey as part of his 'experimental aesthetics', wanted to learn from the public how the two pictures affected them and which of the Madonna heads they preferred.[9] As for the status of the two pictures – original, replica or copy – he left that to the experts to decide. He devised a voting slip to answer his questions: 'Very simple voting scheme: for the (Dresden or Darmstadt) version; for the (Dresden or Darmstadt) Madonna; N. N. (name, title, status, address, date).'[10]

Besides the personal data, Fechner invited further comments on the two pictures and sought as many contributors by a 'generally educated public (including women)' as possible. Of the 11,842 visitors to the exhibition, only 113 – fewer than 1 per cent – answered the survey, which the disappointed Fechner had to accept as a failure. He made a number of suggestions for improving future public surveys. An 'art authority' should encourage the public to take part, fill out some sample replies and exclude connoisseurship problems

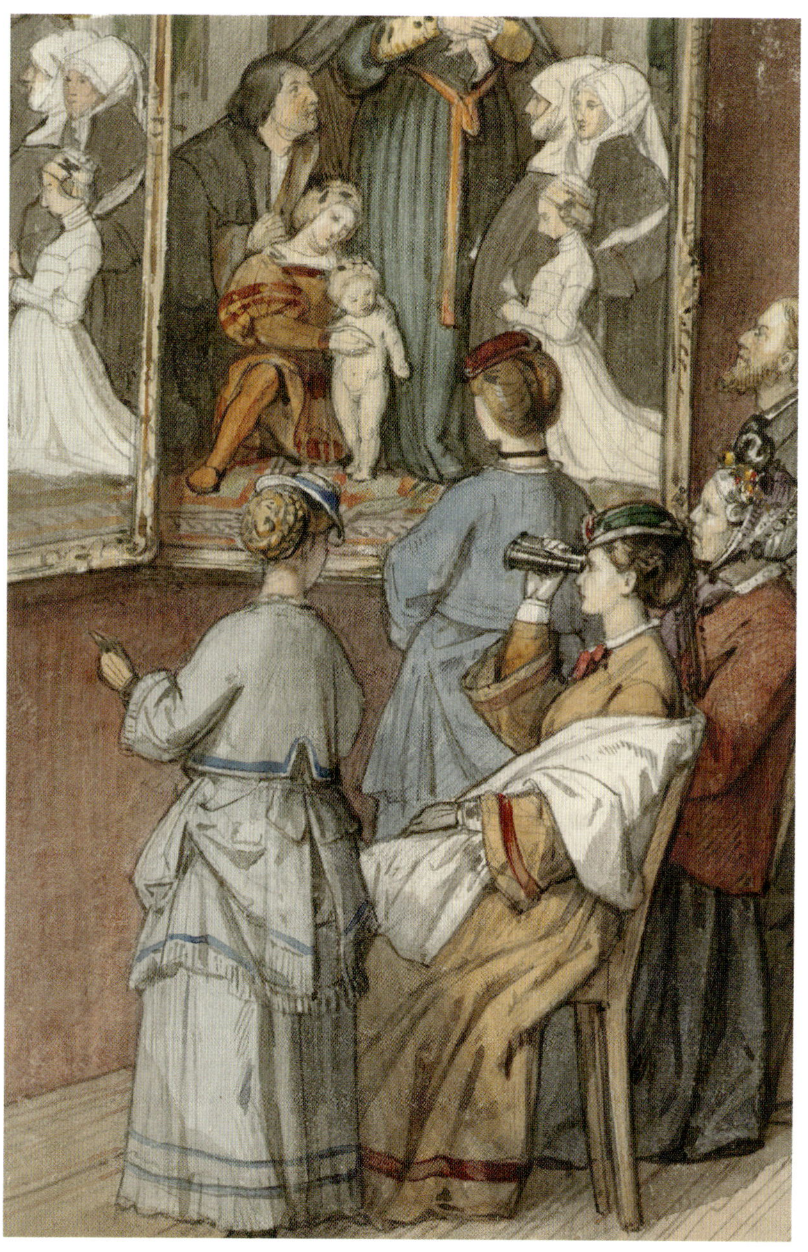

51 Alfred Richard Diethe, *Public Viewing Holbein's The Meyer Madonna in Dresden*, 1871, pencil and watercolour.

from the outset. Fechner published all the replies to his survey and commented on a selection of them. He also identified the author of a sonnet in favour of the Dresden version as the painter and gallery director Julius Hübner, who had participated incognito as a member of the public. The staff censored a sheet with a spiteful poem aimed at Fechner.[11]

The educated public, press and experts continued to discuss the Meyer Madonnas. In 1873 Albert von Zahn listed fifty articles on the Holbein question in journals and the daily press since 1871.[12] The fact that the majority of women voted for the Dresden picture was not considered particularly unusual, and the painter Rudolf Lehmann actually mentioned this finding in his essay 'Les Madones de Darmstadt et de Dresde', published at the end of 1871 in the leading art journal *Gazette des Beaux-Arts*, in which he and 26 co-signatories suggested that both versions were originals.[13]

Fechner's express limitation to two questions of taste was ignored by the public, who also wished to comment on the authenticity. The reaction of the experts to the survey is interesting. They were highly critical of Fechner, believing that it was he who had brought up the question of status with the public. Carl von Lützow, editor of *Zeitschrift für Bildende Kunst*, was outraged by Fechner's public survey and made fun of the visitors' comments.[14] Alfred Woltmann, author of the major Holbein monograph, wrote in the *Nationalzeitung*: 'Professor Fechner . . . in Leipzig wants the decision on the two pictures to be made by universal suffrage.'[15] This was the objection of the arrogant male experts, who believed they had the exclusive right to decide on the two versions. Bayersdorfer wrote in 1872 that he could not refrain from making 'a bitter criticism of Professor Fechner', who had turned before to the 'public at large, as if a mass vote by educated people could help even one jot to resolve a scientific question'.[16] The academic experts reserved for themselves the right to resolve important questions relating to their discipline and to art, while the art public should merely have the role of respectful recipients. Fechner summed up the result of the public survey and the explanation by the academic experts as a 'decisive triumph' for the Darmstadt version, but refused himself to agree with the result and continued to prefer the Dresden version by virtue of its 'more self-assured idealistic majesty and sweetness'.[17]

In 1871 Fechner published his treatise, expanding it in 1876 into an empirical aesthetic theory in his extensive *Vorschule der Aesthetik* as a bottom-up aesthetic based on the experience of 'what is pleasing and what is not', as opposed to a top-down aesthetic based on 'the most general ideas and concepts'.[18]

Art public surveys began with Fechner's modest visitors' book and his invitation to comment on two simple questions. The direct consequences in exhibitions and museums have not yet been studied, but it is likely, given the spiteful comments about Fechner's survey, that museum directors were initially reluctant to invite public comment. It is not known when it became customary to provide visitors' books for commenting in. They are now commonplace, but in many places the way the comments are interpreted is an internal matter and only exceptionally are they publicly presented.[19] Professional public surveys, now with standard and highly sophisticated methodologies, are something completely different.

The closest thing to a bottom-up aesthetic is the project by the Moscow artist duo Vitaly Komar and Alexander Melamid. They appear to take up Martin Disler's idea of the artist fulfilling the wishes of the masses (see Chapter One). Komar and Melamid first launched the project *The People's Choice: The Most Wanted and Most Unwanted Painting* in the USA in 1993. In 1997 the Museum Ludwig in Cologne presented the results of a poll taken in fourteen countries and described the two artists as protagonists of 'subversive and politically driven art infused with irony and surreal wit'.[20] As genuine comics and satirists, the two artists did not join in with the laughter they provoked. A total of 962 people were surveyed in Germany between 4 and 16 December 1996 and a similar number in Austria in May 1998. The professional questionnaire contained 44 questions on taste and seven for statistical purposes (age, birthplace, education and so forth). Almost half of those surveyed never went to museums, a third a maximum of twice a year and less than one-fifth more than twice. Figurative painting was preferred by 14 per cent, while 13 per cent favoured non-objective painting and a further 39 per cent gave no answer to this question. Other questions referred to favourite colours, forms, moods and subjects. The question on purchasing criteria produced a short ranking list of the most famous artists, from Picasso (number 1) to Sigmar Polke (number 12).[21] The poll produced similar results in Austria.[22] The Cologne catalogue includes examples from the USA, Russia, Finland, Italy and Germany. It is striking to note that many of the 'most wanted' were similar: a strip in the foreground, figures in a landscape, a tree, a forest, a lake and mountains and clouds beyond. The difference between Kenya and Iceland, for example, was that the former preferred a hippopotamus and the latter a couple of hoofed animals. The most popular picture in Austria features a couple with a dog on a panorama terrace with a tree and pink-flowered shrub. The view looks out on to a castle, a river and snow-capped mountains, and a small deer can be made out in a field.[23] Komar and Melamid also exhibited 'most unwanted' pictures, abominations consisting of coloured squares, in comparison with the favourite pictures.

The most wanted pictures worldwide are the kind of pictures found in hotel rooms, which Theodor W. Adorno once pilloried as the epitome of kitsch. But the two artists demonstrate that global art wishes tend to feature a sentimental identification in pictures, which is absent from coloured squares. Komar and Melamid established a most wanted list of sentimental works, similar to the most wanted lists of criminals all over the world. Boris Groys believed that the two artists did not intend to look ironically at public taste or to mock the public but to offer an 'allegory of fulfilled wishes'.[24] But the one does not exclude the other.

The artist duo Peter Fischli and David Weiss presented a completely different poll to the public at the Biennale in Venice in 2003 with the installation *Kleine Fragen, grosse Fragen*, and published the results in the ironically and uneasily titled book, *Findet mich das Glück?* (Will Happiness Find Me?).[25] The questions were based partly on everyday decisions, such as 'Should I make myself some soup?', and partly on the temptation to react unkindly to the misery in the world, such as 'Should I sow malice, hate and resentment?' The tendency to subject oneself to external surveillance is reflected in the question 'Should I allow myself to be monitored?' The uneasy fear of being disadvantaged is reflected in 'Am I being exploited?', and the concern for mental and physical well-being in 'Was my bath too hot?' No banality or triviality is omitted, even concerns about the universe with 'Where is the galaxy headed?', and the book concludes with the question to end all questions, 'Am I looking for happiness in the wrong place?'

# 14

# AESTHETIC EDUCATION

In his magazine *Über Künstler und Kunstwerke* in 1865, the literature and art historian Herman Grimm stated that academics should not try to influence artists: 'Giving advice or praising or criticizing a new work should in principle be avoided.'[1] At best, he admitted, academics could be of use to an artist if they gave their judgement in confidence. Grimm explained this reticence by stating that scholarship could not be creative and its only utility for art was to educate the public: 'The scholarly consideration of art has nothing to do directly with the production of modern art. It is aimed not at the artists but at the public, which it seeks to educate, and uses art solely for this purpose.'

Grimm's readers are the 'educated classes' addressed by the *Brockhaus Real-Enzyklopädie* and other serious publications.[2] Heinrich Wölfflin, professor of art history at the University of Basel, addressed the same segment of the population in his 1899 book *Classic Art: An Introduction to the Italian Renaissance*, which begins with a surprising estimation of the 'contemporary public':

> Contemporary public interest, in so far as it is in touch with the visual arts, seems nowadays to desire a return to specifically artistic questions. The reader no longer expects an art-historical book to give mere biographical anecdotes or a description of the circumstances of the time; he wants to be told something

> of those things which constitute the value and the essence of a work of art, and he reaches out eagerly for new concepts.[3]

Wölfflin assumed that the public demanded exactly what he was willing to offer it, in contrast to colleagues who provided biographical and historical data. This book marked a further step in his career, because two years after its publication he was summoned to Berlin and offered the chair of the most important art history faculty in Germany as a successor to Herman Grimm. There he immediately seized on Albrecht Dürer, the 'most German of German artists', as a subject of national importance, and in Munich in 1915 concluded the *Principles of Art History*, in which he proposed five simple pairs of terms that the educated public could easily understand and apply. Wölfflin's *Principles* remained popular for decades and was reprinted several times and translated into over twenty languages.[4]

Like many other art historians and writers, Wölfflin encouraged a more extensive readership. In the last third of the nineteenth century, art publications in Germany, France and Britain reached a wider public than ever before. Following the invention of halftone printing by Georg Meisenbach in Munich in 1881, the reproduction of art illustrations became much cheaper and better.[5] In his 2017 book on changed perception, Pascal Griener shows how illustrated books, alongside visits to museums, stimulated and also satisfied the demand for art among the educated classes in nineteenth-century Germany, Britain and France.[6]

Art books provide a good example of Karl Marx's notion of the connection between production and reception. In the Preface to *Foundations of a Critique of Political Economy* in 1857, he proposed the thesis that the way a commodity is consumed is influenced by its mode of production: 'Production thus produces not only the object but also the manner of consumption.' He continues: 'Production not only supplies a material for the need, but it also supplies a need for the material.' Hence, the need which consumption feels for the object is created by the perception of it, as illustrated by art: 'The object of art – like every other product – creates a public which is sensitive to art and enjoys beauty.'[7]

Art books and illustrated art magazines immeasurably enlarged the art public, encouraging an increase in art writers and art book production. Publishers and authors concentrated initially on celebrated artists such as Raphael, then on those who stimulate patriotic feelings. Dürer, for example, was appropriated by the German people thanks to popular publications and magazines. Friedrich Pecht's magazine *Die Kunst für Alle*, which was first published on 1 October 1885 and was to remain successful for sixty years, mentioned Dürer in practically every issue as the 'most powerful incarnation of the specifically German spirit in the visual arts', comparable with Holbein, Rembrandt and Menzel.[8] The cultural talents are passed on from the top downwards. A striking example of this distribution of gifts from the top is the anecdotal painting *Acquitted* by the Dusseldorf artist Ferdinand Brütt, reproduced in Pecht's magazine in 1885. In the centre of the stairway overlooked by the statue of a lion, the acquitted man is welcomed by his wife and daughter, while members of the ruling class above discuss the case and the common people below learn of the verdict. Pecht wrote that the artist had managed to create 'a number of interesting characters' and depicted a 'touching and heartfelt' picture of the acquitted man and his family, without mentioning the political dimension, which the painter shows as a concession from the top down.[9] The anonymously published bestseller *Rembrandt als Erzieher* by Julius Langbehn in 1890 makes use of a clever strategy, pointing to the decline in the intellectual life of the German people and advocating 'artistic education' as the cure.[10] The transformation is entrusted to a prominent national celebrity

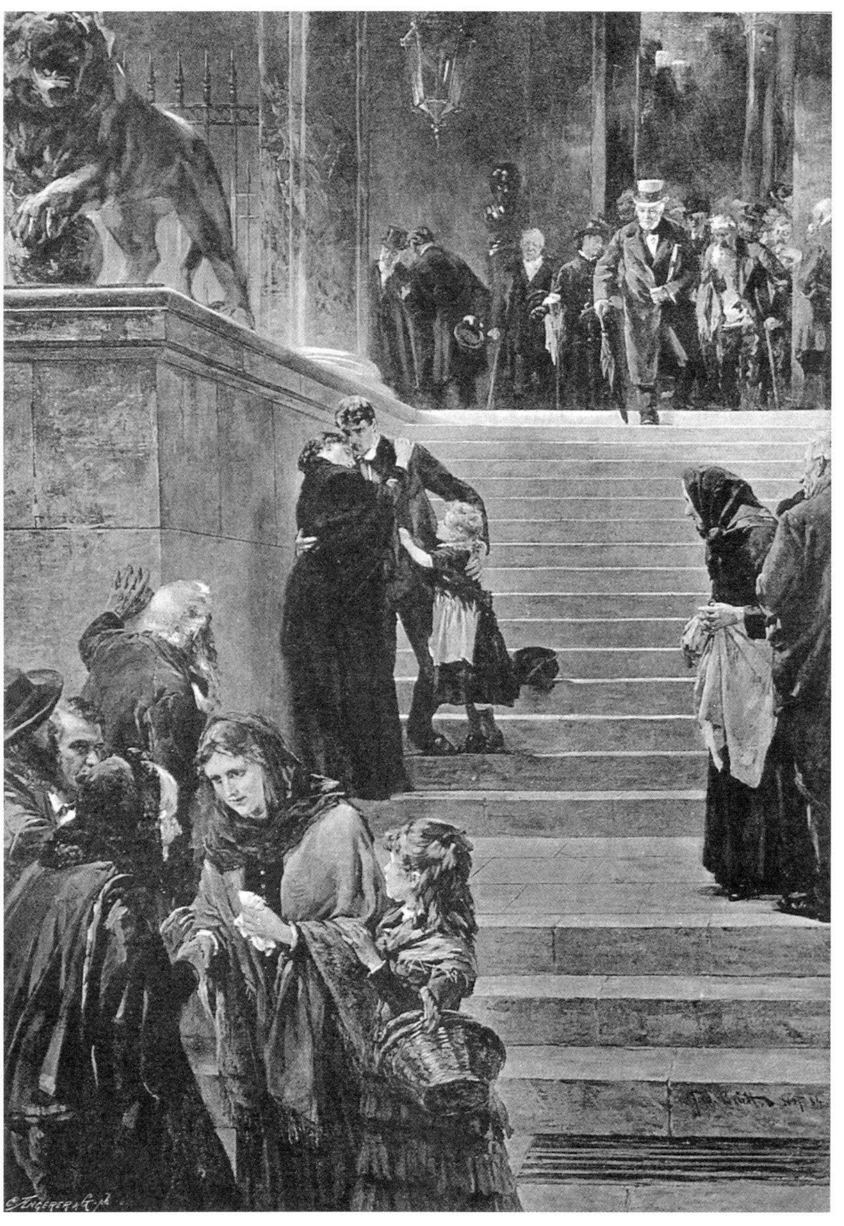

52 Ferdinand Brütt, *Acquitted*, engraving, published in *Die Kunst für Alle*, vol. I (1885).

artist, the 'most German of all German artists', either Dürer or the 'Germanic' Rembrandt, Wagner or Klinger. For the aesthetic education of the public, Hermann Knackfuss, a history painter and art writer, chose the artist monographs by the Velhagen & Klasing publishing company in Bielefeld and Leipzig, of which no fewer than seventeen volumes had appeared by 1896, starting with Raphael in 1895, and followed by Rubens, Rembrandt, Michelangelo and Dürer. It was hoped that the low price of 2 to 3 marks would attract a wide readership. The books instructed readers on how to look at a work of art properly, 'not with long-winded, art-historical explanations but clearly and simply in a way understandable even to a layperson'.[11]

Ferdinand Avenarius, a publisher and writer in Dresden, hoped that the Dürer volume, which he advertised in the September 1901 issue of the magazine *Der Kunstwart*, would foster a widespread cultural revival in Germany. Once again, he noted a decline, this time of the 'aesthetic sensitivity' and of architecture and handicrafts that contrasted with the general economic and scientific boom.[12] Dürer, the celebrated artist from Nuremberg, was the antidote: 'Our people must be worthy of the great Albrecht Dürer, in whose name we should work and for whom nothing in his people and his homeland was too small and nothing in the earthly world and the ever-after was too great.'[13] The appeal was directed at the people, and Avenarius expected thousands of members to join up. Astonishingly, these numbers were indeed achieved in the following year.[14]

The painter Hans Thoma wrote in a talk in 1903 about the relationship of the Germans to Dürer: 'What we recognize and love most of all in Dürer is the quintessential Germanness of his art.'[15] Wölfflin's Dürer book in 1905 was popularized four years after its publication by Johannes Damrich through the slogan 'Die Kunst dem Volke' (art for the people).[16] Based on Wölfflin, he undertook to 'bring the works of the great Nuremberger closer to the hearts and minds of the people'. To this end he also appropriated Grünewald, Holbein the Younger, Raphael and Michelangelo.[17]

But how could the need for art and access to it be stimulated in those who had no relationship to it? All over Europe and in the United States of America, the much disadvantaged workers in industrial societies were supported by all means available in their struggle for better working conditions and hours, wages, social security and housing. Access to art institutions and enjoyment of art were not among the priorities of the labour leaders. But with their sense of social justice, the educated and moneyed classes demanded philanthropically that art be accessible to all. They resorted altruistically to assigning an aesthetic and education function to publicity posters by designing them as works of art in addition to advertising goods and events. In this way, workers were not only to be tempted to buy consumer goods and entertainments, but to receive free aesthetic education into the bargain as they hurried to work in the early morning and dragged themselves back to their homes at the end of the day. The philanthropic aesthetes who indulged their idea of offering the workers an aesthetic education through the artistic representation of unattainable consumer goods did not realize how cynical their endeavours were.[18]

Around 1900, the workers wanted neither religion nor art but bread, as Giovanni Pellizza da Volpedo showed in his monumental painting glorifying their irresistible strength. The two versions of the marching workers were completed in 1895 and 1901. The first, unfinished painting entitled *La Fiumana* shows a woman and child and two men leading a large crowd of agricultural workers leaving a church-like building and their huts behind them and streaming forward irresistibly.[19] In the 1901 version entitled *Il Quarto Stato*, the church building has disappeared and the leaders, unimpressed by

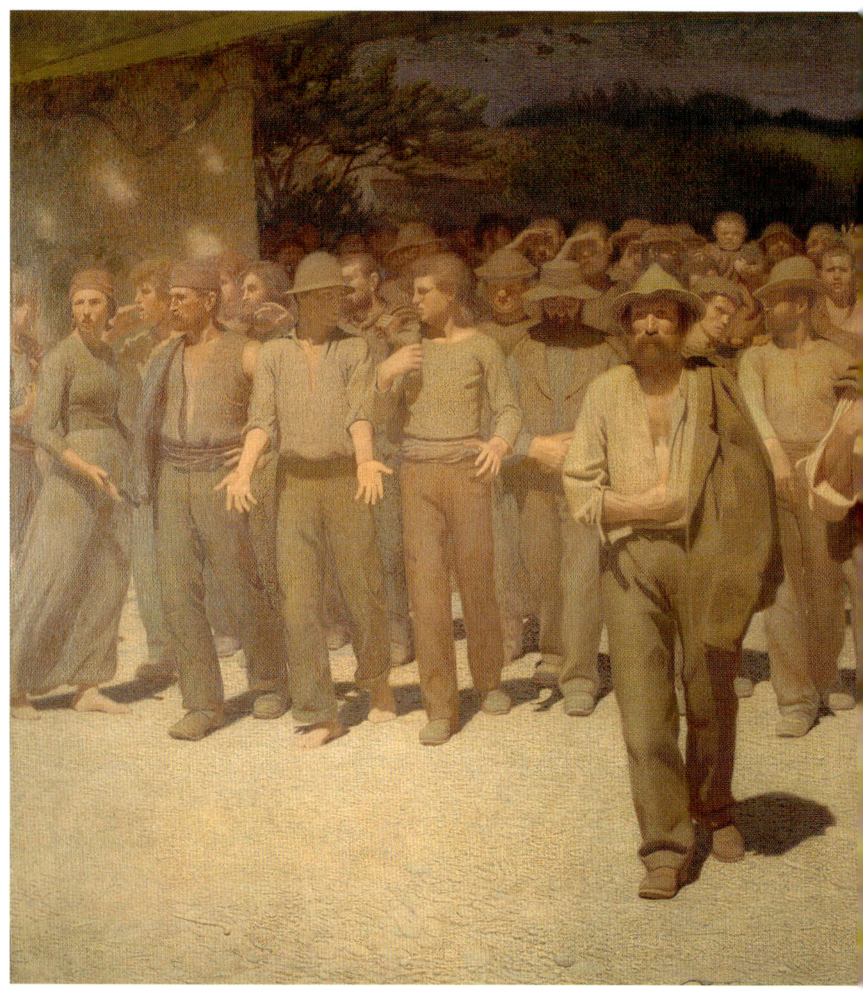

the pleading of the Raphaelite mother and child, fearlessly proclaim their power. Behind them, the men gesture in accusation with their open hands. Pellizza da Volpedo's workers' manifesto, which imposes itself forcefully on the observer, was shown for the first time at an exhibition in Turin but was not to achieve popularity until later.[20] The painting was also used by Joseph Beuys in 1972 for his art propaganda and by Bernardo Bertolucci in 1976 in his film *Novecento*.[21]

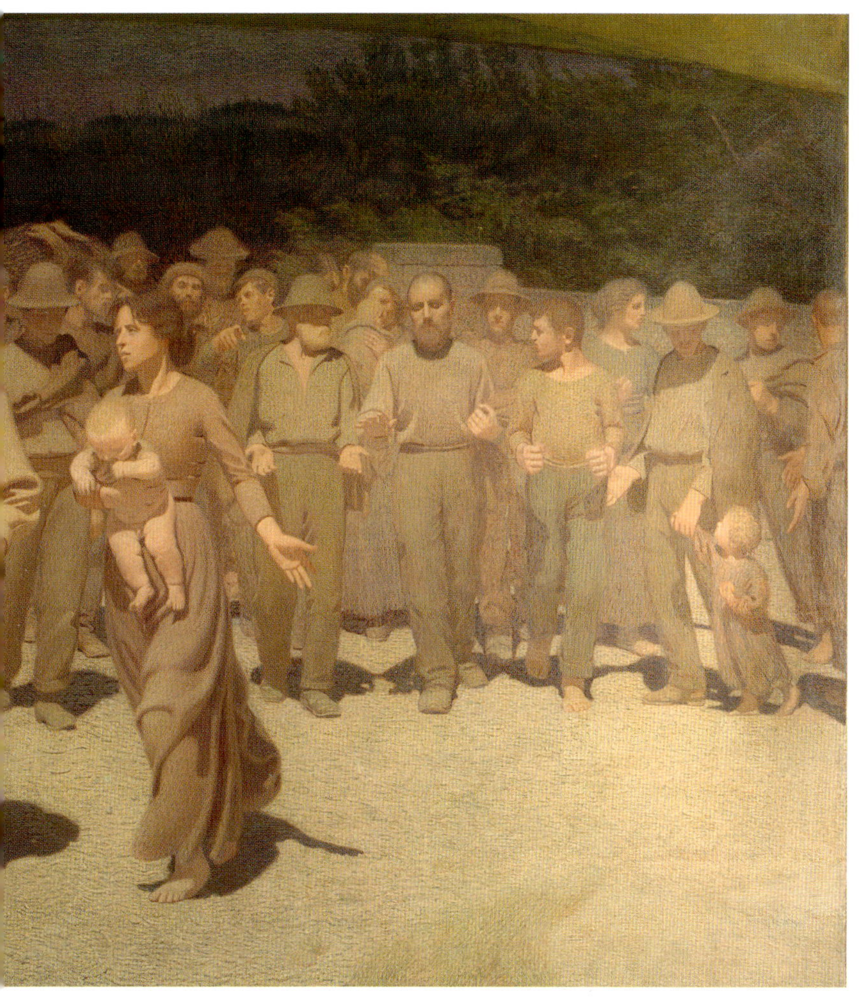

53 Giuseppe Pellizza da Volpedo, *The Fourth Estate*, 1901, oil on canvas.

A typical example of the fostering of the educational effect of posters was Jean Louis Sponsel from Kupferstich-Kabinett Dresden, who in 1897 presented a review of modern poster work 'largely supported by art researchers, art writers and art lovers' and helping to beautify our existence 'through art'.[22] He claimed to note already a positive effect on the public: 'The new poster form is perhaps the most powerful instrument for educating the public to an appreciation of and demand for art. At all events, the modern artistic poster has fostered the discussion in the general public of artistic questions that were hitherto secondary to other interests.'[23]

The author was concerned, however, at the insult to German moral sensitivity by the well-known immoral posters by Jules Chéret and other French artists, so much so that in the chapter 'Frankreich' the author showed only bowdlerized versions, including that of Loïe Fuller's wonderful 'Serpentine Dance' at the Folies-Bergère.[24] German poster art was to adopt the new design principles, but without 'abandoning the way of thinking and sensitivity peculiar to our national character'.[25] Sponsel supported official control, thanks to which the 'poster pollution' was not so widespread in Germany as it was in cities in France, Britain and the United States of America. The technical perfection sought in Germany with multi-coloured lithography nevertheless prevented the transition to modern posters based on Japanese woodcuts.

A major criticism of posters appeared in 1896 in the magazine *La Revue des Deux Mondes* under the title 'L'Âge de l'affiche'. The author, journalist Maurice Talmeyr, described the ubiquitous advertisements as the most brutal and diabolical modernity, characterizing the faster pace of life and all activities in it.[26] Just like people who could be in Paris in the evening and Marseille the following morning, posters were also affixed in the morning and torn down in the evening. In the meantime, however, first in London and now in Paris, they did their damaging work by continuously seducing the public to consume goods and spectacles. Published every month from December 1895 to November 1900, the revue *Les Maîtres de l'Affiche* inaugurated by Jules Chéret presented 256 posters by 97 artists and also appeared in a deluxe edition of one hundred copies printed on Japanese vellum.[27] It included only 'affiches artistiques' from France, Belgium, Britain and the USA. Talmeyr took the widespread coloured, graphic and erotic stimuli as an occasion for unrelenting condemnation.

Koloman Moser criticized Ferdinand Hodler's colouration as 'poster-like': in other words, garish and intrusive. For Hodler, however, the simple composition and flat depiction in intensive colours with repetitive figures served to draw the public's attention directly to the contents. He emphasized another aspect to his biographer, Carl Albert Loosli: 'The effect I am trying to achieve should work directly, through the drawing, the form and the colour, and not through some hidden meaning foisted on me afterwards.'[28] Hodler regarded the 'unbiased public' as the ideal recipient for his art and the art scholars and academics as the artist's 'enemies'.

Max Raphael, who for political reasons was banned from teaching at the Volkshochschule in Berlin, emigrated in 1932 to France, earned a meagre living giving talks and guided tours while writing his major work, *Arbeiter, Kunst und Künstler*, from which he gave readings in the Louvre in 1938 and 1939.[29] In the first sentence, he thanked the public for turning up in such large numbers and asked whether the 'class-conscious proletariat should be interested in art at all', since it was possible that art, like religion, was an opium that 'should disappear after the revolution from the intellectual life of the new society'.[30] Raphael suspected that the confusing experience in museums could demotivate workers from spending 'their free time on Sundays' there. But this conflicted with the class consciousness of the proletariat, which discovered that the 'ruling class' denied it access for fear that it would acquire knowledge and use it for the class struggle. Raphael promised the development of a 'proletarian art perception' as a path in an insecure society for artists: 'The bourgeoisie no longer supports its art, and the proletariat does not support it yet.' Raphael suggested that works of art that corresponded to the means of expression of the ruling class should be seen as materialistic, dialectic and socially critical. The depictions of downtrodden peasants by Louis Le Nain were approved but not the 'sentimental pastoral pictures'.[31] As a Marxist, Raphael would have strongly rejected the idea of seducing workers with poster art showing unattainable goods and events.

The introduction of workers to art became an important project for educational, religious and political groups who wished to spread its influence.[32] In 1910 Richard Keutel's Verlag für Volkskunst in Stuttgart published a quarto volume entitled *Die Gleichnisse Jesu* by the theologian David Koch with illustrations by Eugène Burnand. It was advertised as the 'confirmation book for the German people', cost 15 marks – seven times more than small-format books – but promised high-quality illustrations that fostered the 'unity of religion and art'.[33] Two years later, the same company published *Arbeiter und Kunst* by August Springer with a view to stimulating the need for and appreciation of art in workers in accordance with the human right to art.[34] The illustrated works by Constantin Meunier, Adolph Menzel, Eugène Burnand, Fritz von Uhde and others show workers, a foundry, factories, dockers, grape pickers and the like. The depictions of the working world and the religious instruction were aimed at readers of this missionary brochure, which advocated the right of workers to art and to social reforms, from holidays to housing.[35]

In the last third of the nineteenth century, social reforms in arts and crafts were inaugurated in Britain, and the movement spread to the Continent. The gap between arts and crafts was to be closed, public taste raised and new designs for production and consumption introduced. The aims were diversely defined and pursued, but the different groups – from the Arts & Crafts movement to the Deutscher Werkbund and the Wiener Werkstätte and Bauhaus, to mention but a few – advocated public education through better design of objects or through the 'ideal community of creators and consumers', as Gustav Klimt stated in Vienna in 1908 and proposed as the aim of the Wiener Werkstätte founded in 1903. In the very first sentence of the manifesto, Klimt expounds the problem of the separation of artists and public: 'We do not regard the exhibition as the ideal form for establishing contact between the artist and the public; the completion of great public art projects, for example, would be incomparably more suited for this purpose.'[36]

The dress code for men on the invitation to the 1908 Kunstschau in Vienna called for a 'festive frock coat', a dark knee-length double-breasted coat, rather than the shorter jacket that was starting to become fashionable but was considered unsuitable for the upper classes. Klimt painted the Viennese moneyed aristocracy, and the Wiener Werkstätte produced jewellery, furniture, fabrics and fashion accessories for exclusive tastes and financial resources.

The Volksbildung (popular education) programme proposed in Germany by progressive museum directors such as Alfred Lichtwark, Gustav Pauli and Fritz Wichert offered art education to counter the much bemoaned alienation of the public from art. Lichtwark founded museum education. In 1910 Fritz Wichert, first director of the Kunsthalle in Mannheim, organized the Akademie für Jedermann (Academy for Everyone) and the Der freie Bund zur Einbürgerung der bildenden Kunst (Free Association for the Naturalization of Fine Arts) in Mannheim, two models for popular education and the popularization of museums.[37] Based on Ludwig Justi's museum in the Kronprinzenpalais in Berlin, Alfred H. Barr ensured that the display in the Museum of Modern Art in New York, which opened in 1929, had a strong educational component.[38]

With these museum-education initiatives, the directors clearly showed that they felt responsible both for art and for the public.[39] The Besucherschulen (visitor schools) in the 1960s and 1970s took up this responsibility again, continuing Bazon Brock's demand for two different documentas, one showing works selected by a curator and another showing what the curator did not select, so that the public would be empowered to judge what was shown on the basis of what was not shown. Like other happening and performance artists, Joseph Beuys and Wolf Vostell sought direct contact with the public and acted as their own art educators, as it were. They saw the schooling of the public, also making use of spectacles, as a political activity.[40]

Besucherschulen were offered outside Germany, but not by this name. All museums today have education departments and diverse education programmes for children, adolescents and adults. Museums in the USA offer sophisticated public education orientated towards different interests, a nuanced concept that has also made inroads in Europe. The Guggenheim Museum in Venice, for example, provides comprehensive guidance and instruction to visitors of all categories. Its public programme is 'designed to enrich the experience and understanding of both the permanent collection and the temporary exhibitions'.[41] Parallel to such programmes, digital education is also being developed. Directors of major institutions include initiatives in their programmes for 'opening collections to all of society'.[42]

In the first volume of his *Entwicklungsgeschichte der modernen Kunst* in 1904, the art writer Julius Meier-Graefe wrote a critique of the contemporary art scene that covered all participants and processes: art had no function, artists had no professional ethic, their 'senseless mass production' destroyed the remnants of art awareness, and states used 'stupid means' to promote the senseless production and consumption of commodities presented as art, while the public allowed itself to be deceived by this superficiality:

> The artist manages to deceive the public more easily than any other profession, because, apart from the ready sensitivity of the public for everything shallow, he is helped by his nimbus and a plethora of mediocre supporting institutions that endow this profession with seeming importance and that can be exploited by those with the necessary skill.[43]

It was Meier-Graefe's love of art and his annoyance at the masses that led him to complain about both artists and the public. Concerned about the creation of mass tastes, he advocated an appreciation for art that may be described as 'elitist'. Both the masses, whom he criticized, and the social elite were far from sharing his own preference for contemporary French painting.[44]

Wassily Kandinsky joined Meier-Graefe in criticizing exhibitions and artists, and blamed materialism and the art scene for public indifference in exhibitions. In 1910, he noted: 'The time of alienation of the artist from the public should come to an end. The inseparable internal band between these two elements must also find a form in which it can proclaim itself.'[45] Kandinsky considered asking people for whom art was a necessity about their appreciation of it, their expectations and what they liked. In 1912 he condemned art in its declining phase as 'soulless', while thousands of artists merely sought a 'new fashion', small groups 'entrenched themselves in the positions they had appropriated', the excluded public lost interest in inaccessible art, and the artist could no longer fulfil his function of 'educating the viewer' to his point of view.[46]

Paul Klee, a master in the Bauhaus, expressed his wish for support from the public at his exhibition at the museum in Jena in 1924. In his treatise *On Modern Art* he called for understanding of his works and concluded with a reflection on the situation of artists in view of their remoteness from the public. His dream as an artist was a 'work of really great breadth, ranging through the whole region of element, object, meaning and style'. What was missing was its embedding in a social context, in the 'people', as Klee put it: 'We must go on seeking it. We have found parts, but not the whole. We still lack the ultimate power, for the people are not with us. But we seek a people. We began over there in the Bauhaus. We began there with a community to which each one of us gave what he had. More we cannot do.'[47]

In view of the dispute in the Bauhaus and the growing threat from right-wing parties, this sounds excessively optimistic, but not with regard to the many efforts to narrow the gap between art and the public. The Bauhaus in Weimar was closed on 26 December 1924. On 31 March that year, Lionel Feininger, Wassily Kandinsky, Alexej von Jawlensky and Paul Klee had formed the Blue Four with Galka Scheyer with the aim of 'influencing the youth in North America with a selection of most important works' and of 'communicating this art to the youth of America at universities', as noted by *Der Cicerone*, the magazine for art researchers and collectors.[48] The idea was to attract a new young public in the USA instead of in the Old World and to develop a new market there.

The Weimar Republic and many institutions in Germany undertook new initiatives in the 1920s to foster art for everyone as part of the popular education movement. The expectations were extremely high: the development of 'responsible citizens' through an interest in art, then national integration through German art and recognition of a liberal-minded Germany through international contacts after the destructive war.[49] Radio was also used from the mid-1920s to disseminate information and for popular education, also in the field of art history.[50]

Kandinsky wrote in 1912 that '"understanding" is the training of the viewer to the artist's viewpoint', and at the same time complained that thousands of artists created millions of artworks and sought success while the public remained behind and lost interest.[51] After France was liberated in 1944, the painter André Lhote considered it necessary to admonish the ignorant public not to use the arts for their own amusement: 'It is vital to remind the public of its unworthiness as a judge and to teach it that neither painting nor sculpture nor architecture are "entertainment arts" but sources of infinite torment and considerable annoyance.'[52]

# 15
# MAJOR PLAYERS

Today all participants in the art scene – artists, dealers, collectors, exhibition organizers, media, social media, publishing companies and writers – compete for attention. Those who have succeeded in drawing attention to themselves are often referred to as 'players'. In the penthouse of the art market with their billionaire suites and gold toilet bowls in the style of Maurizio Cattelan, the number of incidents of money laundering, shill bidding, over-invoicing and other criminal or quasi-criminal acts exceeds even the wildest imagination. At stake is an estimated U.S.$70 billion per year.[1] But billionaire art and its sensations should not let us forget that there are still very many serious institutions in the art market that cultivate scholarly tradition, and that there are still serious artists producing work who do not play idle games with art and the public.

The two hundred most important collectors are published every year in the magazine *ARTnews* on the model of the World Billionaires List published since 1987 in *Forbes*, which in 2021 once again listed four hundred billionaires. Some names appear in both lists. In *ARTnews*, portraits of the collectors are included in the list and the origins of their fortunes – luxury goods, investments or inheritance, for example – are briefly mentioned along with the focus of their collections. Contemporary art is the most commonly mentioned, ahead of modern art, which confirms that the majority collect the same items and are in competition with one another.[2] The origins of the fortunes are not questioned and the amounts do not prompt irritation because they are beyond anything that the public could imagine. This list is valuable for the organizers of art events, first to commit exclusive clients and second to titillate the general public with sensational headlines in the mass media. Not wanting to be outdone by the USA, in September 2021 the Italian monthly magazine *Il Giornale dell'Arte* announced its own list, 'Power 100: I top Player dell'arte contemporanea 2.0', with an illustration on the title page of the swollen biceps of four bodybuilders.[3] The list, with photographs and brief descriptions, includes artists, curators, directors, collectors, critics, fashion designers and sponsors. A follow-up with the second one hundred top players has been announced. It is astonishing that all players agree to take part in both the global list and the Italian version.

Not all of us are aware of the destructive effect of competition among the super-rich on the mentality of all involved, on the corruption of the art market and art institutions, on the subjection of the players to ruthless dog-eat-dog competition, and finally on the steady erosion of public art expectations. The significance of public attention can be seen in an announcement on the website of YSI (Yorkshire Sculpture International) for an exhibition of colossal painted figures by Damien Hirst in Leeds, the city in which he grew up. The aim of attracting unlimited attention is clearly stated: 'One of the aims of YSI is to engage a mass audience through sculpture, and Damien's works will play a key role in achieving this. YSI promises to be something special, memorable and game-changing for Yorkshire's growing art scene.'[4] The strategy is relatively simple: an interview by the curator with the eloquent artist in which he answers all of the curator's questions merely with 'yeah'. The number of visitors is the measure of success of such events, as it is with Christie's and Sotheby's, which guarantee exclusivity through the fat bank accounts of the bidders. The art market relies on exclusive offers so as to provoke exorbitant bids, which increase the attention of the media and the masses. The transient sensation demands new and even greater ones, spiralling upwards in the attempt to attract further attention.

The most successful upward spiral to date, through the multiplication of the attention of the global public, began in 2005 in the USA and culminated in New York in 2017. It started with a ruined wooden panel which barely merited the label 'belle croûte'. It was repaired by a skilful restorer, who replaced all missing parts and paint, and gave the picture a mysterious vagueness similar to the effect achieved by Gerhard Richter in his paintings.[5] Then the idea was spread that the painting, sold labelled 'after Leonardo' at an auction in New Orleans in April 2005 for a mere $1,175, was in fact a *Salvator Mundi* by Leonardo himself, whereupon experts were called in to confirm the authorship and investigate the history and provenance.[6] To the amazement of experts and the art world, the specialists commissioned by the owners quickly concurred, since they did not consult critical experts. The expectations of the global public and potential bidders were fuelled by professional rounds of price increases.[7] After a propaganda circuit encircling half of the globe, the exhibition ended up in 2011 in the National Gallery in London, which owned a painting, a cartoon by Leonardo da Vinci and related works, and therefore offered the necessary authentic company for the newly painted wooden panel. The highpoint of its amazing transformation was a hyper-exclusive event on 15 November 2017 at Christie's in the Rockefeller Center in New York, with the outside world following the auction live in the media. The auction room was packed, and celebrities – including the company owner and multibillionaire François Pinault – were thought to be watching from the dark booths in the mezzanine.[8]

Of greater interest than the accompanying deceptions, the skilful disguising of a dealer as an agent, the clandestine connivance of one of the two largest auction houses and the unashamed enrichment is the sensational publicity promoted even by serious media such as the *New York Times* or the *New Yorker*. Auctions in the 2010s increasingly gave rise to dizzying prices that attracted global media attention. The events cleverly staged by auction houses are catapulted by compliant media into global sensations. Christie's auction 3789 of 9 November 2015, at which the price of Amedeo Modigliani's painting *Reclining Nude* was driven up by a skilful auctioneer and aggressive bidders to over $170 million, paved the way for the auction on 15 November 2017. The new owner and holder of the record for just under two years was entitled to feel like the glorious victor of a brutal battle.[9]

One of the reasons for the 2017 Leonardo sensation in New York was the public fascination with the *Mona Lisa* in the Louvre, where the new presentation of the painting since 2005 and the spread of digital cameras have made it possible for visitors to acquire the picture in digital form. The bestseller *The Da Vinci Code* by Dan Brown, filmed by Ron Howard in 2006 with Tom Hanks in the leading role, has served to further enhance interest in Leonardo da Vinci. The film was shot in the Louvre, earning the museum a rumoured revenue of between €15,000 and €24,000 per day. The many negative comments on the book and the film by religious and state organizations fuelled worldwide interest to such an extent that the film grossed $224 million on the first weekend and earned a total of $760 million in 2006, which cranked up the hype even further.[10] For millions of tourists, the *Mona Lisa* became popular again in 2005, when the Louvre finally reopened the Salle des États with the famous painting.[11] For decades it had been barely visible behind green armoured glass in a case on a side wall in the room before being shown in the Grande Galerie during the room's restoration. A huge, almost square

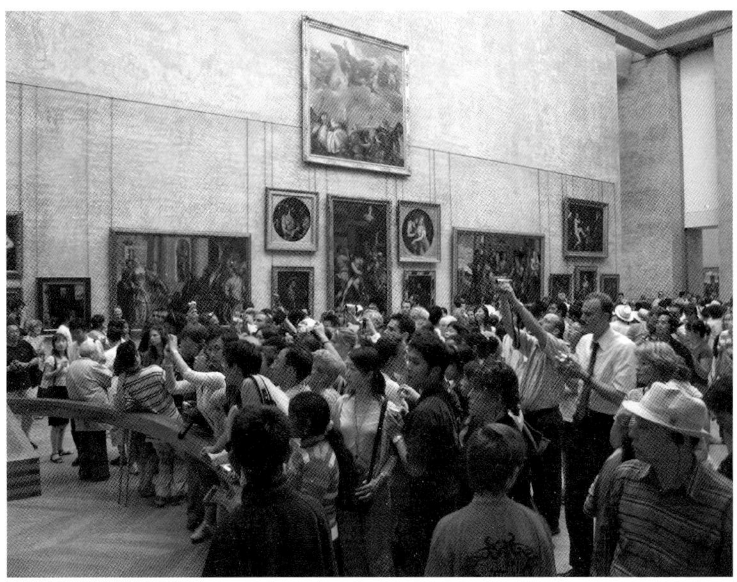

54 Visitors in front of Leonardo's *Mona Lisa*, Musée du Louvre, Paris, 29 June 2005, photograph.

wall has been installed in the Salle des États with a flat rectangular niche for the painting, protected on both sides by armoured glass. The public is kept at a mental, visual and physical distance by a table and a wooden circular segment. In summer 2019 the frame and room were painted dark blue and a new visitor control system was installed allowing a maximum of 50 seconds in front of the picture.

The presentation of Leonardo's painting in the Louvre recalls a picture cult of the past: the table is an altar mensa, the wooden arch adopts the form and function of a choir screen, and Leonardo's painting is presented for admiration like a miracle picture. Without further instruction, the public observing Leonardo's *Mona Lisa* re-enact the behaviour of believers in front of miraculous images of the Virgin Mary (illus. 54). Flocks of visitors raise their arms, hold up a box and stare at the back of it, where the *Mona Lisa* appears as a miniature image. The crowds pause for a few seconds in worship, smile contentedly or take another picture. Some place their partner in front of the painting to capture both of them together. This type of digital appropriation is now being extensively replaced by a selfie with the *Mona Lisa*.

Walter Benjamin points out that the cult veneration of the *Mona Lisa* could be an attempt to make good the loss of aura and cult status.[12] With digital cameras, the public venerates the painting as it used to with miracle pictures of the Virgin Mary and receives this miracle in the form of a miniature photo. The public demand for digital appropriation is overwhelming, and the Louvre and other museums have completely surrendered to it and rescinded the ban on photography.

Institutions are increasingly offering the public at large the possibility of visiting collections and exhibitions online. This has led to a loss of significance of the carefully cultivated public hierarchies and the competition in the public for prominence taking place now at openings, fairs and auctions. For the search term 'vernissage exposition photos', a search engine offers a series of images of the public at the opening of the 'Retour en image sur le vernissage de l'exposition collective' at Galerie Itinerrance in Paris on 27 February 2017.[13] The photos show couples, groups and individual members of the public. Most are looking directly at the camera; many are knee-length portraits with politely smiling subjects. The individual figures, couples and groups are all centred. Some couples are standing in front of a painting, others are approaching the camera, and groups of people can be seen to the left and right of the central figures. One photo shows the public in the room, a group of men smiling and joking in front of the gallery logo.

The social level of the event is evident from the smart winter clothing and the bottles of Desperados, a lager with tequila flavouring drunk from the bottle. The portraits are anonymous – except for the subjects who can see themselves in the pictures. The visitors seem willing to pose for photos, even seeking to stand out from the crowd and to gain prominence in that way. The all-powerful photographer can pick out individuals in the crowd, store the picture, publish it in the media or quietly delete it.

These documentations are frequently published in lifestyle magazines in a deliberately amateurish layout with overlapping, white-edged pictures. They show people holding glasses, laughing and enjoying themselves, and the accompanying text calls the public 'prominent' and the conversation 'sparkling'. The word 'provocative' might also appear in weak memory of the fact that art once existed outside the mainstream. Apart from museum and gallery directors, gallery owners, collectors, moneyed aristocracy and the occasional hereditary peer, artists also sometimes assume jester-like roles.

The bizarre actions of some street artists (or better, if just as ambiguous, 'graffiti artists'), such as Banksy, born in Bristol in 1974, are designed to attract attention. One of his actions caused a worldwide furore and was also commented on extensively on YouTube. The iconoclastic art action took place at Sotheby's in London on 5 October 2018. Lot 67 was a sentimental *Girl with Balloon* from 2006 in a gold frame designed by the artist, offered at a reserve price of £200,000 to £300,000. It was sold for over £1 million, whereupon a whistle blew and a shredder built into the frame by the artist started to cut it into thin strips. The spectators in the packed room looked on in disbelief, amusement or shock, as presumably did the virtual public following the auction in the media. Although the frame was 18 centimetres (7 in.) deep, Sotheby's had apparently failed to notice anything untoward. The auctioneers denied having known anything about the built-in shredder, looked shocked and incredulous, and assumed responsibility for their lack of professionality. The artist claimed that the shredder had created a new valuable work of art called *Love is in the Bin*.[14] The action showed the artist to be a perplexing destroyer but also a cunning producer and self-advertiser.

The worldwide attention that the auction attracted for Sotheby's and the artist in London on 5 October 2018 equalled the attention that Christie's in New York attracted on 15 November 2017 at the auction of *Salvator Mundi*. As at 1 June 2021, the Banksy auction had 43,559 likes and 1,620 dislikes on YouTube, while *Salvator* has just 40,691 likes and 1,690 dislikes. We can take these albeit unverified figures as a measure of the value of an event or an artist. In Banksy's case, his publicity team deals with the financial side. The reactions by the public who followed the auction and its outcome in the media far exceed the comments in visitors' books at exhibitions and in museums. The show was commented on in the October 2018 issue of *Artnet News*: 'In a realm as chockablock with legerdemain as the art world, what matters, at the end of the day, is that the audience enjoyed the show. With his star turn at Sotheby's, Banksy gave us all a command performance.'[15]

Other artists asked how they could exploit Banksy's attention value for themselves. One anonymous artist called 'Burnt Banksy' became known for burning pictures. He bought a Banksy screen-print entitled *Morons (White)* for $95,000 borrowed from investors at Taglialatella Galleries in Chelsea, New York, and proceeded to burn it.[16] He appeared for the performance dressed in black, and a photographer took a picture as a non-fungible token (NFT) and uploaded it onto an online auction platform.[17] The action looked as if it was going to fail because Banksy's print initially refused to burn. The performance was followed by an unverified 50,000 people on Twitter. An anonymous buyer purchased Burnt Banksy's NFT for $380,000 in cryptocurrency.[18] The artist thus succeeded in tapping into Banksy's attention value and appropriating his names, if only for Andy Warhol's famous fifteen minutes.[19] Paradoxically, the NFT recreated an expensive exclusive original from a mass-produced version. There is also the view that 'the act of buying is itself bought' and that the purchased item is merely evidence of the act.[20] The social media made a sensation out of the NFT market, but it is unknown whether the public was impressed or whether people just shrugged their shoulders, as there were no comments on the privatization or accusations of iconoclasm and name theft.

With the aid of NFT and the fractioning of artworks, known as 'tokenization', unsuspected possibilities are created for sharing works of art and exploiting those interested, In July 2021, Artemundi and Sygnum Bank (Switzerland and Singapore) offered shares in a painting by Picasso for CHF 1,000 each so as to permit the buying and selling of blue-chip art without the need to pay the prices demanded by the traditional art market. This also makes it easier for those interested to invest in art, because they no longer have to pay out tens or hundreds of millions for a physical object. The convenience of acquiring tokens of artworks with cryptocurrencies enables the general public to become 'players' with just a relatively small stake and, as in a casino, to gamble with their assets.[21]

# EPILOGUE

The pictures and texts I have used for this book come from the small part of the Earth that for centuries imagined itself to be the centre of the world but is now in fact just known as the 'Western world'. The unintentional limitation results from the non-systematic investigation of pictorial documents and texts. This admission is accompanied by the hope that further examples and questions will enlarge this new research area for art history. The diachronic approach marks an attempt to combine history and analysis while not being just a 'compilateur d'anecdotes'.[1]

I am confident that the research on art publics will continue, be broadened and deepened, and I hope that the visual arts will continue to find an interested public for a long time to come.

# REFERENCES

## Prologue


1 For example, Ken Wilder, *Beholding: Situated Art and the Aesthetics of Reception* (London, 2020), who in 315 pages refers a lot to the 'beholder' and not once to the public. An exception to this trend is Peter Johannes Schneemann, 'Anweisung, Beobachtung und Nachricht: Rollenspiele für eine neue Rezeptionsästhetik', in *Welt, Bild, Museum: Topographien der Kreativität*, ed. Andreas Blühm and Anja Ebert (Cologne et al., 2011), pp. 277–90.

2 Charlotte Klonk, *Spaces of Experience: Art Gallery Interiors from 1800 to 2000* (New Haven, CT, and London, 2009), is an exception.

3 The main work did not appear until 1974: Arnold Hauser, *The Sociology of Art*, trans. K. J. Northcott (Abingdon, 2011); Pierre Bourdieu and Alain Darbel, *L'Amour de l'art: les musées et leur public* (Paris, 1966; translated into English as *The Love of Art: European Art Museums and Their Public* (Cambridge, 1997)); Pierre Bourdieu, *La Distinction: Critique sociale du jugement* (Paris, 1979; translated into English by Richard Nice as *Distinction: A Social Critique of the Judgement of Taste* (London and New York, 1984)).

4 Jürgen Gerhards, ed., *Soziologie der Kunst: Produzenten, Vermittler und Rezipienten* (Opladen, 1997).

5 Hans-Joachim Klein, *Der gläserne Besucher: Publikumsstrukturen einer Museumslandschaft*, Berliner Schriften zur Museumskunde, vol. VIII (Berlin, 1990).

6 See Nora Wegner, 'Besucherforschung und Evaluation in Museen: Forschungsstand, Befunde und Perspektiven', in *Das Kulturpublikum. Fragestellungen und Befunde der empirischen Forschung*, ed. Patrick Glogner and Patrick S. Föhl (Wiesbaden, 2001), pp. 97–152; Patrick Glogner-Pilz, *Publikumsforschung: Grundlagen und Methoden* (Wiesbaden, 2012).

7 Paul Buckermann, *Die Vermessung der Kunstwelt: Quantifizierende Beobachtungen und plurale Ordnungen der Kunst* (Weilerswist, 2020).

8 See Patrick Glogner-Pilz and Patrick S. Föhl, eds, *Handbuch Kulturpublikum: Forschungsfragen und Befunde* (Wiesbaden, 2015), pp. 25–6.

9 Franz Schultheis et al., *Kunst und Kapital: Begegnungen auf der Art Basel* (Cologne, [2015]); English trans. by James Feams as *When Art Meets Money: Encounters at the Art Basel* (Cologne, [2015]) (online, open access).

10 The analysis of mass tourism and cultural overtourism must be left to sociologists, tourism researchers and cultural economists. See Bruno S. Frey, *Venedig ist überall: Vom Übertourismus zum Neuen Original* (Wiesbaden, 2020).

11 Charles-Antoine Coypel, 'Dialogue sur l'exposition des Tableaux dans le Sallon du Louvre, en 1747', *Mercure* (November 1751), p. 59 (BnF Gallica), pp. 5–6.

12 Maurice Malingue, ed., *Lettres de Gauguin à sa femme et à ses amis* (Paris, 1946), p. 298: 'curieux et fou public qui exige du peintre le plus originalité possible et ne l'admet cependant que lorsqu'il ressemble aux autres.'

13 Umberto Eco, *The Open Work*, trans. Anna Cancogni (Cambridge, MA, 1989).

14 For bibliographical information, see Harold Rosenberg, *The Anxious Object: Art Today and Its Audience* (New York, 1964); Hans Belting, *Das Bild und sein Publikum im Mittelalter: Form und Funktion früher Bildtafeln der Passion* (Berlin, 1981); Wilhelm Schlink, *Jacob Burckhardt und die Kunsterwartung im Vormärz*, Frankfurter Historische Vorträge, vol. VIII (Wiesbaden, 1982); Thomas E. Crow, *Painters and Public Life in Eighteenth-Century Paris* (New Haven, CT, and London, 1985); Henrike Junge, *Avantgarde und Publikum: Zur Rezeption avantgardistischer Kunst in Deutschland, 1905–1933* (Cologne et al., 1992); Richard Wrigley, *The Origins of French Art Criticism* (Oxford, 1993), ch. 3, 'In Search of an Art Public', pp. 97–119; Werner Busch, *Das sentimentalische Bild: Die Krise der Kunst im 18. Jahrhundert und die Geburt der Moderne* (Munich, 1993); Peter Johannes Schneemann, *Geschichte als Vorbild: Die Modelle der französischen Historienmalerei 1747–1789* (Berlin, 1994), ch. 3, 'Das Publikum', pp. 55–93; Oskar Bätschmann, *Ausstellungskünstler: Kunst und Karriere im modernen Kunstsystem* (Cologne, 1997); ibid., *The Artist in the Modern World: The Conflict Between Market and Self-Expression* (New Haven, CT, et al., 1997); Antoinette Roesler-Friedenthal and Johannes Nathan, eds, *The Enduring Instant: Time and the Spectator in the Visual Arts – Der bleibende Augenblick: Betrachterzeit in den Bildkünsten* (Berlin, 2003); Joachim Penzel, *Der Betrachter ist im Text: Konversations- und Lesekultur in deutschen Gemäldegalerien zwischen 1700 und 1914* (Berlin, 2007); Eva Kernbauer, *Der Platz des Publikums: Modelle für Kunstöffentlichkeit im 18. Jahrhundert* (Cologne et al., 2011); Wolfgang Kemp, *Der explizite Betrachter: Zur Rezeption zeitgenössischer Kunst* (Konstanz, 2015), ch. 'Der Krieg findet im Saal

statt: Die Lehr- und Prügeljahre des Publikums', pp. 51–63; Beate Fricke and Urte Krass, eds, *The Public in the Picture: Involving the Beholder in Antique, Islamic, Byzantine and Western Medieval and Renaissance Art – Das Publikum im Bild: Beiträge aus der Kunst der Antike, des Islam, aus Byzanz und dem Westen* (Zurich, 2015); Peter J. Schneemann, ed., *Paradigmen der Kunstbetrachtung: Aktuelle Positionen der Rezeptionsästhetik und Museumspädagogik* (Bern et al., 2015); Pascal Griener, *Pour une histoire du regard: l'expérience du musée au XIXe siècle* (Paris, 2017); Anja Weisenseel, *Bildbetrachtung in Bewegung: Der Rezipient in Texten und Bildern zur Pariser Salonausstellung des 18. Jahrhunderts* (Berlin, 2017); Ulrich Pfisterer, *Kunstgeschichte zur Einführung* (Hamburg, 2020), ch. 'Das grosse Publikum', pp. 252–8.

15 Ernst Kris and Otto Kurz, *Legend, Myth and Magic in the Image of the Artist* (New Haven, CT, and London, 1979), ch. 4, 'The Artist and the Public', pp. 99–113.

16 Klonk, *Spaces of Experience.*

## 1 The Public Component

1 Hans Rudolf Reust and James Lingwood, eds, *Texte zum Werke von Thomas Struth* (Munich, 2009); *Thomas Struth: Museum Photographs*, exh. cat., Hamburger Kunsthalle, 1993–4 (Munich, 1993).

2 *Thomas Struth: Museum Photographs*, p. 22: *Stanze di Raffaello I* (Rome, 1990); *Thomas Struth:Museum Photographs*, 2nd edn (Munich, 2005), p. 51.

3 *Thomas Struth: Fotografien 1978–2010*, exh. cat., Zurich, Dusseldorf, London, Porto, 2010–12 (Munich, 2010), pp. 198–9: *Museum Photographs*, p. 1.

4 *Thomas Struth: Museum Photographs*, pp. 44–5: *Kunsthistorisches Museum* III, Vienna, 1989, 145 × 187 cm.

5 Thomas Bernhard, *Old Masters: A Comedy*, trans. Ewald Osers (Chicago, IL, 1992).

6 *Thomas Struth: Museum Photographs*, 2nd edn (2005), p. 85.

7 *Thomas Struth: Fotografien 1978–2010*, p. 47: *Audience 7, Florenz 2004*, chromogenic print, 179.5 × 288.3 cm, Dusseldorf, Kunstsammlung Nordrhein-Westfalen; see also Norman Bryson, 'Not Cold, Not Too Warm: The Oblique Photography of Thomas Struth', *Parkett*, L–LI (1997), pp. 157–65, www.e-periodica.ch.

8 Galleria dell'Accademia di Firenze, Ordine di Servizio, 13 December 2018; see also Le Gallerie degli Uffizi, Regolamento: Qualche regola da seguire (2021): 'Tutti i visitatori sono tenuti a osservare un comportamento conforme alle communi regole di buona educazione.' This is followed by a list of sixteen prohibitions. It is not known how well the rules are enforced.

9 Wolfgang Kemp, 'Kunstwerk und Betrachter: Der rezeptionsästhetische Ansatz', in *Kunstgeschichte: Eine Einführung* (Berlin, 2008), pp. 247–65; Wolfgang Kemp, 'Rezeptionsästhetik', in *Metzler Lexikon Kunstwissenschaft: Ideen, Methoden, Begriffe*, ed. Ulrich Pfisterer (Weimar, 2011), pp. 388–91.

10 Francis Haskell, 'A Turk and his Pictures in Nineteenth-Century Paris', in *Past and Present in Art and Taste: Selected Essays* (New Haven, CT, and London, 1987), pp. 175–85.

11 Oskar Bätschmann, 'The Artist on Show: Gustave Courbet', in *Representation and Show: Studies in Nineteenth-Century Art* (Taipei, 2013), pp. 1–39.

12 Martin Disler, *Die Umgebung der Liebe*, ed. Tilman Osterwold (Stuttgart, 1993).

13 Martin Disler, *Bilder vom Maler*, 3rd edn (Dudweiler, 1983); in the reprint version as *Bilder vom Maler: Roman* (Zurich, 2015) the story of the popular painter is the nineteenth illustration (pp. 85–8) and the text by the painter in the stadium the twentieth illustration (pp. 89–90); Franz Müller, ed., *Martin Disler 1949–1996* (Zurich, 2007); see also Regula Krähenbühl, '"Bilder vom Maler" als Vexierbild vom Schriftsteller', pp. 225–46.

14 For the frontispiece and composite bodies, see Horst Bredekamp, *Thomas Hobbes: Visuelle Strategien – Der Leviathan: Urbild des modernen Staates – Werkillustrationen und Portraits* (Berlin, 1999). Disler was a pupil at the Kapuzinerkollegium in Stans, Switzerland, from 1961 to 1968 and at the Kantonsschule Solothurn in 1969. At the time, philosophy was taught at Catholic secondary schools.

15 Hans Ulrich Gumbrecht, *Crowds: Das Stadion als Ritual von Intensität* (Frankfurt am Main, 2020); translated into English by Emily Goodling as *Crowds: The Stadium as a Ritual of Intensity* (Stanford, CA, 2021).

16 Herbert Killian, *Gustav Mahler in den Erinnerungen von Natalie Bauer-Lechner* with notes and explanations by Knud Martner, revd and expanded edn (Hamburg, 1984), p. 130. With thanks to Johann Layer, Hamburg, for the reference.

17 Jean Cocteau, *Cock and Harlequin: Notes concerning Music*, trans. Rollo H. Myers (London, 1921), p. 49. 'La salle joua le rôle qu'elle devait jouer; elle se révolta tout de suite. On rit, conspua, siffla, imita les cris d'animaux, et peut-être se serait-on lassé, à la longue, si la foule des esthétes et quelques musiciens, emportés par leur zèle excessif, n'eussent insulté, bousculé même, le public des loges. Le vacarme dégénéra en lutte.'

18 Ibid., p. 49; Mélanie de Pourtalès, Comtesse Edmond de Pourtalès, 1836–1914.

19 'Grande Serata Futurista, Firenze, Teatro Verdi, 12 Dicembre 1912', *Lacerba*, 1/24 (15 December 1913), p. 1.

20 Franz Schultheis et al., *Kunst und Kapital: Begegnungen auf der Art Basel* (Cologne, [2015]); English trans. by James Feams as *When Art Meets Money: Encounters at the Art Basel* (Cologne, [2015]) (online, open access), pp. 129–30.

21 Horace, *Ars poetica*, trans. A. S. Kline, 2005, www.poetryintranslation.com, accessed 31 October 2022.

22 Leon Battista Alberti, *De statua, de pictura, elementa picturae – Das Standbild, Die Malkunst, Grundlagen der Malerei*, ed. Oskar Bätschmann and Christoph Schäublin, 2nd edn (Darmstadt, 2011), *On Painting*, trans. Rocco Sinisgalli (Cambridge, 2011), p. 41: 'Fit namque natura . . . ut lugentibus conglugeamus, ridentibus adrideamus, dolentibus condoleamus.'

23 'Fluidum, das' in DWDS *Der deutsche Wortschatz von 1600 bis heute*, since the nineteenth century 'effect or emanation of an object, a person probably triggered by the transfer of the impression to magnetic or electric currents'; see 'Fluidum', in *Wörterbuch der deutschen Gegenwartssprache* (*WDG*), 'imponderable effect emanating from a person or thing: the Fluidum of the artist, the great personality; the Fluidum between the stage and the auditorium'; Christine Göttler, 'Vapours and Veils: The Edge of the Unseen', in *Spirits Unseen: The Representation of Subtle Bodies in Early Modern European Culture*, ed. Christine Göttler and Wolfgang Neuber (Leiden, 2008), pp. xv–xxv.

24 Joachim Bauer, *Warum ich fühle was du fühlst – Intuitive Kommunikation und das Geheimnis der Spiegelneuronen* (Hamburg, 2005).

25 Matthew Pelowski et al., 'Beyond the Lab: An Examination of Key Factors Influencing Interaction with "Real" and Museum-Based Art', *Psychology of Aesthetics, Creativity, and the Arts*, XI/3 (2017), pp. 245–64.

26 There is a large corpus of literature on this subject: see RoseLee Goldberg, *Performance Art: From Futurism to the Present*, revd and expanded edn (London and New York, 2011); Erika Fischer-Lichte, *Ästhetik des Performativen* [2004], 9th edn (Frankfurt am Main, 2014).

27 Marina Abramović and James Kaplan, *The Walk Through Walls* (New York, 2016), pp. 69, 81–5.

28 Ibid., pp. 395–412; see also the video on YouTube; Marcel Bleuler, 'Imaginierter Schmerz: Marina Abramović und die Produktion von Empathie', in *Paradigmen der Kunstbetrachtung: Aktuelle Positionen der Rezeptionsästhetik und Museumspädagogik*, ed. Peter J. Schneemann (Bern et al., 2015), pp. 157–77.

29 Marina Abramović, *Measuring the Magic of Mutual Gaze*, see www.ericforman.com/marina-abramovic-mutual-gaze, accessed 8 July 2022.

## 2 Hierarchical Categories

1 Werner Fuchs-Heinritz et al., eds, *Lexikon zur Soziologie*, 5th revd edn (Heidelberg, 2011), pp. 542–3; John Fiske, *Television Culture* [1987] (London, 2011).
2 See the entry for 'public', in *The Oxford English Dictionary*, 2nd edn, prepared by J. A. Simpson und E.S.C. Weiner (Oxford, 1989), vol. XII, pp. 778–81; and for 'audience' in vol. I, pp. 779–80.
3 *Le Dictionnaire érudit de la langue française* (Paris, 2014), pp. 1529–30.
4 *Grande dizionario italiano dell'uso*, ed. Tullio de Mauro (Turin, 2000), vol. V, p. 264.
5 Jürgen Habermas, *Strukturwandel der Öffentlichkeit: Untersuchungen zu einer Kategorie der bürgerlichen Gesellschaft*, 3rd edn (Neuwied and Berlin, 1968), §5, pp. 46–60 (p. 53).
6 Museum of Modern Art New York: https://membership.moma.org/donor/tiers.
7 See www.instagram.com/themuseumofmodernart/?hl=en.
8 See www.nationalgallery.org.uk/membership.
9 See www.vangoghmuseum.nl/en/about/support-the-museum.
10 For the classification of Art Basel, see Franz Schultheis et al., *Kunst und Kapital: Begegnungen auf der Art Basel* (Cologne, [2015]); English trans. by James Feams as *When Art Meets Money: Encounters at the Art Basel* (Cologne, [2015]) (online, open access), pp. 104–6.
11 Wassily Kandinsky, *On the Spiritual in Art*, ed. Hilla Rebay (New York, 1946), p. 20.
12 Ibid., pp. 20–21.
13 'Most Visited Museums Worldwide in 2019 and 2020', www.statista.com, accessed 8 July 2022. For other rankings, see https://artfacts.net, among others.
14 The website for the Staatliche Museen zu Berlin is www.smb.museum; Zahlen & Materialien aus dem Institut für Museumsforschung, vol. LXXV (Heidelberg, 2021): www.arthistoricum.net, 2021.

## 3 The Apelles Problem

1 For the many mentions of the rivalry, see Christiane J. Hessler, *Zum Paragone: Malerei, Skulptur und Dichtung in der Rangstreitkultur des Quattrocento* (Berlin, 2014), pp. 690–93.
2 Pliny, *Natural History* 35, 84: 'idem perfecta opera proponebat in pergula transeuntibus atque, ipse post tabulam latens, vitia, quae notarentur, auscultabat, volgum diligentiorem iudicem quam se praeferens.'
3 Karl Ernst Georges, *Ausführliches Lateinisch-Deutsches Handwörterbuch*, 8th edn, ed. Heinrich Georges, 2 vols (Hanover, 1918), vol. II, col. 3561:

'Volk, Menge, gemeiner Mann, grosser Haufen, Pöbel, die grosse Masse, der gewöhnliche Schlag'.

4 Pliny, *Natural History* 35, 85: 'ne supra crepidam iudicaret' – he should not judge above the shoe; Magdalena Eickelkamp, 'Apelles an der Kunstakademie: Studien zur Bedeutung des antiken "Malerfürsten" für die akademische Kunst und Kunsttheorie vom 16.–19. Jahrhundert', diss., University of Bonn, 2016, pp. 81–4.

5 Philostratus, *Eikones*, II/6; see Philostratos, *Philostratus the Elder: Imagines – Philostratus the Younger: Imagines – Callistratus: Descriptions*, trans. Arthur Fairbanks (London, 1931), p. 151; see Gottfried Boehm and Helmut Pfotenhauer, eds, *Beschreibungkunst – Kunstgeschreibung* (Munich, 1995), particularly the essays by Fritz Graf, 'Ekphrasis: die Entstehung der Gattung in der Antike', pp. 143–55, and Otto Schönberger, 'Die "Bilder" des Philostratos', pp. 157–76.

6 Mohamed Yacoub, *Splendeurs des mosaiques de Tunisie* (Tunis, 1995), p. 307, fig. 156b; Katharina Preindl, 'Fans und Hooligans in der Antike', *Forum Archaeologiae*, XLIII/3 (2007), pp. 1–19.

7 Publius Vergilius Maro, *Aeneid*, Book I, vv. 453–5.

8 Julia Frick, 'Visual Narrative: The *Aeneid* Woodcuts from Sebastian Brant's Edition of Virgil (Strasbourg 1502) in Thomas Murner's Translation of the *Aeneid* (Strasbourg 1515)', in *Early Printed Narrative Literature in Western Europe*, ed. Bart Besamusca et al. (Berlin, 2019), pp. 241–72.

9 Leon Battista Alberti, *On Painting*, trans. Rocco Sinisgalli (Cambridge, 2011), p. 83.

10 Ibid., p. 61: 'Animos deinde spectantium movebit historia, cum qui aderunt picti homines suum animi motum maxime prae se ferent'; Horace, *Ars poetica*, available at www.poetryintranslation.com.

11 Michael Baxandall, *Giotto and the Orators: Humanist Observers of Painting in Italy and the Discovery of Pictorial Composition, 1350–1450* (Oxford, 1971), pp. 133–4.

12 Leon Battista Alberti, *De statua, de pictura, elementa picturae – Das Standbild, Die Malkunst, Grundlagen der Malerei*, ed. Oskar Bätschmann and Christoph Schäublin, 2nd edn (Darmstadt, 2011), p. 63: 'Denique et quae illi com spectantibus et quae inter se picti exequentur, omnia ad agendam et docendam historiam congruant necesse est.'

13 Martin McLaughlin, 'Alberti's Commentarium to His First Literary Work: Self-Commentary as Self-Presentation in the Philodoxeos', in *Self-Commentary in Early Modern European Literature, 1400–1700*, ed. Francesco Venturi (Leiden, 2019), pp. 28–49.

14 Leon Battista Alberti, *On the Art of Building in Ten Books*, trans. Joseph Rykwert, Neil Leach and Robert Tavenor (Cambridge, MA, 1992), pp. 268–78.

15 Alberti, *De statua, de pictura, elementa picturae*; *On Painting*, pp. 65–6; Volker Saftien, *Ars Saltandi in Renaissance und Barock* (Hildesheim, 1994).
16 Leon Battista Alberti, *Vita: Lateinisch-deutsch*, ed. Christine Tauber (Basel, 2004).
17 Ibid.
18 Ibid.: 'Vituperatoribus rerum quas conscriberet modo coram sententiam suam depromerent gratias agebat, in eamque id partem accipiebat ut se fieri elimatiorem emendatorum admonitu vehementer congratularetur.'
19 Alberti, *De statua, de pictura, elementa picturae*; *On Painting*, p. 84: 'faciem meam in suis historiis pingant'.
20 Heinrich Wölfflin, *Classic Art: An Introduction to the Italian Renaissance*, trans. Peter Murray and Linda Murray (London, 1953), p. 33.
21 Giorgio Vasari, *The Lives of the Artists*, trans. Julia Conaway Bondanella and Peter Bondanella (Oxford, 1991), p. 293: 'Finalmente fece un cartone dentrovi una Nostra Donna ed una Sant'Anna con un Cristo, la quale non pure fece maravigliare tutti gli artefici, ma finita ch'ella fu, nella stanza durarono due giorni d'andare a vederla gli uomini e le donne, i giovani ed i vecchi, come si va alle feste solenni; per veder le maraviglie di Leonardo, che fecero stupire tutto quell popolo.'
22 Susanne Kubersky-Pirotta, '"Et sia ritratto nella stessa forma medesima": Das Florentiner Gnadenbild der SS. Annunziata und seine Repliken', in *Multiples in Pre-Modern Art*, ed. Walter Cupperi (Zurich, 2014), pp. 201–27, esp. p. 205.
23 Luca Landucci, *Diario Fiorentino dal 1450 al 1516*, ed. Iodoco del Badia (Florence, 1883), p. 287; for similar gatherings of curious onlookers, Landucci says 'Vi venne tutto Firenze a vedere', pp. 233–4, but does not mention Leonardo's presentation.
24 Antoinette Roesler-Friedenthal and Johannes Nathan, eds, *The Enduring Instant: Time and the Spectator in the Visual Arts – Der bleibende Augenblick: Betrachterzeit in den Bildkünsten* (Berlin, 2003): 'Introduction: The Times of Spectatorship', pp. 32–5 and n. 43.
25 Leonardo da Vinci, *Sämtliche Gemälde und die Schriften zur Malerei*, ed. André Chastel (Darmstadt, 1990), pp. 378–79 (A108r, A106r); Leonardo da Vinci, *Libro di Pittura (Codice Urbinate lat. 1270)*, ed. Carlo Pedretti, transcription Carlo Vecce, 2 vols (Florence, 1995), vol. I, pp. 180–82, nos. 71, 75.
26 Giorgio Vasari, *Lives of the Most Eminent Painters, Sculptors, and Architects* (London, 1912–15), vol. IV, p. 45 (online): see also Robert Williams, 'Repetition, Variation, and the Idea of Art in Renaissance Italy', *California Renaissance Studies*, VI (2016), pp. 1–20.
27 See the analysis of philosophical representations in Susanna Berger, *The Art of Philosophy: Visual Thinking in Europe from the Late Renaissance to the Early Enlightenment* (Princeton, NJ, 2017).

28 Jacob Burckhardt, *The Cicerone: Art Guide to Painting in Italy*, trans. A. H. Clough (London, 1873), p. 144. Some of the suggestions already mentioned are noted in the comments. The Jesuits designated Cardinal Egidio da Viterbo as an adviser; see the essays by Silvia Ferino Pagden and Matthias Winner in *Raffaello a Roma: Il convegno del 1983* (Rome, 1986), pp. 13–27, 29–45.
29 Wilhelm Schlink, 'Jacob Burckhardts Künstlerrat', *Städel-Jahrbuch*, Neue Folge 11, 1987 (1988), pp. 269–90.

## 4 Public Judgement

1 Giovan Pietro Bellori, *The Lives of Modern Painters, Sculptors and Architects*, trans. Alice Wohl (Cambridge, 2005), p. xxx. In the original edn of 1672: pp. 412–13.
2 [André Félibien], *Entretiens sur les vies et sur les ouvrages des plus excellens peintres anciens et modernes, Quatrième partie, Huitième entretien* (Paris, 1685), p. 254.
3 For an analysis of the documents, see Felix Thürlemann, 'Betrachterperspektiven im Konflikt: Zur Überlieferungsgeschichte der "vecchiarella"-Anekdote', in *Der Betrachter ist im Bild: Kunstwissenschaft und Rezeptionsästhetik*, ed. Wolfgang Kemp (Berlin, 1992), pp. 169–207.
4 Abraham Bosse, *Sentimens sur la distinction des diverses manieres de Peintures, dessein & graveure, & des orginaux d'avec leurs copies* (Paris, 1649).
5 Pablo Schneider and Philipp Zitzlsperger, eds, *Bernini in Paris: Das Tagebuch des Paul Fréart de Chantelou über den Aufenthalt Gianlorenzo Berninis am Hof Ludwigs XIV* (Berlin, 2006), p. 131 (5 September 1665); Chantelou, *Journal de voyage du Cavalier Bernin en France*, ed. Milovan Stanić (Paris, 2001), pp. 156–7: '[le Cavalier] a répété qu'Annibal Carrache voulait qu'on exposât à la censure publique un tableau aussitôt qu'il était fait; que le public ne se trompait pas et ne flattait point, qu'il ne manquait jamais de dire: "Il est sec, il est dur", lorsqu'il l'était, et ainsi du reste.' See the English edition: Chantelou, *Diary of the Cavaliere Bernini's Visit to France*, ed. A. Blunt (Princeton, NJ, 1985).
6 Schneider and Zitzlsperger, eds, *Bernini in Paris*, p. 132; Chantelou, *Journal de voyage*, p. 156; for further aspects of Bernini in Paris, see Heiko Damm, 'Berninis Expertisen: Künstlerurteil und Laienkompetenz im Spiegel der Aufzeichnungen des Paul Fréart de Chantelou', in *Zeigen – Überzeugen – Beweisen: Methoden der Wissensproduktion in Kunstliteratur, Kennerschaft und Sammlungspraxis der Frühen Neuzeit*, ed. Elisabeth Oy-Marra and Irina Schmiedel (Merzhausen, 2020), pp. 111–76 (online).

7 For the brothers Fréart de Chantelou, see Henri Chardon, *Les Frères Fréart de Chantelou, amateurs d'art et collectionneurs manceaux du 17ème siècle* (Le Mans, 1867), esp. pp. 22–66.

8 Roland Fréart de Chambray, *Idée de la perfection de la peinture, démonstrée par les principes* (Le Mans, 1662); Roland Freart, Sieur de Cambray, *An Idea of the Perfection of Painting*, trans. J. E. Esquire (London, 1668).

9 Ibid., dedication, n.p.

10 Ibid., Preface, fol. A2r; edn of 1662, Préface, fol. a recto: 'Il n'y a presque personne qui n'ait quelque inclination pour la Peinture, & qui ne pretende mesme auoir vn jugement naturel & vn sens commun capables de contrôller les Ouurages qu'elle produit. Car non seulement les gens de lettres & de condition, qui sont vray-semblablement toûjours les plus raisonnables, se piquent de s'y connoistre; mais encore le vulgaire se mesle d'en dire son sentiment: si bien qu'il semble qu'elle soit en quelque façon le mestier de tout le monde.'

11 Edn 1668, fol. A2r–A2v; edn 1662, Préface, fol. a-a verso: 'Cette présomption n'est pas un vice particulier des François, ou de nostre Siecle. Il est aussi vieu que la Peinture, & il est né auec celle dans la Grece. On le peut iuger par ce que Pline a remarqué d'Apelles, qu'il avoit acoustumé, avant de mettre la derniere main à ses Tableaux, de les exposer publiquement à la censure de touts les passans, & se tenoit cependant caché derriere, pour escouter ce qu'ils disoient, & pour en faire son proffit: d'où est venu le Prouerbe, *Apelles post tabulam*.'

12 Ibid.

13 Ibid.

14 Edn 1668, fol.5v–fol. A6r; edn 1662, fol. a 3 recto- fol. v verso: 'La Peinture mesme, dont nous regrettons la decadence . . . n'a peut estre jamais esté en plus haute estime parmi nous, ny plus recherchée que maintenant; et cela pourroit bien estre en partie la cause de sa corruption.'

15 Letter of 1 March 1665, in Nicolas Poussin, *Correspondance*, ed. Ch. Jouanny (Paris, n.d.), letter 210, pp. 461–4.

16 Chantelou, *Journal de voyage*; Schneider and Zitzlsberger, eds, *Bernini in Paris*.

17 For the earlier acquaintance, see Jan Blanc, 'Mettre des mots sur l'art: Peintres et connaisseurs dans la théorie de l'art française et néerlandais du XVIIe siècle', *Nederlands kunshistorisch jaarboek*, XXIX (2019), pp. 74–105.

18 [Roger de Piles], *Conversations sur la connoissance de la Peinture et sur le Jugement qu'on doit faire des Tableaux: Où par occasion il est parlé de la vie de Rubens, & de quelques uns de ses plus beaux Ouvrages* (Paris, 1677).

19 Ibid., p. 94: 'Le Spectateur n'est point obligé de sçavoir ce que sçait un peintre, il n'a qu'à s'abandonner à son sens commun pour juger de ce qu'il voit.'

20 République française, Ministère de la culture, ancien hôtel du Cardinal de Richelieu, 21, place des Vosges; for the accessibility of collections not usually mentioned, see the discussion of Viennese collections in Gudrun Swoboda, *Die Wege der Bilder: Eine Geschichte der kaiserlichen Gemäldesammlungen von 1600 bis 1800* (Vienna, 2008); Gudrun Swoboda, ed., *Die kaiserliche Gemäldegalerie in Wien und die Anfänge des öffentlichen Kunstmuseums*, 2 vols (Vienna, 2013); the descriptions take up seventy pages in the print version, de Piles, *Conversations sur la connoissance de la Peinture*, pp. 110–81.

21 De Piles, *Conversations sur la connoissance de la Peinture*, p. 124: 'Ce Tableau, comme vous voyez, est un sujet de desordre'; pp. 169–70; pp. 179–81. It is followed by 'Abrége de la vie de Rubens' recounted by Philarchue, pp. 181–308.

22 [Jean-Baptiste Dubos], *Réflexions critiques sur la poesie et sur la peinture: Nouvelle édition revuë, corrigée & considerablement augmentée*, 3 vols (Paris, 1733), part 2, section XXII, pp. 323–53.

23 Ibid., part 2, section XXII, pp. 334–5: 'Le mot de public ne renferme ici que les personnes qui ont acquis des lumieres, soit par la lecture, soit par le commerce du monde. Elles sont les seules qui puissent marquer le rang des Poëmes & des tableaux, quoiqu'il se rencontre dans les ouvrages excellens des beautez capables de se faire sentir au peuple du plus bas étage & de l'obliger à se récrier.'

24 Friedrich Gottlieb Klopstock, '[Vom Publikum]', in *Der nordische Aufseher*, vol. I, piece 49 (Copenhagen, 1758), pp. 445–51; Dubos, *Réflexions critiques sur la poesie*, part 2, section XXII, pp. 320–22.

25 Klopstock, '[Vom Publikum]', pp. 449–50.

26 Charles-Antoine Coypel, 'Dialogue sur l'exposition des Tableaux dans le Sallon du Louvre, en 1747', *Mercure* (November 1751), p. 59 (BnF Gallica), pp. 5–6: 'Ah, convenez plutôt, Celigni, que dans ces petits ouvrages l'Ecrivain empruntant le nom du public sous une humble, mais fausse apparence, ose s'ériger en Juge souverain. Le grand Corneille demandoit autrefois où logeoit le public? Moi, je soutiens que dans le Salon où l'on expose les Tableaux, le public change vingt fois le jour. Ce qu'admiroit le public à dix heures du matin est blâmé publiquement à midi. Oui, vous dis-je, ce lieu peut vous offrir dans le cours d'une seule journée vingt publics de caractères & de tons differens. Public simple en certains momens, & ce public n'est pas celui qu'on devroit le moins écouter: public partial, public leger, public envieux, public esclave du bel air, qui pour décider veut tout voir, & n'examine rien.'

## 5 Sensational Attractions

1 Stephan Kemperdick and Johannes Rössler, eds, *Der Genter Altar der Brüder van Eyck: Geschichte und Würdigung*, exh. cat., Gemäldegalerie, Berlin (Petersberg, 2014); Sandra Hindriks, *Der 'vlaemische Apelles': Jan van Eycks früher Ruhm und die niederländische 'Renaissance'* (Petersberg, 2019).

2 Volker Herzner, 'Die Inschrift des Genter Altars entstand im 16. Jahrhundert, in *Kunstgeschichte: Open Peer Reviewed Journal* (2021), pp. 1–11; Kemperdick and Rössler, eds, *Der Genter Altar der Bruder van Eyck,* pp. 22–8 (Kemperdick); see also the philological explanations by Christina Meckelnborg, 'Die Inschrift des Genter Altars: Eine philologische Betrachtung', in *Der Genter Altar der Brüder van Eyck*, ed. Kemperdick and Rössler, pp. 112–21.

3 Meckelnborg, 'Die Inschrift des Genter Altars', p. 119.

4 'tueor', in Karl Ernst Georges, *Ausführliches Lateinisch-Deutsches Handwörterbuch,* 8th edn, ed. Heinrich Georges, 2 vols (Hanover, 1918), col. 3248–9.

5 Elisabeth Dhanens, 'La Visite organisée du retable de Gand, xve–xviiie Siècle', *Gazette des Beaux-Arts*, LXXXIX (1977), pp. 153–4, states that permission was probably given to view the altarpiece following a courtesy visit to the donors.

6 Hindriks, *Der 'vlaemische Apelles'*, pp. 299–300.

7 Carel van Mander, *The Lives of Illustrious Netherlandish and German Painters*, 6 vols (Doornspijk, 1994–9); Carel van Mander, *Het Leven der Doorluchtighe Nederlandtsche en Hooghduytsche Schilders*, German trans. by Hanns Floerke as *Das Leben der niederländischen und deutschen Maler*, 2 vols (Munich 1906), vol. 1, pp. 36–7.

8 Hindriks, *Der 'vlaemische Apelles'*, p. 302.

9 Albrecht Dürer, 'Diary of a Journey in the Netherlands', trans. Rudolf Tombo, in *The Humanist's Library*, ed. Lewis Einstein, vol. VI (Boston, MA, 1913), available at www.gutenberg.org.

10 Ibid.

11 Hindriks, *Der 'vlaemische Apelles'*, pp. 298–9.

12 Richard Morris, *Court Festivals in the Holy Roman Empire, 1555–1619* (Turnhout, 2020).

13 Anna Coliva and Sebastian Schütze, eds, *Bernini Scultore: La nascita del barocco in Casa Borghese*, exh. cat. (Rome, 1998), no. 27, pp. 252–75; Andrea Bolland, '*Desiderio* and *Diletto:* Vision, Touch, and the Poetics of Bernini's *Apollo and Daphne*', *Art Bulletin*, LXXXII (2000), pp. 309–30.

14 Ovid,*Metamorphoses* 1.452–568; Wolfgang Stechow, *Apollo and Daphne* (Leipzig, 1932).

15 [Filippo Baldinucci], *Vita del cavaliere gio: Lorenzo Bernino scultore, architetto, e pittore, scritta da Filippo Baldinucci Fiorentino alla Sacra e*

*reale maestà do Cristina Regina di Svezia* (Florence, 1682), p. 9: 'La Dafne del Bernino, senz'altro più; e bastimi solamente il dire, che non solo subito, che ella fu fatta veder finita, sene sparse un tal grido, che tutta Roma concorse a vederla per un miracolo.' (Bibliotheca Hertziana, Digitalisate, Ca-BER 1921-2820 raro). Filippo Baldinucci, *The Life of Bernini*, trans. Catherine Enggass (University Park, PA, 1965).

16 Filippo de' Rossi, *Ritratto di Roma moderna* (Rome, 1652); [Giovan Pietro Bellori], *Nota delli Musei, Librerie, Galerie, et Ornamenti di Statue e Pitture* (Rome, 1664), p. 13; See Giovan Pietro Bellori, *Le vite de' pittori, scultori e architetti moderni*, ed. Evelina Borea (Turin, 1976).

17 For the early reception, see Joris van Gastel, *Il marmo spirante: Sculpture and Experience in Seventeenth-Century Rome* (Berlin, 2013), esp. pp. 192–212.

18 Domenico de' Rossi, *Raccolta di statue antiche e moderne* (Rome, 1704), co. 73, quotes Baldinucci; Filippo de' Rossi, *Descrizione di Roma moderna, formata nuovamente, von le autorità, del Card. Cesare Baronio . . . E d'altri celebri Scrittori . . .*, vol. II (Rome, 1708).

19 Carole Paul, *The Borghese Collections and the Display of Art in the Age of the Grand Tour* (Aldershot, 2008), says nothing of this sensation and Rome's admiration of Bernini.

20 Heinrich Wölfflin, *Renaissance and Baroque*, trans. Kathrin Simon (Ithaca, NY, 1966), pp. 159–60: 'Villae Burghesiae Pincianae/ Custos haec edico:/ Quisquis es, si liber,/ Legum compedes ne hic timeas,/ Ito quo voles, carpito quae voles,/ Abito quando voles./ Exteris magis haec parantur quam hero,/ In aureo Seculo, ubi cuncta aurea/ Temporum securitas fecit,/ Ferreas leges praefigere herus vetat:/ Sit hic amico pro lege honesta voluntas./ Verum si quis dolo malo/ Lubens sciens/ Aureas urbanitatis leges fregerit,/ caveat ne sibi/ Tesseram amicitiae subiratus villicus/ Advorsum frangat.'

21 Filippo de' Rossi, *Ritratto di Roma moderna* (Rome, 1652), pp. 346–8.

22 [Baldinucci], *Vita del cavaliere gio*, pp. 75–8; Baldinucci, *The Life of Bernini*. I am grateful to Tristan Weddigen for this indication; Elena Tamburini, *Gian Lorenzo Bernini e il teatro dell'arte* (Florence, 2012).

23 Mary Beard and John Henderson, *Classical Art from Greece to Rome* (Oxford, 2001), pp. 199–202.

24 Patricia Lee Rubin, *Seen from Behind: Perspectives on the Male Body and Renaissance Art* (New Haven, CT, and London, 2018), ch. 4: 'Models, Motif, and the Migration of Meaning', pp. 111–43; for Goltzius's *Hercules Farnese*, see pp. 138–43.

25 Raphael, *The Ecstasy of St Cecilia*, 1515–16, oil on canvas, Bologna, Pinacoteca Nazionale; Marcantonio Raimondi and Giulio Bonasone engraved Raphael's composition.

26 Huigen Leeflang, ed., *Hendrick Goltzius (1558–1617): Drawings, Prints and Paintings*, exh. cat., Amsterdam and New York (Zwolle, 2003), no. 42, pp. 132–6; see also drawing no. 42.3, *c.* 1592.
27 'Briefe aus Rom', no. 1, in *Der Teutsche Merkur*, 4th quarter 1785, pp. 251–67; no. 2 in *Der Teutsche Merkur*, 1st quarter 1786, pp. 69–82.
28 For David's painting, see *Jacques-Louis David, 1748–1825*, exh. cat., Paris, 1989–90 (1989), cat. 67, pp. 162–7.
29 Ibid., chronology, pp. 562–71; Johann Heinrich Wilhelm Tischbein, *Aus meinem Leben* (Berlin, 1922), pp. 203–5, 211–12.
30 Ibid., p. 204.
31 Ibid., p. 212.
32 Ibid., p. 179.
33 David is referring to the comedy by George Maréchal, Marquis de Bièvre: *Le séducteur: comédie en cinq actes et en vers – représentée à Fontainebleau, devant Sa Majesté, le 4 Novembre 1783, & à Paris le 8 du même mois* (Paris, 1783).
34 Georges Wildenstein, Daniel Wildenstein and Guy Wildenstein, *Documents complémentaires au catalogue de l'oeuvre de Louis David* (Paris, 1973), no. 152, p. 19: 'Il faut que je vous informe, Monsieur le Marquis, du succès inattendu de mon tableau sachant la peine que le peuple Romain a d'accorder quelque mérite à un peintre français. Mais cette fois-ci, ils se sont rendus de bon cœur et il y a un concours de monde à mon tableau presque aussi nombreus qu'à la Comédie du Séducteur. Quel plaisir ce serait pour vous qui m'aimez d'en être témoin, au moins je dois vous en faire la description. D'abord, les artistes étrangers on commencé, ensuite, les Italiens, et par les éloges outrés qu'ils en ont faits, la noblesse a été avertie. Elle s'y est transporté en foule, et on ne parles plus dans Rome que du peintre français et les Horaces. Ce matin, j'ai l'appointement avec l'ambassadeur de Venise. Les cardinaux veulent voir cet animal rare, et se transportent tous chez moi, et, comme l'on sait que le tableau doit partir incessament, chacun s'empresse à le voir'; see also nos 145–60, pp. 18–22.
35 For David's paintings, see *Jacques-Louis David, 1748–1825*, cat. 146–56, pp. 323–53.
36 *Le Tableau des Sabines, exposé publiquement au Palais national des sciences et des arts: salle de la ci-devant Académie d'Architecture, par le C[itoyen] David, Membre de l'Institut National, A Paris, de l'Imprimerie de P. Didot l'Ainé, au Palais National des Sciences et Arts. An VIII* [1800], p. 7: 'Pour moi, je ne connois point d'honneur au-dessus de celui d'avoir le public pour juge. Je ne crains de sa part ni passion ni partialité: ses rétributions sont des dons volontaires qui prouvent son goût pour les arts ses éloges sont l'expression libre du plaisir qu'il éprouve; et de telles récompenses valent bien, sans doute, celles des temps académiques.'

37 Oskar Bätschmann, *Ausstellungskünstler: Kunst und Karriere im modernen Kunstsystem* (Cologne, 1997), pp. 64–6; Karl-Detlef Müller, 'Schiller und das Mäzenat: Zu den Entstehungsbedingungen der "Briefe über die ästhetische Erziehung des Menschen"', in *Unser Commercium: Goethes und Schillers Literaturpolitik* (Stuttgart, 1984), pp. 151–67.
38 Etienne Bréton and Pascal Zuber, *Louis-Léopold Boilly (1761–1845): Le Peintre de la société parisienne de Louis XVI à Louis-Philippe*, 2 vols (Paris, 2019), vol. I, pp. 71–2, vol. II, cat. 761, pp. 674–5: *Le Tableau du Sacre exposé aux regards du Public dans le grand Salon du Louvre*, 1810.
39 Ibid., cat. 2057 E, pp. 880–81.

## 6 Enjoyment, Education and Enlightenment

1 See articles in Carole Paul, ed., *The First Modern Museums of Art: The Birth of an Institution in 18th and Early 19th Century Europe* (Los Angeles, CA, 2012); Bénédicte Savoy, ed., *Tempel der Kunst: Die Geburt des öffentlichen Museums in Deutschland, 1701–1815* (Cologne, 2015).
2 The inscription starts with: 'Obige Erinnerung von der Hand I[hrer] Kais: [erlichen] H.[ohheit] der Frau Erzherzogin Sophie, Mutter S[einer] M.[ajestät] der [sic] Kaiser Franz Joseph I,' signature: SKoller.
3 The question of accessibility to collections is generally neglected; see the stories of the collections for Vienna: Gudrun Swoboda, *Die Wege der Bilder: Eine Geschichte der kaiserlichen Gemäldesammlungen von 1600 bis 1800* (Vienna, 2008); ibid., ed., *Die kaiserliche Gemäldegalerie in Wien und die Anfänge des öffentlichen Kunstmuseums,* 2 vols (Vienna, 2013).
4 Within the wealth of literature, see Micheal Yonan, 'Kunsthistorisches Museum / Belvedere, Vienna: Dynasticism and the Function of Art', in Paul, ed., *The First Modern Museums of Art*, ed. Paul, pp. 166–89.
5 Information from Gudrun Swoboda, Kunsthistorisches Museum, Vienna; see also Annette Schryen, 'Die k. k. Bilder Gallerie im oberen Belvedere in Wien', in *Tempel der Kunst*, ed. Savoy, pp. 443–89.
6 *Die Bildergallerie in München: Ein Handbuch für die Liebhaber, und Kunstfreunde* (Munich, 1787) (Bayerische Staatsbibliothek, online).
7 Sabine Koch, 'Die Düsseldorfer Gemäldegalerie', in *Tempel der Kunst*, ed. Savoy, pp. 183–4.
8 Katharina Pilz, 'Die Gemäldegalerie in Dresden', in *Tempel der Kunst*, ed. Savoy, pp. 272–5.
9 *Liste des Tableaux et des Ouvrages de Sculpture, exposez dans la Grande Gallerie du Louvre, per Messieurs les Peintres, & Sculpteurs de l'Académie Royale, en la presente année 1699* (Paris, 1699), p. 3: 'que les Peintres & Sculpteurs de son Académie Royale, auroient bien souhaité renouveller l'ancienne coûtume d'exposer leurs Ouvrages au Public pour en avoir

son sentiment, & pour entretenir entre eux cette loüable emulation si necessaire à l'avancement des beaux Arts' (BnF Gallica); Udolpho van de Sandt, 'Histoire des expositions de l'Académie royale de peinture et de sculpture 1663–1691', 2019 (for details of access see https://grham.hypotheses.org, accessed 1 November 2022).

10 Mercure galant, September 1699, p. 226, available at https://gallicabnf.fr: 'le peuple a marqué par son concours le plaisir que lui donne l'exposition de tant de chefs-d'œuvres les étrangers les ont admiré et tous sont demeurés d'accord qu'il n'y a que la France capable de produire tant de merveilles.'

11 *Explication des Peintures, Sculptures, et autres Ouvrages de Messieurs de l'Academie Royale* (Paris, 1742), pp. 5–6: 'Comme les suffrages du Public éclairé donnent à chaque genre de travail son veritable prix, c'est de ses suffrages réünis que se forme sa réputation' (BnF Gallica).

12 For the different types of tours, see Thomas Grosser, 'Reisen und soziale Eliten: Kavalierstour – Patrizierreise – bürgerliche Bildungsreise', in *Neue Impulse der Reiseforschung*, ed. Michael Maurer (Berlin, 1999), pp. 135–77; for the classic encyclopaedic description, see Ludwig Schudt, *Italienreisen im 17. und 18. Jahrhundert*, Veröffenlichungen der Bibliotheca Hertziana (Vienna, 1959); for the guides, see Ludwig Schudt, ed., *Le Guide di Roma: Materialien zu einer Geschichte der römischen Topographie – Unter Benützung des handschriftlichen Nachlasses von Oskar Pollak* (Vienna, 1930), Bibliotheca Hertziana (www.biblhertz.it/en/home).

13 Richard Lassels, *The Voyage of Italy; or, A Complete Journey Through Italy*, 2 parts (Paris, 1670).

14 Ibid., part 2, p. 173.

15 Ibid., pp. 198–208.

16 Ibid., pp. 218–24.

17 'The Grand Tour and Princely Collections in Rome', in *The First Modern Museums of Art*, ed. Paul, pp. 1–19.

18 Lassels, *The Voyage of Italy*, part 2, p. 406: 'Taking therefor a gondola, we went to the Arsenal, where after the ordinary formalities of leaving our swords at the door, and paying the porters' fees, we were admitted, and led through this great shop of Mars.'

19 [François Maximilien Misson], *Nouveau Voyage d'Italie, avec un Mémoire contenant des avis utiles à ceux qui voudront faire le mesme voyage, troisième Edition, beaucoup augmentée, & enrichie de nouvelles Figures*, 3 vols (The Hague, 1698), p. xii: 'Ce que j'assure alors, c'est que tous ceux que j'ai vûs en parlent ainsi; c'est la voix & le sentiment du Public! Mais les bruits communs, quoique universellement répandus, ne laissent pas d'être souvent de faux bruits;' the authors point out the different lengths of miles in Italy.

20 Ibid., vol. III, Foreword, fol. 3 r.

21 [François Maximilien Misson], *Voyage d'Italie – Edition augmentée de Remarques nouvelles & interessantes*, 4 vols (Amsterdam, 1718), vol. I, p. xxv.
22 Ibid., vol. IV, pp. 40–41.
23 Ibid., pp. 54–8, quote p. 55: 'Il faut prendre d'abord un bon Antiquaire & régler son temps avec lui, pour visiter les principales raretés de cette célébre ville.'
24 Ibid., pp. 59–70.
25 Ibid., vol. III, p. 248: 'Le David frondant Goliath, l'Enée qui emporte Anchise & la métamorphose de Daphné *(a)*, sont trois pièces modernes du Cavalier Bernin, qui méritent d'être mises au rang des premieres.'
26 Ibid., pp. 250–51.
27 Ibid., pp. 227–9.
28 See Paula Findlen, 'Uffizi Gallery, Florence: The Rebirth of a Museum in the Eighteenth Century', in *The First Modern Museums of Art*, ed. Paul, pp. 72–111. I thank Cecilia Hurley for giving me access to the relevant chapter in her forthcoming book; see also Cecilia Hurley and François Mairesse, 'In the Shadow of the Tribuna', *Studiolo*, 9 (2013), pp. 128–40.
29 Johan Joseph Zoffany, *The Tribuna of the Uffizi*, 1772–7, Royal Collection Trust, www.rct.uk.
30 Desmond Shawe-Taylor, *The Conversation Piece: Scenes of Fashionable Life* (London, 2009), cat. 25, pp. 130–37.
31 See the key plate, ibid., pp. 136–7.
32 Raphael, *Niccolini-Cowper Madonna*, 1508, oil on panel, Washington, DC, National Gallery of Art, inv. 1937.1.25.
33 Joseph Farington, *The Farington Diary*, ed. James Greig (London, 1924), vol. III, pp. 83–4.
34 Mario Praz, *Conversation Pieces: A Survey of the Informal Group Portrait in Europe and America* (University Park, PA, 1971).
35 The gentlemen shown in *Tribuna* are not the members of the Society of Dilettanti, founded in London in 1734 by returnees from the Grand Tour interested in Antiquity. The Society had an important cultural role, among other things by promoting Italian opera, artists and the Royal Academy of Arts: François-Charles Mougel, 'La Société des Dilettanti', in *Le Grand Tour et l'Académie de France à Rome*, ed. Emilie Beck Saiello and Jean-Noël Bret (Paris, 2018), pp. 95–123.
36 Pontus Grate, *French Paintings II: Eighteenth Century* (Stockholm, 1994), cat. 146, pp. 152–5; Anne-Marie Leander Touati and Johan Flemberg, *Gustav III's Antikmuseum* (Stockholm, 2012); Jeffrey Collins, 'Museo Pio-Clementino, Vatican City: Ideology an Aesthetics in the Age of the Grand Tour', in *The First Modern Museums of Art*, ed. Paul, pp. 112–43.
37 Collins, 'Museo Pio-Clementino, Vatican City', p. 113.

38 London, Royal Academy of Arts, Inv. 04/1210; British Museum, photogravure print, inv. 1920,0420.193, and key plate, inv. 1920,0124.4.
39 William Powell Frith, *My Autobiography und Reminiscences* (New York, 1888), pp. 441–5.
40 Ibid., p. 443.

## 7 The Fruitful Public

1 Sabine Schneider, 'Die Laokoon-Debatte: Kunstreflexion und Medienkonkurrenz im 18. Jahrhundert', in *Handbuch Literatur: Visuelle Kultur*, ed. Claudia Benthien und Brigitte Weingart (Berlin, 2014), pp. 68–85.
2 For a detailed history and reaction to the *Laocoön* group, see Christoph Schmälzle, *Laokoon in der Frühen Neuzeit*, 2 vols (Frankfurt am Main, 2018).
3 Paul Klee, *Creative Confession* (London, 2013).
4 Gotthold Ephraim Lessing, *Laocoon: An Essay on the Limits of Painting and Poetry*, trans. E. C. Beasley (London, 1853), p. 101.
5 Ibid., p. 102.
6 Hans Adler, 'Prägnanz – eine Denkfigur des 18. Jahrhunderts', in *Literatur und Geschichte: Festschrift für Wulf Koepke zum 70. Geburtstag*, ed. Karl Menges (Amsterdam, 1998), pp. 15–35, quote p. 18.
7 For details, see also Oskar Bätschmann, '*Laokoon*'s Augenblick: Lessing installiert den fruchtbaren Betrachter', in *Bild und Zeit: Temporalität in Kunst und Kunsttheorie seit 1800*, ed. Thomas Kisser (Munich, 2011), pp. 21–48.
8 Wilhelm Schlink, *Ein Bild ist kein Tatsachenbericht: Le Bruns Akademierede von 1667 über Poussins 'Mannawunder'* (Freiburg, 1996), pp. 46–7, p. 25: 'A cela M. le Brun repartit qu'il n'en est pas de la peinture comme de l'histoire. Qu'un historien se fait entendre par un arrangement de paroles et une suite de discours qui forme une image des choses qu'il veut dire, et représente successivement telle action qu'il lui plaît. Mais le peintre n'ayant qu'un instant dans lequel il doit prendre la chose qu'il veut figurer, pour représenter ce qui s'est passé dans ce moment-là, il est quelquefois nécessaire qu'il joigne ensemble beaucoup d'incidents que aient précédé, afin de faire comprendre le sujet qu'il expose, sans quoi ceux qui verroient son ouvrage se seroient pas mieux instruits que si cet historien, au lieu de raconter tout le sujet de son histoire, se contentoit d'en dire seulement la fin.'
9 Ibid., pp. 25–6, 47–8; for the problem of 'unité', see Thomas Puttfarken, *Roger de Piles' Theory of Art* (New Haven, CT, and London, 1985); Hans Körner, *Auf der Suche nach der 'wahren Einheit': Ganzheitsvorstellungen in der französischen Malerei und Kunstliteratur vom mittleren 17. bis zum mittleren 19. Jahrhundert'* (Munich, 1988).

10 [Anne-Claude-Philippe, Comte de Caylus], *Nouveaux Sujets de peintre et de sculpture* (Paris, 1755), pp. 5–9.
11 Ibid., pp. 13–14: 'Le Spectateur n'ignore pas que ces jeunes gens moururent après une action si remplie de zèle, & dont le Peintre lui présente les plus beaux instants'; Caylus does not cite the source, Herodotus, *Histories*, 1/31.
12 Lessing, *Laocoon*, trans. Beasley, ch. 11, p. 82; for the argument of comprehensibility, see Peter Johannes Schneemann, *Geschichte als Vorbild: Die Modelle der französischen Historienmalerei 1747–1789* (Berlin, 1994), ch. 3, 'Das Publikum', pp. 55–93.
13 Lessing, *Laocoon*, ch. 3, pp. 16–17.
14 W., 'Beschreibung des Torso im Belvedere zu Rom' [1759], in Johann Joachim Winckelmann, *Kleine Schriften, Vorreden, Entwürfe*, ed. Walther Rehm (Berlin, 1968), pp. 169–73, quote p. 172.
15 Oskar Bätschmann, 'Pygmalion als Betrachter: Die Rezeption von Plastik und Malerei in der zweiten Hälfte des 18. Jahrhunderts', in *Der Betrachter ist im Bild: Kunstwissenschaft und Rezeptionsästhetik*, ed. W. Kemp (Berlin, 1992), pp. 237–78; see also the analysis in Matthias Mayer and Gerhard Neumann, eds, *Pygmalion: Die Geschichte des Mythos in der abendländischen Kultur* (Freiburg, 1997).
16 Lessing, *Laocoon*, p. 17.
17 Alberti, *On Painting*, p. 42: 'eaque potissimum pingenda sunt, quae plus animis quod excogitent relinquant, quam quae oculis intuetantur' (and paint things that leave something for the imagination to invent – beyond what is offered for the eye to see).
18 Johann Wolfgang Goethe, 'Upon the Laocoon', in *Essays on Art*, trans. Samuel Gray Ward (New York, 1862), pp. 31–2; Inka Mülder-Bach, 'Sichtbarkeit und Lesbarkeit: Goethes Aufsatz "Über Laokoon"' (29 January 2004), www.goethezeitportal.de, accessed 12 July 2021.
19 Oskar Bätschmann, 'Belebung durch Bewunderung: Pygmalion als Modell der Kunstrezeption', in Mayer and Neumann, eds, *Pygmalion*, pp. 325–70.
20 Bettina Brandl-Risi, *BilderSzenen: Tableaux vivants zwischen bildender Kunst, Theater und Literatur im 19. Jahrhundert* (Freiburg, 2013).
21 Street artists dressed as Egyptians or pierrots, for example, standing motionless on pedestals in order to obtain coins from passers-by are to be found today in many tourist cities.
22 Johann Wolfgang Goethe, *Elective Affinities*, trans. David Constantine (Oxford, 1994), part 2, ch. 5, pp. 144–5; Birgit Jooss, 'Lebende Bilder als Charakterbeschreibungen in Goethes Roman *Die Wahrverwandtschaften*', in *Erzählen und Wissen: Paradigmen und Aporien ihrer Inszenierung in Goethes Wahlverwandtschaften*, ed. Gabriele Brandstetter (Freiburg, 2003), pp. 111–36.

23 For discussion of courtly *tableaux vivants* and their reproduction in a commemorative book, see Ivo Raband, *Vergängliche Kunst und fortwährende Macht: Die 'Blijde Inkomst' für Erzherzog Ernst von Österreich in Brüssel und Antwerpen, 1594* (Heidelberg, 2019), p. 81, B-9.
24 Ibid., Ill. A-9.
25 Zürcher Kunstgesellschaft, ed., *200 Jahre Zürcher Kunstgesellschaft 1787–1987*, with contributions by Christian Klemm and Bernhard von Waldkirch (Zurich, 1987).
26 'History of the Museum', www.staedelmuseum.de; see also contributions by Carolyn Meyding to . . . *zum Besten hiesiger Stadt und Bürgerschaft: 200 Jahre Städel – Eine Festschrift* (Munich, 2015).
27 Corina Meyer, *Die Geburt des bürgerlichen Kunstmuseums: Johann Friedrich Städel und sein Kunstinstitut in Frankfurt am Main* (Berlin, 2014).
28 [Jacob Burckhardt], 'Kunstvereine', in *Allgemeine deutsche Real-Encyklopädie für die gebildeten Stände*, 9th repr. (Leipzig, 1845), vol. VIII, pp. 436–7.
29 Wilhelm Schlink, *Jacob Burckhardt und die Kunsterwartung im Vormärz*, Frankfurter Historische Vorträge (Wiesbaden, 1982), vol. VIII.
30 Ibid., pp. 6–7, with reference to Jürgen Habermas, *Strukturwandel der Öffentlichkeit: Untersuchungen zu einer Kategorie der bürgerlichen Gesellschaft*, 3rd edn (Neuwied and Berlin, 1968), pp. 52–60, 115–17.
31 Ibid., p. 7; see also three articles in Bernd Milla and Heike Munder, eds, *Tatort Kunstverein* (Nuremberg, 2001).

## 8 Sensitive and Moved

1 Gennaro Toscano, ed., *La Mort de Léonard: Naissance d'un mythe*, exh. cat., Château royal d'Amboise (Paris, 2019).
2 *Death of Leonardo da Vinci*, 1818, oil on canvas, 40 × 50.5 cm, Paris, Musée du Petit Palais.
3 [Pierre-Jean-Baptiste Chaussard], *Le Pausanias français: État des arts du dessin en France, à l'ouverture du XIXe siècle – Salon de 1806* (Paris, 1806).
4 Ibid., pp. 85–6: 'Ce Tableau est un de ceux qui remplit le mieux les intentions de la Peinture. Le sujet émeut, intéresse; il exerce sans effort toute la séduction d'un dramatique puisé dans la Nature et dans les grands souvenirs. Le plus sublime génie éclipsé avant son midi; l'hommage rendu au suprême talent par la puissance-elle-même; les larmes de ses rivaux; cette dernière merveille du pinceau suspendue comme un trophée au-dessus du lit funèbre; de si vastes espérances éteintes tout-à-coup dans les regrets d'une perte irréparable, ce deuil de la religion, dont ces mains habiles et aujourd'hui glacées, décoraient naguère l'édifice; ce concours pieux, attendri, de nobles, de lettrés,

d'Artistes, d'élèves, de peuple, frappés avec une énergie diverse, mais profonde d'un sentiment de désolation comme dans une calamité publique, tout porte ice dans l'ame une mélancolie irrésistible, car pour l'éprouver il n'est pas besoin d'être Artiste ou Savant, il suffit d'être sensible..' An outline engraving of the painting helped to understand the text.

5 Pliny, *Natural History*, 35, 73–4; Alberti, *De Pictura,* 42; see also Jennifer Montagu, 'Interpretations of Timanthes' Sacrifice of Iphigenia', in *Sight and Insight: Essays on Art and Culture in Honour of E. H. Gombrich*, ed. John Onians (London, 1994), pp. 305–26; Thomas Kirchner, *L'Expression des passions: Ausdruck als Darstellungsproblem in der französischen Kunst und Kunsttheorie des 17. und 18. Jahrhunderts* (Mainz, 1991); Jennifer Montagu, *The Expression of the Passions: The Origin and Influence of Charles Le Brun's 'Conférence sur l'expression générale et particulière'* (New Haven, CT, and London, 1994); Werner Busch, *Das sentimentalische Bild: Die Krise der Kunst im 18. Jahrhundert und die Geburt der Moderne* (Munich, 1993) expanded this category of emotional works of the eighteenth and nineteenth century in terms of subject-matter and chronology under the general heading 'sentimental pictures'.

6 Chaussard, *Le Pausanias français*, pp. 119–20.

7 Michael Fried, *Absorption and Theatricality: Painting and Beholder in the Age of Diderot* (Berkeley, CA, 1980) sees 'absorption' (denial of a relationship with the public) of the figures as a positive quality and 'theatricality' as a negative one.

8 *Jacques-Louis David, 1748–1825*, cat. 85–91, pp. 194–206.

9 Anselm Gerhard, *Die Verstädterung der Oper: Paris und das Musiktheater des 19. Jahrhunderts* (Stuttgart, 1992), p. 80.

10 Lee Johnson, *The Paintings of Delacroix: A Critical Catalogue,* 6 vols (Oxford, 1981–2002), vol. I, no. 105, pp. 83–91.

11 Stendhal, *Salons*, ed. Stéphane Guégan and Martine Reid (Paris, 2002), pp. 64–5.

12 See *La Grèce en révolte: Delacroix et les peintres français 1815–1848*, exh. cat., Bordeaux, Paris, Athens (Paris, 1996).

13 Wolfgang Drost, *Der Dichter und die Kunst: Kunstkritik in Frankreich – Baudelaire, Gautier und ihre Vorläufer Diderot, Stendhal und Heine* (Heidelberg, 2019), pp. 59–84.

14 See Michael Marrinan, *Painting Politics for Louis-Philippe, 1830–1848* (New Haven, CT, and London, 1988), pp. 27–77.

15 Johnson, *The Paintings of Delacroix*, vol. I, no. 144, pp. 144–51. There is considerable literature on this picture; see Jörg Traeger, 'L'Épiphanie de la Liberté: La Révolution vue par Eugène Delacroix', *Revue de l'Art*, no. 98 (1992), pp. 1–28.

16 Heinrich Heine, 'Französische Maler: Gemäldeausstellung in Paris 1831', in Heinrich Heine, *Historisch-Kritische Gesamtausgabe*, ed.

Manfred Windfuhr (Düsseldorfer Heine Ausgabe, online, vol. xii/1), pp. 9–62, quote p. 51 (addendum 1833); Drost, *Der Dichter und die Kunst*, pp. 85–98.

17 Ibid., quote p. 20. Heine's discussion of the Salon appeared in several forms, first in serial form in *Morgenblatt für gebildete Stände*, 1831; see Ralph Häfner, ed., *Heinrich Heine und die Kunstkritik seiner Zeit: Akten des Internationalen und interdisziplinären Kolloquiums in Paris 2006* (Heidelberg, 2010), esp. Wolfgang Drost (pp. 3–30) and France Nerlich (pp. 101–32).

18 Johnson, *The Paintings of Delacroix*, vol. i, no. 144, pp. 144–51.

19 Théophile Gautier, *Les Beaux-Arts en Europe – 1855*, ed. Marie-Hélène Girard (Alain Montandon, ed., *Œuvres complètes*, vol. vii, iv) (Paris, 2011): 'Cette Liberté . . . étonne et surprend par son aspect fantastique au milieu de personnages d'une réalité crue et brutale.'

20 Heine, 'Französische Maler', p. 21.

21 Ibid., pp. 9–62, quote p. 20.

22 Apart from Delacroix, there was Ary Scheffer, Horace Vernet, Alexandre-Gabriel Decamps, Emile Aubert Lessore, Jean-Victor Schnetz, Léopold Robert and Paul Delaroche.

23 Heine, 'Französische Maler', p. 12.

24 Stendhal, *Salons*, p. 66: 'Négligeant les clameurs du parti contraire, je vais dire au public, avec franchise et simplesse, ce que je sens sur chacun des tableaux qu'il honorera de son attention.'

25 Anonymous, 'Das kunstliebende Publikum', *Morgenblatt für gebildete Leser: Kunstblatt*, xi/5 (1830), pp. 18–20, and no. 6, pp. 22–3 (ub Heidelberg, online); see also the article 'Schorn (Joh. Karl Ludw. von)' in *Allgemeine deutsche Real-Encyklopädie für die gebildeten Stände: Conversations-Lexikon,* 9th repr., vol. xii (Leipzig, 1847), pp. 747–8.

26 Anonymous, 'Das kunstliebende Publikum', p. 19.

27 Ibid.

28 Ibid., p. 20.

29 Stephen Bann,'The Victim as Spectacle: Paul Delaroche's "Lady Jane Grey" and Mademoiselle Anaïs', in *Painting History: Delaroche and Lady Jane Grey*, ed. Stephen Bann and Linda Whiteley, exh. cat., National Gallery, London (2010), pp. 35–45.

30 *Explication des ouvrages de Peinture, Sculture . . . des artistes vivans* (Paris, 1834), no. 503, p. 52, with quote from *Martyrologue des Protestans* (1588). This version could not be found in French libraries, and it is possible that the more widely distributed *Histoire abregée des martirs français du temps de la réformation* (Amsterdam, 1684) was meant.

31 *Painting History*, no. 53, pp. 102–11.

32 Ibid., nos 76–8, pp. 138–9.

33 Heinrich Heine, *Lutetia: Die parlamentarische Periode des Bürgerkönigtums*, xxxvi: Paris, 19 December 1841, available at

www.projekt-gutenberg.org/heine. *Rührungswerk* is formed from *Rührstück*, the melodrama of eighteenth-century literature and musical drama.

34 *La Caricature*, no. 188, *c.* 1833, British Museum, no. 1989,0128.32.

35 British Museum, no. 1989,0128.12.

36 See Guy Cogeval and Beatrice Avanzi, eds, *Dalla scena al dipinto – La magia del teatro nella pittura dell'Ottocento: Da David a Delacroix, da Füssli a Degas*, exh. cat., Marseille, Rovereto, Toronto (Geneva, 2010); esp. Sébastien Allard, pp. 131–9.

37 *Explications des ouvrages de Peinture*, no. 52 (Delaroche) and no. 903 (Granet).

38 Collow, in *Kunstblatt*, 15, no. 35 (1834), p. 137: 'charmant, superbe, admirable, étonnant, capital' – 'finesse, délicatesse, elégance, clarté, harmonie, vérité'.

39 Eduard Collow, 'Briefe über die Kunstausstellung in Paris 1834', in *Kunstblatt*, 15 (1834), no. 32 (22 April 1834), first letter, pp. 125–6.

40 Gustave Planche, *Salon de 1831* (Paris, 1831), pp. 38–40.

41 William Hauptman, *Charles Gleyre, 1806–1874*, catalogues raisonnés of Swiss artists, vol. XVII, 1–2, 2 vols (Zurich, 1996), vol. I, pp. 165–90; vol. II, cat. 545–62, pp. 316–34.

42 Ibid., vol. II, cat. 566, p. 335.

## 9 Grinning, Laughing, Mocking

1 Valentine Green, *A Review of the Polite Arts in France, at the Time of their Establishment under Louis XIVth, Compared with their Present State in England: In Which their National Importance and Several Pursuits, Are Briefly Stated and Considered. In a Letter to Sir Joshua Reynolds, President of the Royal Academy, and F.R.S. by Valentine Green, Fellow of the Society of Antiquaries, Mezzotint Engraver to His Majesty, and to the Elector Palatine; Member of the Royal Academy, London, and Professor of the Electoral Academy, Dusseldorff* (London, 1782), pp. 50–51.

2 John Singleton Copley, *The Death of the Earl of Chatham*, 1781, oil on canvas, 228.5 × 307.5 cm, London, National Portrait Gallery. The etching by Angus was made for a publication that apparently never appeared.

3 Michael P. Costeloe, *William Bullock: Connoisseur and Virtuoso of the Egyptian Hall – Piccadilly to Mexico (1773–1849)* (Bristol, 2008), pp. 57–82.

4 George Cruikshank, 'A scene at the London Museum Piccadilly – or – A peep at the spoils of ambition, taken at the battle of Waterloo – being a new tax on John Bull for 1816 &c &c', London, British Museum, inv. 1853,0112.272.

5 Georg Wilhelm Friedrich Hegel, *Elements of the Philosophy of Right*, trans. S. W. Dyde (Kitchener, ON, 2001), §244, p. 188.
6 Ibid., §245, p. 233.
7 Linda Nochlin, *Misère: The Visual Representation of Misery in the 19th Century* (London, 2018).
8 Charles Dickens, *Oliver Twist; or, The Parish Boy's Progress, By 'BOZ.' Plates designed and etched by George Cruikshank* (London, 1838).
9 Victor Hugo, *Les Misérables* (Neuchâtel, 1862); *Les Misérables,* illustrated by Gustave Brion (Paris, 1867), online BnF Gallica.
10 Ronald Paulson, *Hogarth's Graphic Works*, 3rd edn (London, 1989), no. 130, p. 86.
11 Isaac Cruikshank, *A Peep at the Parisot with Q in the Corner*, 1796, hand-coloured etching, 25.2 × 35 cm, London, British Museum, inv. 1935,0522.4.72.
12 See comments by Dorothy George, *Catalogue of Political and Personal Satires in the British Museum*, vol. VII (1942), copy in British Museum online, inv. 1868,0808.6523.
13 Ibid., *Catalogue*, vol. VIII (1947), copy in British Museum online, inv. 1933,1014.639.
14 Ovid, *Metamorphoses*, 11, 85–193; see Anneke Thiel, 'Midas', in *Mythenrezeption: Die antike Mythologie in Literatur, Musik und Kunst von den Anfängen bis zur Gegenwart*, Der Neue Pauly, supplements, ed. Maria Moog-Grünewald, vol. V (Stuttgart, 2008), pp. 429–32.
15 Jean Michel Massing, *Du Texte à l'image: La Calomnie d'Apelle et son iconographie* (Strasbourg, 1990).
16 Jürgen Müller, *Der sokratische Künstler: Studien zu Rembrandts* Nachtwache (Leiden, 2015), pp. 1–15, with discussion of different interpretations.
17 Oskar Bätschmann, *Ausstellungskünstler: Kult und Karriere im modernen Kunstsystem* (Cologne, 1997), pp. 54–5 with illustration.
18 For Wessel (1688?–1760) from Braunschweig, after 1729 in Geneva, bookseller and bookbinder, see *Répertoire des imprimeurs et éditeurs suisses avant 1800* (online); Rodolphe Töpffer, *Correspondance complète*, ed. Jacques Droin et al., vol. IV (Geneva, 2009), p. 308, n. 10.
19 Constance C. McPhee and Nadine M. Orenstein, eds, *Infinite Jest: Caricature and Satire from Leonardo to Levine*, exh. cat., Metropolitan Museum of Art, New York (New Haven, CT, and London, 2011), nos 20–23, p. 43.
20 Ibid., pp. 13–14, fig. 9.
21 Adolphe Tabarant, *Manet et ses œuvres* (Paris, 1947), p. 67: 'Ils ont tellement ri que les gens qui se préparaient à entrer pestaient contre les lenteurs du tourniquet. "On entrait là comme à Londres, chez Mme Tussaud, dans la chambre des horreurs. On riait dès la porte", a écrit le peintre refusé Charles Cazin.'

22 'Ah pour le coup voilà une composition qui es réellement insensée! et quelle couleur!' – 'Crétin de bourgeois, va!'
23 Charles Baudelaire, 'De l'essence du rire et généralement du comique dans les arts plastiques' [1855], in *Curiosités esthétiques: L'Art romantique et autres œuvres critiques*, ed. Henri Lemaître (Paris, 1962), pp. 241–62.
24 Baudelaire, vol. I, p. 292: 'Le rire est satanique, il est donc profondément humain.' – 'C'est du choc perpétuel de ces deux infinis que se dégage le rire. Le comique, la puissance du rire est dans le rieur et nullement dans l'objet du rire.'
25 Daumier, 'Croquis pris au Salon', *Le Charivari* (1 June 1865), D. 3442, H.D. 1562: 'Les crétins . . . on leur peint un tableau religieux et ils rient . . . ils n'ont même pas la religion de l'art.'
26 Émile Zola, 'Mon Salon', in *Ecrits sur l'art*, ed. Jean-Pierre Leduc-Adine (Paris, 1991), pp. 94–135.
27 Françoise Cachin, ed., *Édouard Manet 1832–1883*, exh. cat., Grand Palais, Paris (1983), cat. 89, 93; Zola, 'Mon Salon', p. 99.
28 *L'Évènement, journal quotidien*, managed by Auguste Dumont: 1st issue to last issue (5 November 1865–15 November 1866).
29 Zola, *Edouard Manet, étude biographique et critique* [1867], in Zola, 'Mon Salon', pp. 137–69; Zola, 'Eine neue Malweise: Edouard Manet', in *Schriften zur Kunst: die Salons von 1866–1896* (Stuttgart, 1988), pp. 47–75.
30 Ludwig Kalisch, 'Die Ritter vom Kronleuchter', *Die Gartenlaube*, no. 49 (1867), pp. 782–4; see also Daumier, *Le Claqueur*, lithograph, in *Le Charivari* (February 1842), p. 19.
31 Zola, 'Mon Salon', pp. 142–3; Zola, *Schriften zur Kunst*, pp. 48–9.
32 Zola, 'Mon Salon', p. 164: 'Mettez dix personnes d'intelligence suffisante devant un tableau d'aspect neuf et original, et ces personnes à elles dix, ne feront plus qu'un grand enfant; elles se pousseront du coude, elles commenteront l'œuvre de la façon plus comique du monde. Les badauds arriveront à la file, grossissant le groupe; bientôt ce sera un véritable charivari, un accès de folie bête.'
33 Ibid., p. 165: 'Et il y a toute une armée dont l'intérêt est d'entretenir la gaieté de la foule, et l'entretient d'une belle façon. Les caricaturistes s'emparent de l'homme et de l'œuvre; le chroniqueurs rient plus haut que les rieurs désintéressés. Au fond ce n'est que du rire, ce n'est que du vent.'
34 Ibid., p. 167: 'Chaque artiste a tiré une foule à lui, la flattant, lui donnant les jouets qu'elle aime, dorés et ornés de faveurs roses. L'art es devenu chez nous une vaste boutique de confiserie, où il y a des bonbons pour tous les goûts.'
35 Paul Klee and Hans Bloesch, *Die Korrespondenz 1898–1940*, ed. Marcel Baumgartner (Göttingen, 2021), pp. 472–81.

## 10 The Masses

1 Adolphe Quetelet, *Sur l'Homme et le développement de ses facultés, ou essai de physique sociale*, 2 vols (Paris, 1835); English trans. by R. Knox as *A Treatise on Man and the Development of His Faculties* (Edinburgh, 1842).

2 On the expansion of the art market in the second half of the nineteenth century, see Elizabeth Gilmore Holt, ed., *The Expanding World of Art 1874–1902*, vol. I: *Universal Exhibitions and State-Sponsored Fine Arts Exhibitions* (New Haven, CT, and London, 1988).

3 Friedericke Vosskamp, 'Die Präsentation der deutschen Kunst auf der Weltausstellung 1878 in Paris: Ausstellungspolitik zwischen nationaler Selbstdarstellung und diplomatischer Rücksichtnahme', *Zeitschrift für Kunstgeschichte*, LXXVII (2014), pp. 241–56.

4 Ibid., pp. 254–6.

5 Brian R. Mitchell, *International Historical Statistics, 1750–2000*, 3 vols (Basingstoke, 2003), vol. I.

6 Gustave Doré and Blanchard Jerrold, *London: A Pilgrimage* (London, 1872).

7 Ibid., p. 65.

8 Ibid., p. 74.

9 Ibid., pp. 78–9.

10 For Poe's short story, see Kevin J. Hayes, 'Visual Culture and the Word in Edgar Allan Poe's "The Man of the Crowd"', *Nineteenth Century Literature*, LVI (2002), pp. 445–65.

11 Poe writes 'fiend', which in connection with Retzsch may be understood as referring to Satan or the Devil; see *Umrisse zu Goethe's Faust gezeichnet von Retsch* [*sic*] (Stuttgart, 1816). For Moritz Retzsch's Goethe illustrations, see Eva Krüger, *Bilder zu Goethes 'Faust': Moritz Retzsch und Dante Gabriel Rossetti* (Hildesheim, 2009).

12 Gustave Le Bon, *Psychologie des foules* (Paris, 1895), published in English as *The Crowd: A Study of the Popular Mind* (Mineola, NY, 2002), p. 2.

13 Ibid., p. xiii.

14 Ibid., pp. 12–13: 'Pour l'individu en foule, la notion d'impossibilité disparaît. L'individu isolé sent bien qu'il ne pourrait à lui seul incendier un palais, piller un magasin, et, s'il en est tenté, il résistera aisément à sa tentation. Faisant partie d'une foule, il a conscience du pouvoir que lui donne le nombre, et il suffit de lui suggérer des idées de meurtre et de pillage pour qu'il cède immédiatement à la tentation.'

15 Rolf Winau, 'Ansteckung – medizinhistorisch', in *Ansteckung: Zur Körperlichkeit eine ästhetischen Prinzips*, ed. Mirjam Schaub, Nicola Suthor and Erika Fischer-Lichte (Munich, 2005), pp. 61–72.

16 Le Bon, *The Crowd*, p. 39: 'Le héros que la foule acclame est véritablement un dieu pour elle. Napoléon le fut pendant quinze

ans, et jamais divinité n'eut de plus parfaite adorateurs. Aucune n'envoya plus facilement les hommes à la mort.'

17 Dieter Schwarz, ed., *Kunstmuseum Winterthur, Katalog der Gemälde und Skulpturen,* vol. II (Winterthur, 2008), cat. 44, pp. 52–4 (Lukas Gloor).

## 11 Mourning Crowds

1 Under 'Trauerfeier für Künstler', the Kubikat database lists the announcement in February 1901 by the Künstlergenossenschaft in Munich of the funeral of Arnold Böcklin, but no works or publications.

2 Tabea Schindler, *Bertel Thorvaldsen – Celebrity: Visualisierungen eines Künstlerkults im frühen 19. Jahrhundert* (Berlin, 2021), pp. 365–72.

3 Hans Christian Andersen, 'Albert Thorwaldsen: A Biographical Sketch', trans. C. Beckwith, in *Bentley's Miscellany*, vol. XXII (London, 1847), p. 428.

4 Ibid., p. 417.

5 Tabea Schindler, 'Bertel Thorvaldsen, Celebrity: Visualisierungen eines Künstlerkults im frühen 19. Jahrhundert', habilitation thesis, University of Bern, 2017, ch. IV.1, pp. 251–7.

6 Eugène Plon, *Thorvaldsen: His Life and Works,* trans. I. M. Luyster (Boston, MA, 1874), p. 170.

7 Hans Christian Andersen, *Bertel Thorwaldsen: Eine biographische Skizze,* German trans. by Julius Reuscher (Berlin, 1845), p. 37.

8 Ibid., p. 69.

9 Ibid., pp. 71–3; see also Schindler, 'Bertel Thorvaldsen, Celebrity', ch. IV.3, ms. pp. 306–11.

10 David Bindman, *Warm Flesh, Cold Marble: Canova, Thorvaldsen and Their Critics* (New Haven, CT, and London, 2014).

11 Sven Oliver Müller, *Richard Wagner und die Deutschen: Eine Geschichte von Hass und Hingabe* (Munich, 2013), pp. 9–11.

12 See the extensive media coverage of Makart's life, illness and death: Ralf Behrens, *Hans Makart ist tot! Der wahre Vorreiter von 'Sex sells!' – Der Farbenzauberer seiner Zeit und dessen Nachklang in einer Presseschau* (behrens_r@t-online.de), version 28 January 2019, addition 1 October 2020, pp. 276–385.

13 *Die Presse*, Vienna, 28 April 1879, pp. 2–5 (Österreichische Nationalbibliothek, Historische österreichische Zeitungen und Zeitschriften); for the phenomenon of the 'painter princes', the nineteenth-century star artists celebrated by practically all segments of the population, see Doris Lehmann and Katharina Chrubasik, eds, *Malerfürsten*, exh. cat., Bundeskunsthalle, Bonn (Munich, 2018), esp. the essay by Michael Stockhausen, pp. 82–9.

14 *The Spring*, 1883–4, oil on canvas, 370 × 630 cm, Salzburg, Museum Carolino Augusteum.

15 Quoted from the press cuttings in Behrens, *Hans Makart ist tot!*, pp. 281–346; see also *Die Gartenlaube*, no. 43 (1884), pp. 709–10.

16 Anonymous, 'De uitvaart van Sir Laurens Alma Tadema', *Algemeen Handelsblad* (Saturday, 6 July 1912).

17 rma, 'Abschied von Jean Tinguely', *Neue Zürcher Zeitung* (5 September 1991), p. 22.

18 Play SRF Sendungen, 'Beerdigung von Jean Tinguely', www.srf.ch, no. 205 (4 September 1991).

## 12 Esteemed Public

1 Hilaire Sazerac, *Lettres sur le Salon de 1834* (Paris, 1834), pp. 38–9: 'Hier la chambre était complète, c'était comme à *Don Juan*. L'aspect du Musée en était tout autre; on s'y sentait plus à l'aise au milieu de ce tribunal d'hommes et femmes de goût et d'esprit si divers.'

2 Ibid., pp. 39–40: 'Il en est de la solennité d'une exposition de tableaux comme d'une représentation théâtrale: c'est le public qui anime, qui fait vivre l'une et l'autre. Sans le public toute est mort! Que le drame est représenté devant les banquettes, les plus beaux morceaux ne sont pas même applaudis.'

3 Ibid.: 'C'est de la foule assemblée que sortent presque toujours les jugements les plus impartiaux.'

4 Werner Busch, *Adolph Menzel: Auf der Suche nach der Wirklichkeit* (Munich, 2015), pp. 181–5.

5 Thomas W. Gaehtgens, 'Menzels "Théâtre du Gymnase"', *Jahrbuch der Berliner Museen*, 41, supplement: Adolph Menzel (1999), pp. 105–15; see also Edgar Degas's long interest in the stage, dancers and spectators in *Degas à l'Opéra*, exh. cat., Musée d'Orsay and Grand Palais, Paris (2019).

6 See the corresponding painting *The Drama* in the Bayerische Staatsgemäldesammlungen, Neue Pinakothek, Munich, inv. 8697.

7 *Catalogue des Tableaux de M. Edouard Manet, exposés Avenue de l'Alma* (Paris, 1867), p. 4: 'Sans cela, le peintre serait trop facilement enfermé dans un cercle dont on ne sort plus. On le forcerait à empiler ses toiles où à les rouler dans un grenier.'

8 George Heard Hamilton, *Manet and His Critics* (New York, 1969), p. 106: 'L'admission, l'encouragement, les récompenses officielles sont en effet, dit-on, un brevet de talent aux yeux d'une partie du public prévenue dès lors pour ou contre les œuvres reçues ou refusées. Mais, d'un autre côté, on affirme au peintre que c'est l'impression spontanée de ce même public qui motive le peu d'accueil que font les divers jurys à ses toiles.'

9 Ibid., pp. 106–7: 'Montrer est la question vitale, le sine qua non pour l'artiste'; pp. 6–7: 'Il ne s'agit donc plus, pour le peintre, que de se concilier ce public dont on lui a fait un soi-disant ennemi.'

10 Oskar Bätschmann, *Edouard Manet* (Munich, 2015), ch. 3: 'Schaustellen: Manet und das Publikum'.

11 See *Edouard Manet, Le Déjeuner – Un Bar aux Folies Bergère*, exh. cat., Courtauld Institute of Art and Neue Pinakothek, Munich (2004).

12 Louvre, Département des Antiquités grecques, étrusques et romaines, inv. Cp 5194.1, c. 520–510 BCE, 114 × 194 × 69.5 cm.

13 Martin Schwander, ed., *Edouard Vuillard: Im Louvre – Bilder für eine Basler Villa*, exh. cat., Kunstforum Baloise Park, Basel (2021).

14 Guillaume Faroult, ed., *La collection La Caze: chefs-d'œuvre des peintures des XVIIe et XVIII siècles* (Paris, 2007), Sophie Eloy, 'La Salle la Caze au Louvre', pp. 177–83.

## 13 The 1871 Survey in Dresden

1 Oskar Bätschmann and Tristan Weddigen, eds, *Benedetto Varchi, Paragone: Rangstreit der Künste*, intro., trans. and commentary by Oskar Bätschmann and Tristan Weddigen (Darmstadt, 2013).

2 Gustav Theodor Fechner, *Bericht über das auf der Dresdner Holbein-Ausstellung ausgelegte Album: Mit einigen persönlichen Nebenbemerkungen* (Leipzig, 1872), p. 6.

3 Gustav Theodor Fechner, *Ueber die Aechtheitsfrage der Holbein'schen Madonna: Discussion und Acten* (Leipzig, 1871), pp. iii–iv.

4 Adolf Bayersdorfer, *Der Holbein-Streit: Geschichtliche Skizze der Madonnenfrage und kritische Begründung der auf dem Holbein-Congress in Dresden abgegebenen Erklärung der Kunstforscher* (Munich, 1872), p. 8n.

5 'Erklärung', *Zeitschrift für Bildende Kunst*, 6 (1871), p. 355.

6 'Zur Holbeinfrage', *Zeitschrift für Bildende Kunst*, 7 (1872), p. 28.

7 Fechner, *Bericht über das auf der Dresdner Holbein-Ausstellung ausgelegte Album.*

8 Lena Bader, *Bild-Prozesse im 19. Jahrhundert. Der Holbein-Streit und die Ursprünge der Kunstgeschichte* (Paderborn, 2013), pp. 105–8.

9 Gustav Theodor Fechner, *Zur experimentalen Aesthetik* (Leipzig, 1871).

10 Fechner, *Bericht über das auf der Dresdner Holbein-Ausstellung ausgelegte Album*, p. 6.

11 Ibid., pp. 6–35.

12 Albert von Zahn, 'Die Ergebnisse der Holbein-Ausstellung zu Dresden', *Jahrbücher für Kunstwissenschaft*, 5 (1873), pp. 147–70, 193–220, esp. 218–20.

13 Robert Lehmann, 'Les Madones de Darmstadt et de Dresde', *Gazette des Beaux-Arts* (1871), pp. 516–19.

14 Fechner, *Bericht über das auf der Dresdner Holbein-Ausstellung ausgelegte Album*, p. 12.
15 Ibid., p. 13.
16 Bayersdorfer, *Der Holbein-Streit*, p. 33n.
17 Fechner, *Bericht über das auf der Dresdner Holbein-Ausstellung ausgelegte Album*, p. 29.
18 Fechner, *Zur experimentalen Aesthetik;* Gustav Theodor Fechner, *Vorschule der Aesthetik*, 2 parts (Leipzig, 1876), p. 1; Christian G. Allesch, *Fechner: Vorschule der Ästhetik*, 2 vols (Berlin, 2018); see also the essays in Ulla Fix and Irene Altmann, eds, *Fechner und die Folgen ausserhalb der Naturwissenschaften* (Tübingen, 2003); and in Marie Guthmüller and Wolfgang Klein, eds, *Ästhetik von unten: Empirie und ästhetisches Wissen* (Tübingen, 2006).
19 See the analysis of the visitors' books for documenta 5 in Christian Saehrendt, *Kunst im Kreuzfeuer, documenta, Weimarer Republik, Pariser Salons: Moderne Kunst im Visier von Extremisten und Populisten* (Stuttgart, 2020), pp. 108–16.
20 Evelyn Weiss, ed., *Komar and Melamid: The Most Wanted – The Most Unwanted Painting*, exh. cat., Museum Ludwig, Cologne (Ostfildern, 1997), pp. 6–7.
21 Ibid., pp. 12–24 (questionnaire and evaluation by Christian Heiliger).
22 *Komar and Melamid 'Schön – Hässlich': Das beliebteste und das unbeliebteste Bild Österrreichs*, exh. cat., Kunsthalle, Vienna (Klagenfurt, 1998), pp. 33–43.
23 Ibid., p. 31.
24 Boris Groys, 'Bilder der erfüllten Wünsche', ibid., pp. 77–81.
25 Peter Fischli and David Weiss, *Findet mich das Glück?* (Cologne, 2002); English trans. as *Will Happiness Find Me?* (London, 2003).

## 14 Aesthetic Education

1 Herman Grimm, *Über Künstler und Kunstwerke*, no. 1 (January 1865), pp. 1, 3 (Digitalist UB Heidelberg); for information about Grimm, see Wilhelm Schlink, 'Herman Grimm (1828–1901): Epigone und Vorläufer', in *Aspekte der Romantik: zur Verleihung des Brüder-Grimm-Preises der Philipps-Universität Marburg im Dezember 1999*, Schriften der Brüder-Grimm-Gesellschaft Kassel 32 (2001), pp. 73–93.
2 *Allgemeine deutsche Real-Encyklopädie für die gebildeten Stände*, 9th edn (Leipzig, 1843–8).
3 Heinrich Wölfflin, *Classic Art: An Introduction to the Italian Renaissance*, trans. Peter Murray and Linda Murray (London, 1952).
4 Evonne Levy and Tristan Weddigen, eds, *The Global Reception of Heinrich Wölfflin's Principles of Art History* (Washington, DC, 2020).

5 Otto F. W. Krüger, *Die Illustrationsverfahren: Eine vergleichende Behandlung der verschiedenen Reproduktionsarten, ihrer Vorteile, Nachteile und Kosten* (Leipzig, 1914), pp. 74–127.

6 Pascal Griener, *Pour une histoire du regard: l'expérience du musée au XIXe siècle* (Paris, 2017), ch. V: 'Le match Angleterre/France: deux pratiques du livre d'histoire de l'art pour le grand public', pp. 158–86; Joseph Imorde and Andreas Zeising, eds, *Billige Bilder: Populäre Kunstgeschichte in Monografien und Mappenwerken seit 1900 am Beispiel Albrecht Dürer* (Berlin, 2019).

7 Karl Marx, *Foundations of a Critique of Political Economy*, trans. Martin Nicolaus (London, 1973), pp. 25–6.

8 See https://digi.ub.uni-heidelberg.de/diglit/kfa; see also Michael Bringmann, *Friedrich Pecht (1914–1903): Massstäbe der deutschen Kunstkritik zwischen 1850 und 1900* (Berlin, 1982); Friedrich Pecht, 'Weihnachtsbücherschau', *Die Kunst für Alle*, no. 5 (1 December 1890), p. 73.

9 Friedrich Pecht, 'Über die deutsche Malerei der Gegenwart', *Die Kunst für Alle*, no. 1 (1 October 1885), p. 4.

10 [Julius Langbehn], *Von einem Deutschen, Rembrandt als Erzieher* (Leipzig, 1890), pp. 1–3.

11 Publisher's catalogue for the series Künstler-Monographien in Verbindung mit Anderen herausgegeben von H. Knackfuss, Velhagen & Klasing, subscription list, 1895, p. 2.

12 Ferdinand Avenarius, 'Zum Dürer-Bunde! Ein Aufruf', *Der Kunstwart*, no. 24 (1901), pp. 469–74; see also Gerhard Kratzsch, *Kunstwart und Dürerbund: Ein Beitrag zur Geschichte der Gebildeten im Zeitalter des Imperialismus* (Göttingen, 1969); Gerhard Kratzsch, '"Der Kunstwart" und die bürgerlich-soziale Bewegung', in *Ideengeschichte und Kunstwissenschaft*, ed. Ekkehard Mai (Berlin, 1983), pp. 371–96.

13 Avenarius, 'Zum Dürer-Bunde! Ein Aufruf', pp. 471–2.

14 Ibid., 'Der Dürerbund', *Der Kunstwart*, XVI/3 (November 1903), pp. 97–8.

15 Susanne Heiland, *Dürer und die Nachwelt* (Berlin, 1955), p. 232.

16 Johannes Damrich, *Albrecht Dürer* (Munich, 1909).

17 Ibid., p. 3n.

18 There is a good deal of literature on this subject: Barbara Wagner, 'Zwischen Repräsentation und Sozialkritik: die Kunst als Begleiterin der Industrialisierung', in *Karl Marx, 1818–1883: Leben, Werk. Zeit*, ed. Beatrix Bouvier and Rainer Auts, exh. cat., Trier (Darmstadt, 2018), pp. 234–51; Dieter Marcos, 'Eine soziale Bestimmung der Kunst? Marx, Proudhon, Morris und die Kunst ihrer Zeit', ibid., pp. 253–61; Patrick Brantlinger, '"News from Nowhere": Morris's Socialist Anti-Novel', *Victorian Studies*, XIX/1 (September 1975), pp. 35–49.

19 Giovanni Pellizza da Volpedo, *La Fiumana – Human Flood,* 1895, oil on canvas, 255 × 438 cm, Milan, Pinacoteca di Brera, inv. 5555.
20 Michael F. Zimmermann, 'Labour, Art and Mass Media: Giuseppe Pellizza's "Il Quarto Stato" and the Illustrated Press', in *Pittura italiana nell'Ottocento*, ed. Martina Hansmann and Max Seidel (Venice, 2005), pp. 331–48.
21 On the use and misuse of pictures, see Federico Valerio, 'Il "Quarto Stato": La forza di un immagine', 2 December 2012, www.youtube.com; and www.pellizza.it/index.htm, 'Fortuna' del Quarto Stato.
22 Jean Louis Sponsel, *Das moderne Plakat* (Dresden, 1897), p. v.
23 Ibid.
24 Ibid., after p. 30.
25 Ibid., p. vi.
26 Maurice Talmeyr, 'L'Âge de l'affiche', *La Revue des deux Mondes,* CXXXVII/1 (September 1896), pp. 201–16; see also Maurice Talmeyr, *La Cité du Sang (Tableaux du siècle passé)* (Paris, 1901), pp. 255–88 (BnF Gallica).
27 *Les Maîtres de l'affiche*, 1896–1900, published by L'imprimerie Chaix, see BnF Gallica.
28 Carl Albert Loosli, *Ferdinand Hodler: Leben, Werk und Nachlass,* 4 vols (Bern, 1921–4), vol. I, pp. 153, 204–13.
29 Published posthumously: Max Raphael, *Arbeiter, Kunst und Künstler* (Frankfurt am Main, 1975); see also Ulrike Wendland, 'Raphael, Max', *Neue Deutsche Biographie*, XXI (2003), pp. 150–51; Ulrike Wendland, ed., *Biographisches Handbuch deutschsprachiger Kunsthistoriker im Exil*, 2 vols (Munich, 1999).
30 Raphael, *Arbeiter, Kunst und Künstler*, p. 7.
31 Ibid., p. 33.
32 On art education, see Michael Matile, ed., *Zeichenunterricht: Von der Künstlerausbildung zur ästhetischen Erziehung seit 1500*, exh. cat., Graphische Sammlung der ETH, Zürich (Petersberg, 2017).
33 David Koch and D. Hesselbacher, *Die Gleichnisse Jesu,* illustrated by Eugène Burnand (Stuttgart, 1910), p. 9.
34 August Springer, *Arbeiter und Kunst* (Stuttgart, 1911), pp. 65, 82–9.
35 Ibid. From 1933 to 1945 the Nazis in Germany appropriated the subject of workers and art as part of the 'Kraft durch Freude' (strength through joy) programme, which subjected all leisure activities by the German people to a political diktat. Various authors have studied the effect of the new posters on the public: *NS-Kraft durch Freude: Der Arbeiter und die bildende Kunst – System und Aufgabe der Kunstausstellungen in den Betrieben (Werkausstellungen, Fabrikausstellungen)* (Berlin, 1938); on propaganda, suppression, ideologization and all the terrible consequences that cannot be discussed here, and the indoctrination and persecution by other totalitarian regimes, see Forschungsstelle

'Entartete Kunst' at the Freie Universität Berlin (Klaus Krüger, Meike Hoffmann), 'Entartete Kunst' database, fsek@campus.fu-berlin.de.

36 Gustav Klimt, 'Rede bei der Eröffnung der *Kunstschau Wien*', in *Kunstschau Wien 1908*, exh. cat. (Vienna, 1908), pp. 2–5.

37 Barbara Becker, '"Ein künstlerischer Erzieher für eine ganze Stadt . . ." Eine biografische Annäherung an Fritz Wichert', in *Teilhabe am Schönen: Kunstgeschichte und Volksbildung zwischen Kaiserreich und Diktatur*, ed. Joseph Imorde and Andreas Zeising (Weimar, 2013), pp. 261–84.

38 Charlotte Klonk, *Spaces of Experience: Art Gallery Interiors from 1800 to 2000* (New Haven, CT, and London, 2009), ch. 4, 'The Spectator as Educated Consumer', pp. 135–71.

39 Bazon Brock calls them 'Beispielgeber' (role models); Paolo Bianchi, 'Beispielgeber im Beispiellosen: Ein Gespräch mit Künstler-Kritiker-Kurator Paolo Bianchi', *Kunstforum International*, CLXXXI (2006), pp. 262–79.

40 See Peter Weibel's comprehensive documentation: Peter Weibel, ed., *Beuys Brock Vostell: Aktion Demonstration Partizipation 1949–1983*, exh. cat., ZKM, Karlsruhe (Ostfildern, 2016).

41 See Peggy Guggenheim Museum, Venice, www.guggenheim-venice.it/en/learn.

42 Dagmar Hirschfelder, appointed director of the Gemäldegalerie of the Staatliche Museen zu Berlin on 29 June 2021 (information on 30 June 2021).

43 Julius Meier-Graefe, *Entwickelungsgeschichte der modernen Kunst: Vergleichende Betrachtung der bildenden Künste, Als Beitrag zu einer neuen Aesthetik*, 3 vols (Stuttgart, 1904), vol. I, pp. 20–22.

44 *Julius Meier-Graefe: Grenzgänger der Künste*, ed. Ingeborg Becker and Stephanie Marchal (Berlin, [2017]); Meier-Graefe's relationship to the public is not discussed either in this most recent extensive study.

45 Wassily Kandinsky, *Gesammelte Schriften 1889–1916*, ed. Helmut Friedel (Munich, 2007), pp. 387–8: 'An das Publikum'; see also Wassily Kandinsky, *Über das Geistige* (Munich, 1922), p. 8.

46 Wassily Kandinsky, *Concerning the Spiritual in Art*, trans. M.T.H. Sadler (Boston, MA, 2006), pp. 6–15.

47 Paul Klee, *On Modern Art*, trans. Paul Findlay (London, 1948), pp. 54–5.

48 *Der Cicerone*, XVI (1924), p. 385: 'Verschiedenes'; see also Vivian Endicott Barnet and Josef Helfenstein, eds, *Die Blaue Vier: Feininger, Jawlensky, Kandinsky, Klee in der Neuen Welt*, exh. cat., Bern and Dusseldorf (Cologne, 1997).

49 See Kristina Kratz-Kessemeier, '"... um uns zu einer wirklich höheren Kultur emporzuarbeiten": Kunstvermittlung als republikanische Bildungskonzept des Weimarer Preussen', in *Teilhabe am Schönen:*

*Kunstgeschichte und Volksbildung zwischen Kaiserreich und Diktatur*, ed. Joseph Imorde and Andreas Zeising (Weimar, 2013), pp. 29–46, esp. pp. 30–31.

50 Andreas Zeising, *Radiokunstgeschichte: Bildende Kunst und Kunstvermittlung im frühen Rundfunk der 1920er bis 1940er Jahre* (Cologne, 2018).

51 Kandinsky, *Concerning the Spiritual in Art*, pp. 9, 15.

52 André Lhote, 'Les attractions du Salon d'Automne' [1944], André Lhote, *La peinture libérée* (Paris, 1956), p. 20: 'Il est essentiel de rappeler le public à son indignité en tant que juge et de lui apprendre que ni la peinture ni la sculpture, pas plus que l'architecture, ne sont des "arts d'agrément", mais bien des sources d'infinis tourments, de désagréments considérables.'

## 15 Major Players

1 For an estimate and collection of incidents, see Monika Roth, *Kunst und Geld – Geld und Kunst: Schattenseiten und Grauzonen des Kunstmarkts* (Bern, 2020).

2 *ARTnews*, 'Top 200 Collectors', 14 February 2021; Franz Schultheis et al., *When Art Meets Money: Encounters at the Art Basel*, trans. James Feams (Cologne, 2015).

3 'Power 100: I top Player dell'arte contemporanea', *Il Giornale dell'Arte*, September 2021, pp. 16–24.

4 Jane Bhoyroo, Curator and Producer of YSI, Leeds, United Kingdom, https://yorkshire-sculpture.org, 2019.

5 See Oskar Bätschmann, 'Landscape at One Remove', in *Gerhard Richter: Landscapes*, ed. Dietmar Elger, exh. cat., Sprengel Museum, Hanover (Ostfildern, 1998), pp. 24–38.

6 Margaret Dalivalle, Martin Kemp and Robert B. Simon, *Leonardo's Salvator Mundi and the Collecting of Leonardo in the Stuart Courts* (Oxford, 2019).

7 Ben Lewis, *The Last Leonardo: A Masterpiece, a Mystery and the Dirty World of Art* (London, 2019), pp. 241–78.

8 Ibid., pp. 293–321.

9 Christie's auctions, live auction 3789, 9 November 2015; the proceeds amounted to over $491 million.

10 *The Da Vinci Code* (film), from Wikipedia (20 April 2021).

11 On the *Mona Lisa*, see Frank Zöllner, *Leonardo da Vinci: Mona Lisa – Das Porträt der Lisa del Giocondo: Legende und Geschichte* (Frankfurt am Main, 1994); on the theft of 22 August 1911, see Jérôme Coignard, *On a Volé la Joconde* (Paris, 1990).

12 Walter Benjamin, 'Das Kunstwerk im Zeitalter seiner technischen Reproduzierbarkeit' [1935], in W. B., *Gesammelte Schriften*,

ed. R. Tiedemann and H. Schweppenhäuser, vol. 1/2 (Frankfurt am Main, 1974), pp. 471–508.

13 Galerie Itinerrance, 24b boulevard du Général d'Armée Jean Simon, F-75013 Paris.

14 See 'Behind the Banksy Stunt', The Art Assignment, www.youtube.com, 1 November 2018.

15 Lenny Schachter, 'What did Sotheby's know about the headline-grabbing stunt, if anything?', *Artnet News*, 17 October 2018.

16 Adam Iscoe, 'Ars Longa: Up in Smoke', *New Yorker*, 17 May 2021, pp. 14–16; see also Kolja Reichert, *Krypto-Kunst: NFTs und digitales Eigentum* (Berlin, 2021), www.digitale-bildkulturen.de.

17 NFT: non fungible token, a certificate of authenticity and ownership.

18 NFT Art: non-exchangeable tokens, the digital works are forgery-proof.

19 See Cristina Criddle, 'Banksy Art Burned, Destroyed and Sold as Token in "Money"', www.bbc.co.uk, 9 March 2021; Iscoe, 'Ars Longa: Up in Smoke'.

20 Reichert, *Krypto-Kunst*, pp. 54–5.

21 See www.artemundi.com.

## Epilogue

1 But see the rescue of the anecdote by Werner Busch, *Die Künstleranekdote 1760–1960: Künstlerleben und Bildinterpretation* (Munich, 2020).

# SELECT BIBLIOGRAPHY

Abramović, Marina, and James Kaplan, *The Walk through Walls* (New York, 2016)
Alberti, Leon Battista, *De statua, de pictura, elementa picturae – Das Standbild, Die Malkunst, Grundlagen der Malerei*, ed. Oskar Bätschmann and Christoph Schäublin, 2nd edn (Darmstadt, 2011)
——, *Vita: Lateinisch-deutsch*, ed. Christine Tauber (Basel, 2004)
[Baldinucci, Filippo], *Vita del cavaliere gio: Lorenzo Bernino scultore, architetto, e pittore, scritta da Filippo Baldinucci Fiorentino alla Sacra e reale maestà do Cristina Regina di Svezia* (Florence, 1682)
Bätschmann, Oskar, *The Artist in the Modern World: The Conflict between Market and Self-Expression* (New Haven, CT, London and Cologne, 1997)
——, *Ausstellungskünstler: Kunst und Karriere im modernen Kunstsystem* (Cologne, 1997)
Baxandall, Michael, *Giotto and the Orators: Humanist Observers of Painting in Italy and the Discovery of Pictorial Composition, 1350–1450* (Oxford, 1971)
Belting, Hans, *Das Bild und sein Publikum im Mittelalter: Form und Funktion früher Bildtafeln der Passion* (Berlin, 1981)
Bourdieu, Pierre, *La Distinction: Critique sociale du jugement* (Paris, 1979; English trans. by Richard Nice as *Distinction: A Social Critique of the Judgement of Taste* (London and New York, 1984))
——, and Alain Darbel, *L'Amour de l'art: Les Musées et leur public* (Paris, 1966; translated into English as *The Love of Art: European Art Museums and their Public* (Cambridge, 1997))
Busch, Werner, *Das sentimentalische Bild: Die Krise der Kunst im 18. Jahrhundert und die Geburt der Moderne* (Munich, 1993)
Chantelou, *Journal de voyage du Cavalier Bernin en France*, ed. Milovan Stanić (Paris, 2001)
Crow, Thomas E., *Painters and Public Life in Eighteenth-Century Paris* (New Haven, CT, and London, 1985)

[De Piles, Roger], *Conversations sur la connoissance de la peinture et sur le jugement qu'on doit faire des tableaux: Où Par Occasion il est parlé de la vie de Rubens, & de quelques uns de ses plus beaux ouvrages* (Paris, 1677)

Disler, Martin, *Bilder vom Maler*, 3rd edn (Dudweiler, 1983); new edn *Bilder vom Maler: Roman* (Zurich, 2015)

Drost, Wolfgang, *Der Dichter und die Kunst: Kunstkritik in Frankreich – Baudelaire, Gautier und ihre Vorläufer Diderot, Stendhal und Heine* (Heidelberg, 2019)

[Dubos, Jean-Baptiste], *Réflexions critiques sur la poesie et sur la peinture: Nouvelle édition revuë, corrigée & considerablement augmentée*, 3 vols (Paris, 1733)

Fischer-Lichte, Erika, *Ästhetik des Performativen* [2004], 9th edn (Frankfurt am Main, 2014)

Fréart de Chambray, Roland, *Idée de la perfection de la peinture, démonstrée par les principes* (Le Mans, 1662)

Frey, Bruno S., *Venedig ist überall: Vom Übertourismus zum Neuen Original* (Wiesbaden, 2020)

Fricke, Beate, and Urte Krass, eds, *The Public in the Picture: Involving the Beholder in Antique, Islamic, Byzantine and Western Medieval and Renaissance Art – Das Publikum im Bild: Beiträge aus der Kunst der Antike, des Islam, aus Byzanz und dem Westen* (Zurich, 2015)

Fried, Michael, *Absorption and Theatricality: Painting and Beholder in the Age of Diderot* (Berkeley, CA, 1980)

Glogner-Pilz, Patrick, and Patrick S. Föhl, eds, *Das Kulturpublikum: Fragestell-ungen und Befunde der empirischen Forschung* (Wiesbaden, 2001)

—, *Handbuch Kulturpublikum: Forschungsfragen und -Befunde* (Wiesbaden, 2015)

Goldberg, RoseLee, *Performance Art: From Futurism to the Present* [1979], rev. and expanded edn (London and New York, 2011)

Griener, Pascal, *Pour Une Histoire du regard: L'Expérience du musée au XIXe siècle* (Paris, 2017)

Gumbrecht, Hans Ulrich, *Crowds: Das Stadion als Ritual von Intensität* (Frankfurt am Main, 2020); English trans. by Emily Goodling as *Crowds: The Stadium as a Ritual of Intensity* (Stanford, CA, 2021)

Habermas, Jürgen, *Strukturwandel der Öffentlichkeit: Untersuchungen zu einer Kategorie der bürgerlichen Gesellschaft*, 3rd edn (Neuwied and Berlin, 1968)

Junge, Henrike, *Avantgarde und Publikum: Zur Rezeption avantgardistischer Kunst in Deutschland, 1905–1933* (Cologne, 1992)

Kandinsky, Wassily, *Concerning the Spiritual in Art*, trans. M.T.H. Sadler (Boston, MA, 2006)

Kemp, Wolfgang, *Der explizite Betrachter: Zur Rezeption zeitgenössischer Kunst* (Konstanz, 2015)

Kernbauer, Eva, *Der Platz des Publikums: Modelle für Kunstöffentlichkeit im 18. Jahrhundert* (Cologne, 2011)

Klonk, Charlotte, *Spaces of Experience: Art Gallery Interiors from 1800 to 2000* (New Haven, CT, and London, 2009)

Pelowski, Matthew, et al., 'Beyond the Lab: An Examination of Key Factors Influencing Interaction with "Real" and Museum-Based Art', *Psychology of Aesthetics, Creativity, and the Arts*, XI/3 (2017), pp. 245–64

Penzel, Joachim, *Der Betrachter ist im Text: Konversations- und Lesekultur in deutschen Gemäldegalerien zwischen 1700 und 1914* (Berlin, 2007)

Pfisterer, Ulrich, *Kunstgeschichte zur Einführung* (Hamburg, 2020)

Philostratos, *Eikones – Die Bilder*, Greek–German, trans. Ernst Kalinka and Otto Schönberger (Munich, 1968)

Pliny the Elder, *Natural History*, vol. IX, books 33–5, trans. H. Rackham (Cambridge, MA, 1992)

Reichert, Kolja, *Krypto-Kunst: NFTs und digitales Eigentum* (Berlin, 2021)

Roesler-Friedenthal, Antoinette, and Johannes Nathan, eds, *The Enduring Instant: Time and the Spectator in the Visual Arts – Der bleibende Augenblick: Betrachterzeit in den Bildkünsten* (Berlin, 2003)

Rosenberg, Harold, *The Anxious Object: Art Today and Its Audience* (New York, 1964)

Schlink, Wilhelm, *Jacob Burckhardt und die Kunsterwartung im Vormärz*, Frankfurter Historische Vorträge, vol. VIII (Wiesbaden, 1982)

——, 'Jacob Burckhardts Künstlerrat', *Städel-Jahrbuch*, n.s. XI (1987), pp. 269–90

Schneemann, Peter Johannes, *Geschichte als Vorbild: Die Modelle der französischen Historienmalerei, 1747–1789* (Berlin, 1994)

——, 'Anweisung, Beobachtung und Nachricht: Rollenspiele für eine neue Rezeptionsästhetik', in *Welt, Bild, Museum: Topographien der Kreativität*, ed. Andreas Blühm and Anja Ebert (Cologne, 2011), pp. 277–90

——, ed., *Paradigmen der Kunstbetrachtung: Aktuelle Positionen der Rezeptionsästhetik und Museumspädagogik* (Bern, 2015)

Schneider, Pablo, and Philipp Zitzlsperger, eds, *Bernini in Paris: Das Tagebuch des Paul Fréart de Chantelou über den Aufenthalt Gianlorenzo Berninis am Hof Ludwigs XIV* (Berlin, 2006)

Schultheis, Franz, et al., *Kunst und Kapital: Begegnungen auf der Art Basel* (Cologne, [2015]; English trans. by James Feams as *When Art Meets Money: Encounters at the Art Basel* (Cologne [2015]))

*Thomas Struth: Fotografien 1978–2010*, exh. cat., Zurich, Dusseldorf, London, Porto (Munich, 2010)

Weisenseel, Anja, *Bildbetrachtung in Bewegung: Der Rezipient in Texten und Bildern zur Pariser Salonausstellung des 18. Jahrhunderts* (Berlin, 2017)

Wilder, Ken, *Beholding: Situated Art and the Aesthetics of Reception* (London, 2020)

Wrigley, Richard, *The Origins of French Art Criticism* (Oxford, 1993)

# LIST OF ILLUSTRATIONS

*statue antiche e moderne* (Rome, 1704), photo Archäologisches Institut, Universität zu Köln.

10 Johann Wilhelm Baur, *View of Villa Borghese*, 1636, tempera on parchment, 30 × 45 cm. Galleria Borghese, Rome (Inv. 519).

11 Hendrick Goltzius, *Hercules Farnese*, *c.* 1592, engraving dated 1617, 42.1 × 30.4 cm. The Metropolitan Museum of Art, New York (Acc. no. 17.37.59).

12 Jacques-Louis David, *Oath of the Horatii*, 1784, oil on canvas, 330 × 425 cm. Musée du Louvre, Paris (Inv. 3692).

13 Louis-Léopold Boilly, *The Public Viewing David's 'Coronation' at the Louvre*, 1810, oil on canvas, 61.6 × 82.6 cm. The Metropolitan Museum of Art, New York (Acc. no. 2012.156).

14 Louis-Léopold Boilly, *The Picture Enthusiasts*, 1823, hand-coloured lithograph, 26 × 21 cm. Minneapolis Institute of Art, MN (Acc. no. P.17,510).

15 Anonymous, *Aristocratic Visitors in the Gallery of Prince Eugene in Belvedere Palace, Vienna,* 18th century, gouache on parchment, mounted on wood panel. Private collection.

16 Johann Joseph Zoffany, *The Tribuna of the Uffizi*, 1772–7, oil on canvas, 123.5 × 155 cm. Royal Collection Trust/© His Majesty King Charles III 2023 (RCIN 406983).

17 Bénigne Gagneraux, *Pius VI Showing King Gustav III the Vatican Galleries*, 1785, oil on canvas, 164 × 262 cm. Nationalmuseum, Stockholm (NM 829), photo Erik Cornelius.

18 William Powell Frith, *A Private View at the Royal Academy, 1881*, 1883, oil on canvas, 103 × 195.5 cm. Private collection.

19 Nicolas Beatrizet, *Speculum Romanae Magnificentiae: Laocoon*, 16th century, engraving, 50 × 33 cm. The Metropolitan Museum of Art, New York (Acc. no. 41.72 (2.78)).

20 *Belvedere Torso*, 1430s, engraving in Domenico de Rossi and Paolo Alessandro Maffei, *Raccolta di statue antiche e moderne* (Rome, 1704), photo Archäologisches Institut, Universität zu Köln.

21 Benjamin Zix, *Napoleon and Empress Marie-Louise Visit the Laocoön Room at Night*, *c.* 1810–11, pen and ink and brown wash on paper, 26 × 29 cm. Musée du Louvre, Paris (Cabinet des dessins, inv. 33406-recto).

22 Adolphe Mouilleron, after Eugène Delacroix, *Liberty Leading the People, 28 July 1830*, 1831, lithograph, 31 × 39.5 cm. Musée Carnavalet, Histoire de Paris.

23 Paul Delaroche, *The Execution of Lady Jane Grey*, 1833, oil on canvas, 246 × 297 cm. The National Gallery, London (NG1909).

24 Charles Gleyre, *The Execution of Major Davel*, 1850, oil on canvas, 300 × 270 cm (now destroyed). Formerly Musée cantonal des Beaux-Arts, Lausanne (Inv. 1387).

39 Félix Vallotton, *Fireworks*, plate VI from *The World's Fair* (*L'exposition universelle*), 1901, woodcut, 16.4 × 12.2 cm. Musée d'art et d'histoire, Geneva (Est 1208-0006).

40 Camille Pissarro, *Boulevard Montmartre, Mardi Gras, Sunset*, 1897, oil on canvas, 54 × 65 cm. Kunst Museum Winterthur (Inv.-Nr. KV 756).

41 Joel Ballin, *Memorial of Thorvaldsen on the Occasion of His Funeral*, 1844, lithograph, 44 × 27.5 cm. Thorvaldsens Museum, Copenhagen (Inv. no. E2285), photo Jakob Faurvig.

42 Adolph Menzel, *Théâtre du Gymnase*, 1856, oil on canvas, 46 × 62 cm. Nationalgalerie, Staatliche Museen zu Berlin (Inv.-Nr. A I 901).

43 Honoré Daumier, 'The Actor and the Street Urchin', lithograph, 24.3 × 22.4 cm, published in *Le Charivari*, 18 April 1864. The Metropolitan Museum of Art, New York (Acc. no. 53.650.2).

44 Édouard Manet, *Au Paradis* (*In the Balcony*), 1877, lithograph, *c.* 24 × 34 cm. National Gallery of Art, Washington, DC (Acc. no. 1943.3.5764).

45 Édouard Manet, *Lola from Valencia*, 1862, oil on canvas, 123 × 92 cm. Musée d'Orsay, Paris (RF 1991).

46 Benjamin Vautier, *Peasants at the Museum*, 1867, oil on canvas, 84 × 104 cm. Musée cantonal des Beaux-Arts, Lausanne (Inv. 694).

47 Edgar Degas, *Mary Cassatt in the Louvre: The Etruscan Gallery*, *c.* 1879, etching and aquatint on laid paper, 26.8 × 23.7 cm. The Clark Art Institute, Williamstown, MA (No. 1955.1407)

48 Édouard Vuillard, *At the Louvre, la Salle La Caze*, 1921, distemper on canvas, 170 × 140 cm. Villa Bauer, Basel.

49 Gustav Theodor Fechner, notice for poll in Dresden, 1871. Hochschule für Bildende Künste Dresden.

50 Adolph Menzel, 'Holbein Exhibition, plebiscite table', 1871, pencil, 14 × 8.2 cm. Kupferstichkabinett, Staatliche Museen zu Berlin (Inv.-Nr. SZ Menzel Skb.36, pp. 59–60).

51 Alfred Richard Diethe, *Public Viewing Holbein's The Meyer Madonna in Dresden*, 1871, pencil and watercolour, 14.1 × 9.6 cm. Staatliche Kunstsammlungen Dresden, Kupferstich-Kabinett (Inv.-Nr. C 1985-84).

52 Ferdinand Brütt, *Acquitted*, engraving, published in *Die Kunst für Alle*, vol. I (1885), photo Universitätsbibliothek Heidelberg.

53 Giuseppe Pellizza da Volpedo, *The Fourth Estate*, 1901, oil on canvas, 283 × 550 cm. Museo del Novecento, Milan.

54 Visitors in front of Leonardo's *Mona Lisa*, Musée du Louvre, Paris, 29 June 2005, photograph. © Archive OB.

# ACKNOWLEDGEMENTS

I am grateful to many friends and colleagues for their interest and expert advice: Marieke von Bernstorff, Rome; Andreas Beyer, Basel; Bernhard U. Bischoff, Bern; Jan Blanc, Geneva; Küngolt Bodmer, Bern; Birgitt Borkopp-Restle, Bern; Sebastian Buchmann, Stockholm; Teresa Ende, Dresden; Elena Filippi, Vicenza; Cecilia Hurley, Neuchâtel/Paris; Julia Gelshorn, Fribourg/Rome; Sandra Gianfreda, Zurich; Loa Haagen Pictet, Geneva; Marcus Andrew Hurttig, Leipzig; Joseph Imorde, Cologne/Siegen; Susanne Kubersky-Pirotta, Rome; Ulf Küster, Basel; Claus Lamm, Vienna; Daria Lanzuolo, Rome; Johann Layer, Hamburg; Catherine Lepdor, Lausanne; Christine Göttler, Bern; Eva-Lena Karlsson, Nationalmuseum Stockholm; Matthew Pelowski, Vienna; Adrian Porikys, Berlin; Wolfgang Pross, Munich; Jennifer Rabe, Rome; Christoph Schäublin, Bern; Tabea Schindler, Zurich; Wilhelm Schlink†, formerly Freiburg i.Br.; Manuel Schmid, Zurich; Peter Johannes Schneemann, Bern; Corinne Linda Sotzek, Zug; Gabriele Strobel, Munich; Thomas Struth, Berlin; Gudrun Swoboda, Vienna; Christine Tauber, Munich; Bernadette Walter, Biel-Bienne; Tristan Weddigen, Rome/Zurich; Christian Weiss, Zurich; Andreas Zeising, Dortmund.

The author and publisher would like to thank the Ernst Göhner Foundation, Zug, for its considerable contribution to the printing of this volume.

# INDEX

Illustration numbers are indicated by *italics*